Sri Sathya Sai Gita

ALL ABOUT
SPIRITUALITY
IN
Q's & A's

(Culled from Bhagawan Baba's Discourses)

P. P. ARYA

PRASANTHI NILAYAM

SRI SATHYA SAI BOOKS & PUBLICATIONS TRUST

Prasanthi Nilayam P.O. 515 134 Anantapur District,
Andhra Pradesh, India
STD: 08555   ISD: 91-8555
Phone: 287375   Fax: 287236
email: enquiry@sssbpt.org

International Standard Book No. 81 - 7208-363-7

First Edition   : October 2004
Reprint   : September 2005

Published by
The Convener,
Sri Sathya Sai Books & Publications Trust
Prasanthi Nilayam, India - Pin Code 515 134
STD : **08555** ISD : **91- 8555**
Phone : **287375** Fax : **287236**
email: enquiry@sssbpt.org

Printed at :
INDIGO PRESS
Red Hills, Lakdi ka pool,
Hyderabad-500 004.

CONTENTS

PREFACE

God is the source of life. We are alive because of His living presence within us as life itself. He is *Sat-Chit-Ananda* – Existence, Consciousness, Bliss Absolute. He is existence; so, we exist. We, think, feel, move about, work and are vitally alive because God exists within us as Consciousness. And, if only we will keep and preserve the purity of this inner divine essence of our being, and learn to abide and be aware of our being, we will find that we too abide in Him. The Self or *Atma*, the pure *Sat* (Existence) and *Chit* (Consciousness) existing in us is not anything but the Essence of the Absolute Bliss, that exists both within and outside every creature, being all-pervasive.

All other dual experiences we undergo are relative only, pertaining to the dimension of the body, mind and intellect, to the planes of the physical and the psychological, which are always subject to change because this is a phenomenal world, a feverish flux of relative change, the *Samsara*, wherein we are bound to experience the pairs of opposites – pleasure and pain, joy and sorrow,

sweetness and bitter taste, likes and dislikes etc. –
whereas the essence of our being has nothing to do with
this dimension of duality, for It, the *Atma*, is beyond
dualities, beyond time and space, beyond the *gunas*,
beyond *maya*. It is Pure Existence, Pure Consciousness,
Bliss Absolute. It is *Satyam, Jnanam, Anantam Brahma*.
It is Self-luminous. It is embodiment of Knowledge.
Nothing is hidden from It. It is Omniscient precisely
because of this truth about its Being.

Self-realisation is the realisation of that God who
illumines within the chambers of our spiritual heart as
the very essence of our being, as our own true, essential
real Self, our eternal, divine identity – beyond this
temporary, passing, changeful human identity which is
only a seeming, relative reality. Our real identity is
covered by aspects of this temporary reality. And, no
matter in what aspect this temporary reality is present
as a sheath covering and hiding our true reality, it has
to be gradually torn asunder, set aside and transcended.
It is a cage denying us freedom. It is bondage. It has to
go. It must go. It may be beautiful to look at, but it is a
cage nevertheless, because it binds us to the cycle of
birth and death. We are attached to this cage and take it
as our reality and are suffering from birth to birth. This
attachment must go because this is binding.

The goal of life is liberation from this bondage.
It is illumination. Unless it is attained we are
unenlightened, living our life in darkness, ignorance

and bondage, forgetful of our true reality. Until we are emancipated we are in bondage. Until we are enlightened we are in a state of slumber, in darkness.

We are not aware of the ocean of Bliss hidden within us, we are not experiencing the Immortal Soul, God residing in the cavity of our heart because of our preoccupation with the little 'I'. We are so much involved with it, so much overpowered and obscured by it, wrapped up with this little 'I'. It is like a lampshade completely covered by layers of thick black soot hiding the light. Bhagawan Baba has said that "I" and "Mine" are the causes of this bondage of man. Ego is the trap. This is *maya*, this is *samsara* and this is *Prapancha*. So, liberation commences with the clear perception and recognition that we have to rise up from this unreality of ego-characterised personality holding us in prison, to the realisation of our Reality, to be aware of our being part and parcel of the Cosmic Soul, divine in nature, beginning-less, beyond name and form, beyond birth and death, Immortal.

The separation of the Self from the non-Self, of *Atma* from the *An-atma*, is not something that suddenly happens. We have to be gradually led upto it by a constant non-stop process of rejecting the *An-atma*, the non-Self, and affirming our identity with the *Atma*, the Self, by engaging ourselves in an unbroken spiritual *sadhana*.

In the *Upanishadic* times the science of the soul

and God, and the great spiritual secrets of realising the sacred Divinity were taught by the ascetic sages to the few selected dispassionate seekers. In the *Dwapara Yuga*, through His disciple Arjuna, Lord Krishna gave the same sacred knowledge of the pure *Atma Tattwa* and the means of attaining it, to the entire mankind for seeking deliverance from the cycle of birth and death. In this *Kali* age, the *Yuga Avatar* Bhagawan Sri Sathya Sai Baba, through His infinite Grace, has been showering His Love through His Divine Discourses for the last more than six decades, imparting His divine teachings to the whole humanity, for recreating and reforming man on the true basis of *dharma*, and helping the mankind to tread the path of *sadhana* for attaining success in the search for lasting peace, illumination and liberation. Bhagawan exhorts the devotees: "*utilise the opportunity of association with Me as much as possible, and endeavour as quickly and as best as you can, to follow the directions that I have been giving. Obeying My instructions is enough. Resolve to keep those ideals before you ever, in all your thoughts, words and deeds. That can confer on you the summum bonum of mergence in the Supreme Substance of Divinity.*"

Bhagawan's teachings incorporated in Questions and Answers form in this book titled "Sri Sathya Sai Gita", are culled from His Divine Discourses delivered by Him to the devotees over a period of more than six decades from the time He gave His first lesson to the devotees when He declared His identity at Uravakonda:

"*Manasa   Bhajare   Gurucharanam,   Dustara Bhavasagara Taranam*" . These are meant for all classes of devotees from the novices to the *Mumukshus* – the seekers of *Moksha*. The great spiritual teachings given by Swami for the inspiration and guidance of the seekers on the Godward path, shine with His full glory in this book.

Bhagawan has said that God is not somewhere high up in the heavens; He is in us, with us, beside us, behind us, before us. He is in every cell as life. He is in every atom as activity. He is all this and more besides. Every human being is equipped with intelligence by means of which he can inquire, investigate and experience this Truth. *Sadhana* on the spiritual journey leads us to inner path away from the objective world where the senses mislead and misinterpret.

Bhagawan has come for the redemption of the mankind and we can save ourselves and proceed smoothly and safely to the Bliss of Self-Realisation, following His directions, teachings and lessons on spirituality, unfolded by Bhagawan contained in this book. It is hoped that this book will surely help the devotee to tread the spiritual path safely and with confidence until triumph crowns him, as He Himself who has given these gemlike secrets of spirituality contained herein, is the Guide, Guardian and God.

Placed at the Lotus Feet
P. P. Arya

SAI WORDS AND SAI PATH

All the scriptures you study diligently will reveal
that the Sai path is the truth.
Exploring the purport of all the *Vedas* you will find
the true path in Sai's words.
All the science and scriptures will testify
to the truth of Sai's words.
Chanting the *Gayatri* full-throatedly will prove
the truth of Sai's message.
Of what avail is all your striving
if the mind remains polluted?

[SSS Vol. 20, P 118]

1

GOD AND CREATION

■ Nature Of Divinity

Q 1. How can we understand the principle of Brahman – the Divine principle?

A. *The Upanishads elaborate on the principle of Brahma through three names: **Viraat: Hiranyagarbha and Avyaakruta.** These three forms of Divinity relate to Sthoolam (gross), Sookshmam (subtle) and Kaaranam (cause) and to the three states of waking, dream and deep sleep.*

[Summer Showers 1991, P 131]

Q 2. How do we explain these three aspects of Brahman?

A. VIRAAT

The Atma principle which personifies the waking state, is Viraat. Viraat is that form of the Atma that dons a physical body, lives a long life and embodies the waking state. He assumes various forms and is known by various names ... The entire visible universe including the five elements is a form of Viraat, without exception, without any distinction of "this" or "that".

Therefore, Viraat is that principle which manifests as the external, gross, visible world.

Viraat has two other names – Vaishvanara and Vairaajasuta.

Vaishvanara is He who appears as 'I' consciousness in each individual.

Vairaajasuta is one who exists in a mysterious form. He exists in everyone but is undetected. He performs all actions but behaves as if He does not. He experiences everything but does not reveal it.

Viraat, Vaishvanara and Vairaajasuta are three names of the same being.

HIRANYAGARBHA

The second form of Brahman is Hiranyagarbha, the basis, the source of all wisdom. All knowledge: worldly, ethical, dharmic, spiritual, scientific – has emanated from Hiranyagarbha. Therefore, He is also called Jnana Bhaskara – the Sun of Knowledge. When the Sun rises, He appears golden (Hiranya) and colours the world with a golden hue. *Creation emerged from Hiranyagarbha, which is oval in shape, a golden egg, like the one I materialised a few days ago. The mouth was the first to emerge from this shape. From the mouth, sound. Then, the nose, through which air began flowing. Eyes came next, with fire emanating through them. Ears arrived next. Therefore Hiranyagarbha is the origin of the human form.*

All beings evolved from Hiranyagarbha, who also bestowed Vijnana, Sujnana and Prajnana to them to facilitate discrimination between the temporary and the permanent. What should be attained, what is not worth pursuing? What deeds should be done, what should not? ... What is the purpose of life? Hiranyagarbha granted all wisdom to man to clarify such issues.

*Hiranyagarbha, like Viraat, has two other names – **Sutraatmaka** and **Praana**. Just as thread (sutra) passes through a necklace of gems, Sutraatmaka is that principle which underlies all beings, and gives bliss to them. **This unifying thread like principle is also called Brahma Sutra.** The thread called God is present in equal measure in all humans without distinction, promoting unity of mankind - This is the principle of Hiranyagarbha. **Hiranyagarbha assumes a subtle (sookshma) form during the dream state – the form of Atma. This means that Hiranyagarbha is one who is awake during the dream state.***

Viraat creates everything in the waking state. Hiranyagarbha creates everything in the dream state by mere willing. Every object is created by (Divine) Will alone. Whatever is seen in dreams is created by Hiranyagarbha.

(The Upanishads reveal that Hiranyagarbha is the sum-total or aggregate of all the Jivas, Samashti. Macrocosmic aspect of Brahman is Hiranyagarbha. Microcosmic aspect of Brahman is Jiva, individual soul. Jiva and Hiranyagarbha are the two aspects of Brahman. Hiranyagarbha abides in the body, which is made up of five elements. Hiranyagarbha having created the bodies of Devas and men, also entered the heart of every living being.)

AVYAAKRUTA

The third form of Brahman is Avyaakruta. He is absolutely formless – unmanifested. He exists in the causal body and enjoys the state of deep sleep. He has no limbs, but does all actions. He travels to distant places. He has no eyes, but sees everything. He has no ears but listens to everything. He performs every act in creation, but possesses no form.

Avyaakruta also has two additional names – Antaraatma and Easwara. Notice that the three forms of Brahman – Virat, Hiranyagarbha and Avyaakruta – have, in turn, three names each. What is the significance of these names? Antaratma motivates and influences everything from Himself. Every motive, urge, inspiration comes from the Antaraatma. This is 'inner voice' (antarvaani). All sounds that man produces also emerge from Antaraatma.

Next, Easwara. He is the embodiment of all forms of prosperity (sakala aisvarya swaroopa). In addition, He bestows results of actions (karma-phala). He has the power of action (Kriya-shakti) with which He assesses good/bad actions and grants corresponding results. He is also called Laya-Kaarak (the destroyer). Easwara bestows prosperity (aisvarya). What is prosperity? Both good and bad are prosperity. Since Easwara represents all forms of prosperity, He judges man's actions and grants the corresponding wealth.

[Summer Showers 1991, P 131-134]

Q 3.   Where does God abide and how is one to experience Him?

A. *"Antar Bahischa Tath Sarvam Vyaapya Narayana Sthitaha"* – *God is present inside, outside, everywhere.* *"Vedaaha metham Purusham Mahaantam, Aditya Varnam Tamasah Parastaat"* – *I have seen (experienced) that Great Person, brilliant like the Sun who is beyond verbal description. Where is He present? Beyond darkness (tamas). Unless we transcend the darkness of ignorance, we cannot experience Him.*

[Summer Showers 1991, P 19]

Q 4. **What are the means of attaining awareness of this Divinity?**

A. *There are some clearly defined methods for achieving this aim.* **Man's vision, which is now turned outward towards the phenomenal universe, should be turned inwards towards the Indwelling Spirit. One should manifest the Divine consciousness inherent in him.** *He should submit himself to that Consciousness as a Spiritual discipline. This is called "Conscious Realisation of the Inner Divine".*

[SSS Vol.21, P 44]

Q 5. **What are the different stages of attaining awareness of the Divinity?**

A. *The first task is to develop awareness of the Divinity within . The next stage is the realisation of the truth that the Divinity that is within one's self is equally present in all others. One must recognise that the veil or barrier that appears to separate him from others is born out of delusion and every effort has to be made to remove it. Only then will it be possible to experience the oneness of all living things.* **"Atma eva idam Sarvam"**, *says the Sruti* **(I am indeed all this).** *The realisation dawns: "All this is contained in Me." And then there is the consciousness,* **"I am Divine.**

The Divine is Me. I am Brahman. Brahman is Myself.
There is no distinction between Brahman and Me."
[SSS Vol. 21, P 44-45]

Q 6. What is the relationship between man and God?

A. *Narada described the relationship between man and God in these words:*

"Yallabdhwa Puman, Iccharamo Bhavati,
Tripto Bhavati, Matto Bhavati, Atmaramo Bhavati" – *(After attaining God, man gets total satisfaction, fulfilment, ecstasy and bliss).*

[Sanathana Sarathi – Nov.2000, P, 349]
[Summer Course Discourse, 18-05-2000]

Q 7. Even though divinity resides in his heart, why does man consider himself weak?

A. *Human being is the repository of divine energy.* **Durga** *(goddess of power),* **Lakshmi** *(goddess of wealth) and* **Saraswati** *(goddess of wisdom) are present in man. He is not poor, weak and lonely in any sense. He has all the capacity to experience divine bliss.* **In spite of being endowed with all powers, man considers himself weak. This is the effect of his evil company.** *By associating himself with bad company, man is developing bad thoughts and bad feelings.*

[Sanathana Sarathi – Nov. 2002, P 326]

Q 8. How to cultivate sacred feelings that will instill faith in the inherent divinity, impart strength and foster truth, righteousness, justice and sacrifice?

A. *"Tyaja Durjana Samsargam,*
Bhaja Sadhu Samagamam;
Kuru Punyam Ahoratram,
Smara Nityam Anityatam." – **(Shun bad company, seek**

good company and perform righteous deeds day and night; discriminate between permanent and ephemeral).

[Sanathana Sarathi – Nov. 2002, P 326]

Q 9. Man's heart is full of sweetness. Having been blessed with such sacredness, what is man supposed to do?

A. *Firstly, make sacred use of the eyes given by God. Only then your life will be sanctified. Your netra (eye) is the sastras (scripture) given by God. Understand this sastras and conduct yourself accordingly. Once you have control over your vision, you will have control over your speech. Speak only truth, there is nothing greater than truth. Samyak drshti (pure vision) and samyak vak (pure speech) will lead to samyak sravanam (pure hearing) and samyak bhaavam (pure feeling). Maanava (human being) becomes Madhava (God), once he understands the importance of human values and puts them into practice.*

[SSS Vol. 35, P 153]

Q 10. What is the difference between the perception of a scientist and a spiritualist (sage) regarding God's creation?

A. *Take, for instance, a handful of sand from seashore in a plate. The scientists can determine its place and country of origin by examining its colour, weight etc. But the sages do not think in this manner. They say that it is God's creation and God's maya. Thus, there is a gulf of difference between the perceptions of the scientists and the sages. Science is like a semi-circle. It starts at some place and ends at some other place. It is not a perfect whole. But spirituality ends at the same point from where it begins. It is a full circle.* **The wholeness is the sign of Divinity.**

Poornamadah   Poornamidam   Poornat
Poornamudachyate, Poornasya Poornamadaya
Poornameva Avashishyate (That is the whole, this
is the whole. When the whole is taken out of the
whole, what remains is again the whole).

[Sanathana Sarathi – Feb. 2003, P 45-46]

Q 11. **How can one understand this atomic power and
how to understand divinity connected with this?**

A. *Atom is not visible to the physical eye but it is*
present everywhere. The water we drink, the food we
eat, the words we utter, the sound we hear, everything is
permeated with atoms. Though man treads on atoms, eats
atoms, drinks atoms, he is unable to understand their
mystery. He thinks that only scientists can investigate
into the nature of atoms. **Atomic process is highly**
sacred. By conducting a proper enquiry into this, one
can understand Divinity. This was the teaching of
Sage Kanada.

[SSS Vol. 35, P 191]

Q 12. **Where from did the Atomic energy originate and
how long does it take for the atom to go back to its
source?**

A. *The body will be respected so long as there is so-*
ham (life-breath) in it. That is the sound of Pranava.
That is the energy contained in an atom. This energy
has its origin in Divinity. None can create it. This
truth was propagated by Sage Kanada. It is very difficult
to understand the power of the atom. God is present in
every atom. The entire world is the manifestation of the
atom. The space and sound are the expressions of the
atom. Therefore, do not neglect the principle of atom. It

has mighty power in it. It takes something like twenty-two thousand crore of years for an atom to go back to its source.

[SSS Vol. 35, P 193]

Q 13. **One desires to merge in God and achieve liberation (Moksha). How is one to realise such an important Divinity having so many potencies?**

A. *Water can integrate with water. Air can combine with air. Fire can merge with fire. As God is formless, to become one with God one has to become formless. What does this imply? It means that one has to get rid of the attachment to the body.*

[Sanathana Sarathi – Jan. 2001, (back title page)]

Q 14. **What are the various kinds of potencies that have been attributed to God?**

A. *Eight kinds of potencies have been attributed to God. He is the source of all sound, all motion, all light, all speech, all bliss, all excellence, all illusion (Maya) and all prosperity.*

[Sanathana Sarathi – Jan. 2001, (back title page)]

Q 15. **Where does divinity exist in man?**

A. *The divinity, which fills the entire cosmos, exists in man as 'Hridaya'. The Vedas name this 'Hridaya' (spiritual heart) as 'Atma'. Atma has another name 'Easwara'. 'Easwara Sarva Bhutanam (God dwells in all beings).*

[Sanathana Sarathi – Aug. 2000, P 249-250]
[Summer Course Discourse on 16-5-2000 at Brindavan]

Q 16. **Why is mind known as *Vishnu Swarupa* and where are the three aspects of Godhead present in man?**

A.   *The mind originates from the Atma and is known as Vishnu Swarupa, as stated in the axiom Vishwam Vishnumayam (the universe is pervaded by Vishnu). It is said, Brahma originated from the navel of Vishnu. So, speech, which originates from the mind, represents Brahma. Therefore Easwara is Atma Swarupa, Vishnu is Mano Swarupa and Brahma is Vak Swarupa. The three aspects of Godhead, viz., Brahma, Vishnu and Maheshwara are intimately interrelated.*

[Sanathana Sarathi – Aug. 2000, P 250]
[Summer Course Discourse on 16-5-2000 at Brindavan]

Q 17. **Does God ignore or relax His own code or *vidhan* at times?**

A.   **The *Divine cannot act against His own moral code. So, on different occasions, God waits for the appropriate time to enforce the code.* ** *On that account, you cannot say God is powerless or incompetent. God is omnipotent, but that does not mean He can act arbitrarily. He acts according to the cosmic code.*

[Sanathana Sarathi - April 95, P 89 (Discourse on 28-5-95)]

■ Aspects Of Divinity

Q 18. **What is the clear distinction between *Nirguna*, *Saguna* aspects of Divinity?**

A.   *The Sarvantharyami Paramatma and the gross form and name which Paramatma assumes and through which He is realised are not separate entities; they are identical.*

When this All-pervasive All-inclusive Pure Existence is described, the matter and the method depend on the principles of the speaker and the tastes of the listener. When the individual name and form are transformed into the Attributeless and the Formless, it is referred to as Brahman; when this same Brahman appears with attributes and forms, it is referred to as Rama, Krishna, Vishnu or Siva...When this Subtle Omnipresence is systematically worshipped through a gross form and as having attributes, the devotee will clearly realise its nature through the Sadhana itself. To vouchsafe the knowledge of this Sadhana and that Truth, and to bless the Bhaktas with that Bliss, the Attributeless Paramatma incarnates in this world, assuming name and form, and gives scope for all embodied beings to have concrete experience and joy. Through these experiences, the Incarnations facilitate the realisation that Paramatma is Sarvantharyami and Sarvabhoothanthraratma, All-pervasive, the Inner Atma of every thing in Creation. Lord Krishna showed in His own form the entire Creation. Until he saw with his own eyes how Lord Krishna had contained in His gross form the entire creation, even Arjuna failed to understand that Krishna was Sarvantharyami.

[Prema Vahini, P 61-62]

Q 19. Do the goddesses Lakshmi, Saraswati and Parvati, really exist? What is Nature and how does it delude?

A. *When a referece is made to Devi (Shakti), it signifies the united form of Durga (Parvati), Lakshmi and Saraswati. The three together represent Shakti. Shakti is the energy that accounts for all the phenomena of Prakriti (Nature).*

Nature is energy and the controller of that enery is the Lord. Prakriti (Nature) is made up of the three qualities, Satva, Rajas and Tamas. Saraswati represents the Satva guna. Lakshmi represents the Rajo guna and Parvati represents the Tamo guna. As Prakriti (Nature) is made up of these three (Satva, Rajas and Tamas), to get control over Nature, man has been offering worship to Durga (Parvati), Lakshmi and Saraswati. These are not goddesses but deified symbols of the three qualities.

The human body emerged from Nature. Nature has two forms: Apara Prakriti and Para Prakriti. Apara Prakriti (lower Nature) includes Ashta Aishvaryas (eight forms of wealth), and Kama, Krodha, Lobha, Moha, Mada, Matsarya and the three mental faculties in man: Manas (mind), Chitta (subconscious mind) and Ahamkara (ego). Para Prakriti (the higher Nature) represents the consciousness in man. True humanness consists in controlling the five elements, which make up the Apara Prakriti (lower Nature) and merge in the higher Nature represented by the life force and Chaitanya (consciouness).
[SSS Vol. 25, P 321, 323]

Q 20. How are the two aspects – Parameswara and Sakti, related to each other?

A. *The word swadha has also given a meaning to Prakriti as if it was a feminine and a meaning to Para Brahma as if He was a Purusha. If the aspect of Parameswara and of Sakti cannot combine, there cannot be creation in the world. Especially these two aspects are such that one cannot exist without the other. In this context, there is no objection to regard the whole of Prakriti as feminine and the aspect of Para Brahma as Purusha.*
[Summer Showers 1974, P 83-84]

Q 21. How best can one understand the limitless aspect of God?

A. *If we want to understand this well, we must realise that religions are all different but all of them lead to the same goal. The cloth may be different but the basic material, namely the thread, which makes the cloth of different kinds is the same. Ornaments are all different but the gold which goes into making the ornaments is the same. The colour of the cattle may vary from one to another but the milk that comes from these cattle is the same. Human beings have missed the essential point and are unable to understand this as a result of their ignorance and men have submitted themselves to great many difficulties because of such ignorance. God is one but each individual should be able to create a form for himself according to his taste.*

When salt is in the sea, it is not distinct from the sea. It is a part of the ocean. One drop of water is enough to tell us that the ocean water is salty. In the same manner, even if you experience a small part of the aspect of Brahman, which is in your heart, you can understand the entire divine aspect of God. There is only one God all over and He is not different in different persons.

[Summer Showers 1974, P 49-50]

Q 22. In what form is God present in the human body?

A. *All that you see and enjoy in the material world, the life force in the world, have all been described by one comprehensive word 'Purusha' in the Veda. This word signifies the shining and self-effulgent Brahman. This self-effulgent Brahman is present in the human body in three different names, that is,*

Vishwa, Taijasa and Prāgya (Prajna). In the world the same Brahman is present in three different aspects of Virat, Hiranyagarbha and Avyakruta.

[Summer Showers 1974, P 207]

Q 23. Who represents these three aspects of Divinity in the Universe?

A.   *Indra is one who has the form of Virat and gives all Aishwaryas or wealth. Surya the sun will have the form of Hiranyagarbha. Vasu stands for one who eradicates sorrow.*

[Summer Showers 1974, P 207]

Q 24. What does Brahma stand for?

A.   *Brahma means the vast, infinite principle. The element of Akasa (sound) emanated from this infinite expanse of Brahma. From akasa emerged vayu (air), tejas (fire) from vayu, wind from tejas, prithvi from wind, ocean from earth, food from oceans and finally humans from food. Ponder this sequential cycle and you will arrive at the truth that man (Purusha) has emerged from the infinite Brahma.*

[Summer Showers 1991, P 130]

Q 25. God has the appellation *Suhrid*. What does it mean?

A.   *It means a good-hearted friend. In every human relationship, there is an element of selfishness in the display of affection. God alone showers His Love with no trace of selfishness.*

[SSS Vol. 26, P 65]

Q 26. God is also called *Nivaasah*. What does it mean?

A.   *Nivaasah is the Supreme Abode. Our aim should be to dwell in the Lord. This cosmos is the abode of the Lord.*

The sacred feeling that we are living in the abode of the Lord should be cherished by everyone.

[SSS Vol. 26, P 66]

Q 27. God is described as "*Acharam chara meva cha*"? What does it signify?

A.   *It means that He is both non-moving and moving. That is, though appearing to be moving, but He can grasp everything. He has no feet but He can move everywhere. He has no eyes but He can see everything. This is the significance of "Acharam chara meva cha".*

[SSS Vol. 26, P 72]

Q 28. God is addressed as Eesha, Gireesha, Naresha, Paresha and Bilvesha. What do these terms mean?

A.   *(i)   Eesha: Eesha means sakala aishwarya sampanna (master of all types of wealth). Aishwarya includes not only property, movable and immovable, but also strength, knowledge, skill, intelligence and prosperity. Easwara is the master of all wealth.*

(ii)   Gireesha: Gireesha means master of Giri or Hill. People go to Thirupathi Hills and offer their hair in fulfilment of vows. The inner significance of this sacrifice of hair must be understood. The head is the peak of the human body. Ignorance or Thamasic quality is supposed to be dark or black. The black hair is enveloping the peak of the human body that is the head. By removing the hair on the head you expose the white surface of the peak. This is symbolic of surrendering the dullness or tamasic quality. Since God is the master of light of wisdom, as opposed to dullness on the head at the top of the human body, He is termed as Gireesha.

(iii) Naresha: In the term Naresha (master of Narah) "Na"

means 'no', 'Ra' means ignorant of one's sacredness. Narah means man who is not ignorant. He is not a sinner. He is the embodiment of pure Atma. The master of man is Naresha.

(iv) **Paresha:** *'Para' means 'above all'. God transcends all. He is Akhanda (limitless) and Anir-vachaneeya (beyond description by words). As God transcends the three stages of time – past, present and future – and transcends space, pervading everywhere, He is termed Paresha.*

(v) **Bilvesha:** *He is termed Bilvesha – the lover of the Bilva leaf which has triple leaves in a single stalk, Thri-nethra – one with three eyes and Thrigunateeta – transcending the three gunas (qualities of Sathva, Rajas and Thamas). His weapon is Thrishul, the three-pointed Javelin. One should offer the three qualities to God, symbolised by the offer of the triple-leaf Bilva for worship. One should do worship with full understanding of the inner significance of the rituals.*

[SSS Vol. 26, P 133-134]

Q 29. God is described as *Jnana Bhaskara*. What does this term mean?

A. *It means the embodiment of Wisdom or shining with the Light of Wisdom.*

[SSS Vol. 26, P 136]

Q 30. We describe God as *Ananta*. Does it mean endless?

A. *Ananta is endless like the sky or fathomless like the ocean. God is said to be of blue colour. It does not mean that His skin is bluish. It means He is infinite and fathomless because He is Jnana Bhaskara also.*

[SSS Vol. 26, P 136]

Q 31. Why Easwara (Shiva) is known as 'Bhola Shankara'? And how did Vinayaka get Gajaasura's (elephant's) head?

A. *Once upon a time there was an Asura (demon) named Gajaasura. He performed penance. Easwara, pleased with his penance, offered him a boon whatever he desired. Easwara is a deity who is easily propitiated. Hence He is known as Bhola Shankara. When He is pleased with a devotee, He gives the devotee whatever he asks. Sometimes He gets into a difficult situation, as in the case of Bhasmasura, who was granted by Shiva the boon to turn into ashes anyone on whose head he placed his hand. Immediately after getting the boon Bhasmasura wanted to test his power by trying to place his hand on Shiva's head itself! (Hence also the name Aasuthosh - easily propitiated)*

And what was the boon Shiva gave to Gajaasura? The demon desired that fire should go forth from him continuously so that no one dare approach him. Shiva granted him the boon. Gajaasura continued to do penance and Shiva used to appear before him off and on. Once Shiva asked him what he wanted. The demon said: "I want you to dwell in my stomach." Shiva granted the boon and lodged himself in the demon's stomach. Shiva's consort Parvathi, searched for Shiva everywhere and could not find Him. As a last resort, she went to her brother, Vishnu and appealed to Him to trace the whereabouts of her husband. The all-knowing Lord assured her: "Don't worry. Your husband is Bhola Shankara. He grants readily whatever boon His devotee prays for, without considering the consequences. I suspect that He must have got into some trouble, I shall find out what has happened."

Vishnu staged a minor drama. He converted Nandi (Shiva's bull) into a dancing bull and led it before Gajaasura, while Himself assuming the role of a piper

*playing music on the pipe while the bull did the dancing.
Gajaasura was in ecstasy over the dancing of the bull. He
asked the piper (Vishnu) what he wanted. The piper
replied: "If that is so, release from your stomach Shiva
who is dwelling there." Gajaasura then realised that the
piper was none other than Vishnu Himself, who alone
could know the secret of Shiva's presence inside his
stomach. He fell at the feet of Vishnu, released Shiva from
his stomach and prayed to Him for a boon. He said: "I
have been blessed by many boons from you. My last
request is that all should cherish my memory by
worshipping my head after I pass away." Shiva thereupon
brought his son and placed Gajaasura's head on him.*

*Ever since, the tradition has prevailed in Bharath that
every auspicious function of any kind commences with
worship of Ganapati.*

[SSS Vol. 30, P 182-183]

**Q 32. What are the 8 appellations of God demonstrating
the Divine Principle in the Veda?**

A.   *The Veda permeates the universe. It is the embodiment
of Truth. It flows in eight streams:* **Sabdabrahmamayee**
(manifesting as all-pervading Cosmic sound);
Charaacharamayee *(pervading all moving and
unmoving objects);* **Jyotirmayee** *(all-pervading
effulgence);* **Vaangmayee** *(sacred speech);*
Nityanandamayee *(eternal bliss);* **Paraatparamayee**
(embodiment of Omniwill); **Mayamayee** *(manifestation
of Maya) and* **Srimayee** *(the embodiment of all
prosperity).*

[SSS Vol. 19, P 77]

**Q 33. Is Prakriti feminine? What is the concept of *Ardha-
naareeswara*?**

A.   *Every being in the cosmos, whatever may be the gender, in external form, is essentially feminine. Prakriti (Nature) is feminine. She represents one half of the Lord – Ardhaangi. The Paramatma (the Supreme Self) is the Purusha (the Supreme Godhead). Together Prakriti and Purusha represent the concept of Ardha-naareeswara – the Divine conceived of half male and half female. This union of male and female is found in every human being.*

[SSS Vol. 27, P 117]

Q 34. **Do Brahma, Vishnu and Maheshwara have forms and do they exist both in the macrocosm and the microcosm?**

A.   *In a way, they do have a form. This is not a physical form, but the form of consciousness. Vishnu is Sarva-vyapaka (one who is omnipresent); so is the mind. Manomoolam Idam Jagat (the mind pervades the world). The mind can go anywhere at any time. It is not bound by time, space and circumstances.* **Brahma is Brihat-swarupa** *(one with cosmic form), which signifies vastness. Similarly, Vak (sound), which represents Brahma, has limitless vastness. Brahma is addressed as Sabda-Brahmamayi (Brahma is the primordial sound).*

Brahma, Vishnu and Maheshwara are limitless, infinite and all-pervasive. The Trinity of Brahma, Vishnu, Maheshwara, thus, permeates the entire cosmos. But it is also present in its microscopic form in human body. They exist at the smallest of the small and also as the vastest of the vast (Anoraneeyan Mahatomaheeyan).

[Sanathana Sarathi – Aug. 2000,P 250][Summer Course Discourse on 16-5- 2000 at Brindavan]

Q 35.   Is it possible for man to see this Trinity?

A.   *It is not possible for anyone to see the infinite cosmos and the Trinity that pervades it. But it is possible to realise Brahma, Vishnu and Maheshwara who reside in the human body.* You can attain the knowledge of their cosmic form only when you realise them within yourself.

[Sanathana Sarathi – Aug. 2000, P 250]
[Summer Course Discourse on 16-5-2000 at Brindavan]

Q 36.   How is Easwara described?

A.   *Hridaya stands for Easwara.* One who realises this should not harbour evil thoughts and evil feelings. *Easwara is described as Niguna, Niranjana, Sanathana, Niketana, Nitya, Shuddha, Buddha, Mukta, Nirmala Swarupi (attributeless, pure, final abode, eternal, unsullied, conscious, free and embodiment of sacredness).* Man's conduct should therefore be according to the attributes of Easwara.

[Sanathana Sarathi – Aug. 2000, P 250]
[Summer Course Discourse on 16-5-2000 at Brindavan]

Q 37.   Why is the trifoliate Bilva leaf offered to Lord Shiva? Why Lord Shiva is depicted having three eyes?

A.   *Easwara is symbolic of the heart. "Tridalam, Trigunakaram, Trinetram Cha Triayudham, Trijanma Papa Samharam, Eka Bilvam Sivarpanam"* (we offer the trifoliate Bilva leaf which is symbolic of the body with three attributes to the three-eyed Shiva, who carries the trident and has the potency to destroy the sins accumulated over three births).

[Sanathana Sarathi – Aug. 2000, P 252]
[Summer Course Discourse on 16-5-2000 at Brindavan]

Q 38.   *Why is Lord Shiva depicted having the third eye? What does the third eye signify?*

A. *Shiva is depicted as the one with the third eye. The third eye does not refer to the physical eye. It is symbolic of wisdom and foresight. Man has only two eyes as he can visualise only past or present. But God knows the future also. That is why He is depicted as having the third eye.*

[Sanathana Sarathi – Aug. 2000, P 252]
[Summer Course Discourse on 16-5-2000 at Brindavan]

Q 39. What does the word 'Bhagawan' stand for?

A. *In the word 'Bhagawan' (God), the letter 'Bha' stands for effulgence. An ordinary electric bulb illuminates only a limited area, but God who is all-pervasive illumines the entire creation.* Divinity shines in everybody. So, do not hate anybody…Hurting others amounts to hurting God Himself. Our hatred will certainly rebound on us.

[SSS Vol. 33, P 162]

Q 40. Is God above the Trinity of Brahma, Vishnu and Mahesh?

A. *In the word "GOD", you have three letters: G, O, D. 'G' refers to "Generation" (or creation). 'O' refers to "Organisation" (that is, keeping creation going). 'D' stands for destruction. "God" combines the three aspects of Generation, Organisation and Destruction…*

[SSS Vol. 28, P 47]

The three presiding deities over creation, protection and dissolution are the Trinity – Brahma, Vishnu and Siva. But there is a fourth entity – Shironayaka (the Overlord), who is above these three. He is God.

[SSS Vol. 28, P 53]

Q 41. Can God overrule the Trinity? How is one to attain the Omnipotent God?

A.   *He can overrule the Trinity. How? By mitigating the magnitude of the consequences of karma. He can counteract any kind of situation. That is the Divine prerogative of God. He can create anything, protect anything. He creates and brings about its dissolution. Therefore, God should be regarded as having control over Generation, Organisation and Destruction. **To realise God, you have to surrender yourself completely. When the surrender is total, a direct link with God is established. Without such surrender, propitiating the lesser deities is a waste of time**.*

[SSS Vol. 28, P 53]

Q 42. Who is Purushothama?

A.   *While the individual Person or Purusha is God installed in that body which is thereby a temple, the Purushothama, the Supreme Sovereign Person, is the sum-total of all the Purushas and so has in Him all of them.*

[SSS Vol.16, P 109]

Q 43. What is the concept of God or Easwara?

A.   *When the unmodifiable transcendent and immanent Brahman, instead of being just 'being', decides on 'becoming', it is best designated as 'God', or 'Easwara' ('Almighty'). The Divine ground of everything is the spiritual Absolute, called Paramaathman (Supreme Absolute Self). It is also the ground, the base, the reality of man.*

[SSS Vol. 14, P 157]

Q 44. What is the relation between Easwara (God) and Brahman?

A.   *Easwara (God) is the sathvic reflection of Brahman. The jiva (individual) has the emotional, passionate and*

active qualities in his composition. The quality that is
inferior is thamasic and that which is superior is sathvic.
Easwara is the sathvic reflection of Brahman. Therefore
man must strive to rise higher into the sathvic realm. He
must be ever vigilant not to slide down into the lower
realm – the thamasic realm of matter and material pursuits.

[SSS Vol. 14, P 162]

Q 45. Who is Brihaspathi?

A.   *Brihaspathi is the preceptor (Guru)of the Gods.*

[SSS Vol. 6, P 11]

**Q 46. How is Niraakara manifesting as *Saakara* in the
world?**

A.   **There are two birds sitting on one tree, the
Upanishad says, the jivatma and Paramatma, on
the tree of this body, this world. One bird eats the
fruits of the tree, while the other simply looks on,
as a witness. But, the wonder is, the two birds are
really one, though they appear as two; they cannot
be separated, since they are two aspects of the same
entity. Niraakara and Saakara are just two ways
in which the One manifests itself.**

[SSS Vol. 4, P 5]

**Q 47. Krishna is named as Yogeswara in the Gita. What
does that mean?**

A.   *Yoga is defined by Patanjali as the nirodha (control) of
the vrittis (agitations) of the chitta (mind-stuff). **If the
mind is stilled and free from waves produced by the
wind of desires, then he becomes a Yogi and the Lord
is the highest Yogi, for He is the ocean that is
unaffected by the waves which agitate the surface.***

[SSS Vol. 9, P 27]

Q 48. **Lord is also called** *chitta-chora.* **What does it mean?**

A.   *There is a song used in Bhajans – "Badaa chitta-*
chora" – where God is said to be a "big thief", who
steals the hearts of persons! The whole world is
God's. All of you belong to Him, though you may
not know it. Therefore, He can take anything from
anyone. He is the master of the ether, wind, fire,
water and earth. He can change the sky into the earth
and the earth into the sky. So, He can take hold of
the hearts of people and fill them with Love. Once
people know how great is the Love that God gives,
they will not desire any thing else. That is why He
is called chitta-chora (heart-thief).

[SSS Vol. 9, P 45]

Q 49. **What are the different names in which the Divine**
functions in the cosmos?

A.   *Divinity has five names. The first is Para-naamam.*
Second, Vyuha-naamam. Third, Vibhava-naamam.
Fourth, Antharaathma-naamam and fifth, Archana-
naamam. The Divine functions in the cosmos in these
five names.

Para-naamam refers to the abode of the Supreme,
Vaikunta. There the Supreme Lord dwells under the name
Para-naamam. The Lord dwells there as an effulgence.
He oversees everything. But, He is not visible to anyone
and no one can see His form.

The second is: Vyuha-naamam. This name refers to
the Lord who reclines on a serpent on the ocean of
milk. The Lord in this form can be seen only by Devas
(the various deities). Ordinary beings cannot do so. The
Lord in His Vyuha form fulfils the desires of the Devas.

Third is: Vibhava-naamam. This refers to the various human forms in which the Lord incarnates on earth as Avatar of Rama and Krishna etc.

The fourth is: Antharaathma-naamam. In this form, the Lord pervades every part of a human being as an indwelling spirit. This indwelling spirit is Divine.

The fifth is: Archana-naamam. This refers to the form in which the Divine can be worshipped, praised and adored for securing His grace.

[SSS Vol. 29, P 301-303]

Q 50. Has God any attributes?

A. *It is due to attachment that you acquire attributes. Divinity has no attributes. Divinity is described as* **Nirguna, Niranjana, Sanathana, Niketana, Nitya, Buddha, Shuddha, Mukta, Nirmala Swarupi,** *(attributeless, pure, final abode, eternal, unsullied, aware, free and embodiment of sacredness). You are unable to recognise its real nature due to your excessive attachment to the body.*

[SS – Nov. 2000, P 326-327]
[Dasara Discourse 1, on 1-10-2000]

■ Prana (Life Principle)

Q 51. Where does *Prana* (life principle) function in the body? At what level the *prana* and the *buddhi* (intellect) function in the body with reference to the mind?

A. *In the human being, the Antahkarana (the inner psychosomatic instrument) is made up of mind, the intellect, the Will and the ego. The ego is linked to the prana (life principle). It is encased in the*

Vijnanamaya Kosha (the sheath of integrated awareness). The mind is linked to the Chitta (Will) and is encased in the Manomaya Kosha (the mental sheath). Thus between individual soul and the prana (vital principle), the mind functions. The life principle functions between the mind and the body. The buddhi (intellect) functions above the level of the mind. The vital principle functions below the mind.

[SSS Vol. 21, P 218]

Q 52.   What is responsible for the heat in the body?

A.   *Both the intellect and the prana are surcharged with Agni (heat). It is their combined presence in the body that accounts for the heat in the body.*

[SSS Vol. 21, P 219]

Q 53.   Why does the mind of man melt so easily and gets swayed?

A.   *Man comprehends the world through the mind and hence its working should be closely watched. Because the mind is located between the buddhi (intellect) and the prana (vital principle) — both of which are filled with the fire principle — it tends to melt.*

[SSS Vol. 21, P 219]

Q 54.   Wherefrom does the Life Force (*Prana*) get the power to sustain the body?

A.   *The invisible Vital Force (Prana) is the basis for the visible body. Prana has no form, while the body has a form. There is, however, **the Atmic principle, which confers all the potencies for the Prana (Life Force). It is because of the power imparted by the Atma that the Life Force is able to activate the body.** The body inherently*

*is inert. It is made up of different kinds of material
substances.*

[SSS Vol. 28, P 238]

**Q 55. How does the Life Force operate in the body to
sustain it?**

A. *The Vedas declare: "Prajnanam Brahma" (Constant
Integrated Awareness is Brahman). It is by the
presence of Prajnana that the Life Force is able to
animate the body. The body represents inert matter.
The Life Force operates in the body as a vibration.
This Vibration derives its power from Prajnana,
which finds expression in radiation.*

[SSS Vol. 28, P 238]

**Q 56. What happens to the five *Prana* when we go to
sleep?**

A. *When a living being sleeps, the five vital airs – Prana,
Apana, Vyana, Udana, Samana – do function along with
the five fires in the body conferring warmth. The
inhalation and exhalation of the breath proceed serenely.
The 'Prana' vital air energises us in the same steady
manner. Udana enables the person to experience the taste
of mergence with the Supreme... during sleep and derive
Bliss. But this experience does not last; it is quite temporary.
Only the person who has gained the purification of the
mind and the clarification of Buddhi (intellect) will have
the unchanging Bliss of Mergence in Param-Atma.*

[Sutra Vahini, P 78-80]

■ Universe (Cosmos), Creation, Prakriti

Q 57. Are creation and God two distinct things?

A. *No, creation and God are not two distinct things. In our* *own ignorance we regard what really is a projection of God's maya as the world and material creation. It will appear as the manifestation of the spirit of the Divine if we act wisely and with knowledge. It is only when we can think of both and discriminate between them will we see the difference...We should recognise the truth that God alone cannot separately exist without His own creation and without creation, there is no God.*

[Summer Showers 1977, P 152,153]

Q 58.   How to relate the meaning of the words " I, World and God"?

A.   *In the aspect of the jiva (individual soul), we should experience the Brahman or the God in it. You must recognise the oneness of the Brahman that is present in all of us. You may have many different vessels of different colours, of different forms and made up of different metals, but the reflection of the Sun in all these vessels is of the same sun. In the same manner, we should recognise that what we find as reflection in all the jivas is the reflection of only the one Paramatma...*

The aspect of I, which is present in everyone, is the aspect of Brahman. When we ask the question 'who am I', it will be appropriate to give the answer 'I am I'. This is the correct interpretation of Adwaita. Contrary to this, even if we say 'Aham Brahmasmi', I am Brahman, we see an amount of duality. In that statement, two things appear to us. One is the 'I' and the other is Brahman. It is this dualistic concept in man that gives rise to several misinterpretations and several doubts.

[Summer Showers 1977, P 153 -154]

Q 59. **If the Reality is one, why do we see other things of varied forms?**

A. *In the spiritual sphere, it has been said "Ekam Eva Adwiteeyam". What exists in reality is only One, there is no parallel second that exists. All other things that we see in this world are manifestations arising out of changing time.* Man is one, but changes come in him because of changes in time. When he is 10 years old, we call him a boy. When he is 30 years old, we call him a man; when he is 75 years old, we call him a grandfather. The different stages described as child, boy, man and grandfather have come about because of changes in time. At all times, there is only one aspect of this individual, which is common. *So also, it is by the change in time that good and bad appear. There do not exist two separate things called good and bad. Good is simply the opposite of bad. Absence of good may appear as bad.*

[Summer Showers 1977, P 22]

Q 60. **What is the basis of *Prakriti* – the material creation? What is *Maya*?**

A. *In this context, we see that Maya or illusion and avidya or lack of knowledge (ignorance, ajnana) and Karma or work have been explained as the basis for creation.* Here, illusion and ignorance are synonymous. It is not possible for us to undertake work without a basis. For work, desire is the basis. For desire, ignorance is the basis. Here, we see that the basis of all work is desire and the basis for desire is ignorance and for all these things, the Parameswari Sakti is the basis. This Parameswari Sakti is no doubt the basis but this Sakti does not by itself

*independently do anything. Parameswara is the one who
has Maya as his instrument. This Maya is taking the form
of ignorance. Ignorance also occasionally takes the form
of illusion. The body that is Maya and Parameswara who
is resident in the body are closely connected with each
other.*

[Summer Showers 1974, P 83]

**Q 61.   What does the statement "*Sarvam Brahmamayam
Jagat*" mean?**

A.   *This means that the aspect of Brahma is the basis of all
the work that we do and having this in mind, we should
not be disappointed with any result we may get. If we
understand correctly the basis of creation, then we will
understand the spirit of Siva-Sakti Atma of the world.
We have to recognise the oneness of the experience and
the experiencer himself. In a manner, the mother of the
universe is Maya (Parameswari Sakti) and the father of
the universe is Para Brahma. If there is no Maya, we will
not even attempt to understand the aspect of Para Brahma.
Maya is the form of God whereas Para Brahma is the name
for God Himself. The form and name are related with each
other in an inseparable manner.*

[Summer Showers 1974, P 84]

**Q 62.   How is the creation projected by Para Brahma and
Parameshwari Shakti or *Maya*?**

A.   *Either for the creation or for the existence of the
world, Maya and Para Brahma remain as the basis.
If we examine this carefully, we will come to the
conclusion that Para Brahma alone cannot be
responsible for creation that we see around us.
Creation is possible only when Para Brahma and*

*Sakti or maya come together. This becomes the basis
for creation. Para Brahma Sakti and Para Brahma are
interdependent and are both needed for creation like the
mud and water for a potter. Such a Para Brahma is also
pictured as wearing the ignorance or the maya sakti on
Him as His form.*

[Summer Showers 1974, P 85,86]

Q 63. **What is the role of *sankalpa* or Divine Will in
creation of the universe?**

A. *The entire Universe, that is to say, the moving and the
unmoving, everything formed from the five primordial
elements and hence named Prapancha, has been projected
by the Divine Will. It is the result of Bhagavad Sankalpa,
the Will of God, which is the Cause. No consequence can
happen without a precedent Cause.*

[Sutra Vahini, P 71]

Q 64. **Is *Prakriti* inert?**

A. ***Prakriti pulsates with Chaitanya (Consciousness).
It is the union of these two that contributes to the
oneness of humanity.***

[Summer Showers 1993, P 42]

Q 65. **It is said that the *Jagath* (Cosmos) is *Mithya*
(illusory) and *Brahman* (Absolute) alone is real. Is
it correct?**

A. *This is not correct. The Jagath (Cosmos) is also real. When
you have the love-filled vision, the whole cosmos appears
Brahmamayam (permeated by the Absolute). When you
see the world with the physical eye, it appears as a bundle
of miseries from birth to death. Love of God is the only
way out of the misery.*

[SSS Vol. 25, P 115]

Q 66. **What are the characteristics of this seen objective Universe?**

A. *In the Upanishads and the Vedantha (Vedic philosophy), five characteristics of the universe are mentioned: Asti (Being), Bhaati (Awareness), Priyam (will Bliss), Naama (Name) and Rupa (Form).* Of these, the last two are temporary, and therefore, trivial. The first three are the three facets of the everlasting truth, the Atma. The categories of Sat-Chit-Ananda are also co-related in Vedantha with bhootha akasa, chittha akasa and chida akasa respectively.

[SSS Vol. 14, P 228]

Q 67. **What are the inherent characteristics of the material world?**

A. *Janma-mrthyu-jaraa-vyaadhi-dukha-doshaanudarsanam, which means: the awareness of the inevitable cycle of birth and death, of senility and disease, of grief and evil and other signs of the temporariness of this created world, and life in it.* Though people see these things happening to them as well as others, they do not investigate the reasons for these and the methods of escaping from them. That is the great mystery, the wonder.

[Geetha Vahini, P 249]

Q 68. **What are the meanings of the terms *Prakriti* and *Para-prakriti*? What do they denote?**

A. *Prakriti consists of earth, water, fire, air, ether, mind, intellect and ego. **Beyond this Prakriti, however, there is a higher realm known as Para-prakriti. It is through Para-prakriti that man becomes Divine. Prakriti binds man to the world. Para-prakriti***

divinizes him. Prakriti is concrete, corporeal and intangible. The Immanent Atma, also is incorporeal and intangible. It is subsistent beyond mind, space and time.

[Summer Showers 1979, P 105]

Q 69. Can *Para-prakriti* be experienced? If so, how?

A. *It can be experienced intuitively and mystically by following the path of Yoga. Prakriti is a vessel; sadhana is the churning rod and jnana is the rope wound round the churning rod of sadhana. Pull the rope of jnana and churn Prakriti with the churning rod of sadhana, and the Divinity that is latent in Prakriti will show forth.*

[Summer Showers 1979, P 105]

Q 70. What is meant by the material and efficient cause of the creation?

A. *Earth, water, fire, ether, mind, intellect and ego are the primal substances out of which the universe has been created. Mud or clay is the basic substance out of which the pot is made and is, therefore, the material cause for the pot. The potter without whose sankalpa (thought) and involvement the pot cannot arise in its efficient cause. Similarly, **Prakriti is the material cause for the universe and Brahman is its efficient cause. It is the Will of Brahman that has created the myriad facets of this dynamic universe with its multifarious forms and innumerable objects.***

[Summer Showers 1979, P 110-111]

Q 71. 'The universe is the body of God', what does this term mean?

A. *One blood-stream circulates through all limbs; one Divine principle circulates through all the lands and peoples. **The universe is the body of God; He knows and feels***

every twitch, every pang, be it from a black man or
white, from land or sea or air or space.

[SSS Vol. 8, P 81]

Q 72. **What was the experience of Sage Kanada regarding creation of the universe?**

A. *Earlier nothing existed in the universe. In the beginning, the sun, the moon, the stars, the earth, the sky, etc., did not exist. There was only pitch darkness all around. The combination of atoms resulted in the formation of hard matter of a very high density. As a result, a lot of heat was generated. Then all of a sudden, the hard matter exploded with a big bang into pieces and spread all over. This was the basic cause of creation. This was the perception of Sage Kanada.*

[SSS Vol. 35, P 190]

Q 73. **What is the fundamental basis of the creation?**

A. **The combination of atoms resulted in the formation of hard matter of a high density. The hard matter exploded with a big bang...This was the cause of creation. Sound that emanated when the big bang took place is "Pranava". That is Omkara, the primordial sound.** *It is from the Pranava that the sun, the moon, the earth, the sky, etc., originated. The atom is the fundamental basis of the entire creation. Every human being is a combination of atoms. There is no matter without atoms.*

[SSS Vol. 35, P 190]

Q 74. **What other aspects of the creation were observed by Sage Kanada? Can we understand divinity through the mystery of the aspects of creation?**

A. Twenty thousand years ago...*Kanada recognised the*

principles of Hydrogen and Oxygen. The scientists observed that hydrogen represented the water principles, while oxygen represented the fire principle...Atom is not visible to the physical eye but it is present everywhere. The water we drink, the food we eat, the words we utter, the sound we hear, everything is permeated by atoms. Though man treads on atoms, eats atoms, drinks atoms, he is unable to understand their mystery. Atomic process is highly sacred. By conducting proper enquiry into this, one can understand divinity.

[SSS Vol. 35, P 191]

Q 75. How does the creation come into existence?

A.   *There is no basic difference between the human and the Divine. They are integrally related to each other like the object and the image. Take, for instance, a seed. There are two halves in it. It is only when the two halves are unbroken that the seed can sprout when planted in the soil. Likewise the tree of Creation comes into existence when the Paramatma (the Omni-will) and the Jivatma (the individual soul) come together. Man alone is endowed with this capacity to give a name and form to God and to realise It.*

[SSS Vol. 19, P 146]

Q 76. Which was the initial impulse (force)in the Prakriti at the time of its creation; how did the subsequent impulses or elements come into existence and how are they held within the initial impulse?

A.   *The whole Cosmos is made up of Pancha Bhoothas (five basic elements: Space, Air, Fire, Water and Earth). Their subtle qualities are represented by sound, touch, form, taste and smell. All these have emerged from Sath-Chith-Ananda (Being-Awareness-Bliss), the Primal Source.*

Akasa (Space or ether) provides the initial impulse. It is comparable to an infinite container. The other four elements – air, water, fire and earth – are contained in it. These elements vary in their subtlety. Water is subtler than earth and is more expansive and lighter than earth. Fire is subtler than water and air is subtler than fire and more pervasive. Akasa is subtler than air and is all-pervasive. Each of these elements is covered by a kosha (sheath). The mind, the intellect, the Will and the ego are enveloped by these sheaths.

[SSS Vol. 21, P 217-218]

Q 77. What are *Padartha* and *Parartha*?

A.   *Every material object 'Padartha' in the world is filled with the spirit of 'Parartha'. Though matter and spirit appear to be different, they are in reality one only. Matter is gross and derives its energy and sustenance from spirit. Hence matter and spirit are intertwined and inter-related. This 'Parartha' and 'Padartha', 'Adhara' and 'Adheya' have been described as 'Kshetrajna' and 'Kshetra'. This fact has been sustained by the aphorism in Brahmasutra 'Tat Jalan'. It means that the world which emanates from 'Tat' is sustained by it and merges in it.*

[Summer Showers 1993, P 41-42]

■ Divine Will

Q 78. What was the first effect of the Divine Will as it emerged?

A.   *When the Will emerged, Brahman became Easwara, God. And by that Will alone, God created the Cosmos or Jagath.*

[Sutra Vahini, P 57]

Q 79. Is Divine Will Conscious?

A.   *The Jagath is ever in movement; the Lord of the Cosmos (Jagadiswara) is the mover...Chara and Achara (the apparently moving and unmoving, active and inert) are both willed by the Divine (Daiva Sankalpa). That Will is Chetana, a Conscious Act. It is not A-chetana, a form of inertia. The truth that Daiva Sankalpa is the root of everything stands unshakable.*

[Sutra Vahini, P 59]

Q 80. What are the forms of the Divine Will?

A.   *Srishti, Sthithi and Laya (creation, sustenance and dissolution) are the three forms of the Divine Will.*

[SSS Vol. 4, P 193]

Q 81. How are the three forms of the Divine Will – *Srishti*, *Sthiti* and *Laya* comprehended?

A.   *You have to penetrate the inner meaning of Srishti by means of Karma Yoga; you have to grasp the significance of Sthithi by means of Bhakti Yoga and when you master the Jnana Yoga, you arrive at the experience of Laya, of manifoldness in the One.*

[SSS Vol. 4, P 193]

Q 82. How was the Universe created by God?

A.   *The entire Universe has been projected by the Divine Will. It is a consequence of Bhagavath Sankalpa, the Will of God, which is the Cause. No consequence can happen without a precedent Cause. The Cause has, however, two aspects, **the material cause (Upadana Karana) and the efficient cause (Nimitta Karana)**...God is the material Cause of Creation, of the Cosmos, the Universe. He is the substance, the*

basis, the Upadana Karana. He is the efficient cause,
too, the Nimitta Karana. He is both transcendental
and phenomenal, both Being and Becoming. He has been
manifesting Himself as all this. He has Willed to become
all this.

[Sutra Vahini, P 71-72]

Q 83. What is responsible for the rotation and revolution of the earth?

A.   *The earth rotates on its axis and revolves around the sun.*
Who is responsible for this phenomenon? Nobody can
explain this. As earth rotates on its axis, we have days
and nights. As it revolves around the sun, we have various
seasons, which help us to grow food required to sustain
our body. It is the Divine Will that is responsible for
all this. It is God's master plan for the benefit of the
world.

[SSS Vol. 35, P 195]

Q 84. What are the three modes of the Divine Primal Will and how does it work?

A.   *Maya is the Divine Will that inaugurated the*
manifestation of the cosmos (Ekoham, Bahusyam—
I am one; I will be many). Maya (apparent deluding
reality) inheres in every being and every activity of
that being; it has three aspects of achievement
through the three modes and moods of that Will—
the sathwic, the rajasic and the thamasic (the calm,
contented, equanimous mood; the potent, passionate
mood; the inert, slothful, sluggish mood)…The facets
of that Will are called Jnana sakthi, Iccha-sakthi
and Kriya-sakthi.

[SSS Vol. 14, P 159]

Q 85. **What single pursuit on the part of the *sadhaka* can make his life immortal?**

A. *You must strive to earn the great wealth of God's love. Only then will you enjoy the experience of unity.*

[SSS Vol. 32 Part 2, P 48]

■ Heavens, Lokas, Yugas

Yugas

Q 86. **How is *Kali Yuga* different from other *Yugas*?**

A. *Kali Yuga is often described as Kalaha Yuga (the age of discord) in which there will be misunderstanding and quarrels between husband and wife, father and son, preceptor and disciple...We find people indulging in cruel deeds, devoid of even a trace of compassion and behaving worse than birds and beasts...Man neglects swadharma (his rightful duty) and relies on transient body behaving like a beast. He does not make any effort to realise that in the changing body there is the changeless and eternal Atma (Spirit).*

[SSS Vol. 27, P 101]

Q 87. **How have the human beings differed in respect of physical aspects through the aeons (*yugas*)? And what kind of life did they lead?**

A. *In the **Kritha Yuga,** human beings used to live for hundreds of years. Moreover, their bodies were not as small as in this age. They were gigantic figures, with arms as long as six feet. In the **Kritha Yuga**, life remained in the body as long as the bones were intact. All other parts* of the body may disintegrate, but life remained in the skeleton.

In **Tretha Yuga**, the height of human beings was less. The longevity was also less. Life remained as long as muscles and flesh remained in the body.

In **Dwapara Yuga**, life remained as long as blood circulated in the body. As you may know, Bheeshma lay on a bed of arrows after he had been wounded in the Kurukshetra war. As long as blood remained in his body, he lived. His life lasted for 56 days in this bed of arrows.

In the present **Kali Yuga**, life lasts as long as there is food in the body. Without food man cannot survive.

In **Kritha** and **Tretha Yugas**, men had intimate relationship with God. Food was not so important. In **Dwapara Yuga**, the head became important. In **Krita** and **Treta Yugas**, Dharma was all-important. "**Dharma moolam idam jagath**" (The cosmos is based on Dharma). In **Dwapara Yuga**, the decline started and wealth became all important. "**Dhana moolam idam jagath**" (The world is founded in wealth). The war between Kauravas and Pandavas was over property rights.

In the **Kali Yuga**, neither Dharma nor Dhana (wealth) is as important as Daya (compassion). It is because of the absence of compassion that the world today is afflicted with so many troubles.

[SSS Vol. 29, P 303-304]

Q 88. What is meant by *Sukla-paksha* or the Bright Fortnight?

A.   *It is the half-month when the light of the moon increases day by day...The moon is the symbol of the mind of* man…*The bright half of the moon therefore signifies the progress of the mind spiritually, in Divine discipline. The full moon signifies the fullness of that achievement. The bright half is thus the period when spiritual progress is attained.*

[Geetha Vahini, P 189]

Q 89. And what is *Uttarayana?*

A. *Uttarayana is the period when no dot of cloud contaminates the vast dome (sky) and the Sun shines in all its Glory. This is the gross meaning, but there is a subtle one too. The heart is the inner sky. There, the Sun that shines is intelligence (buddhi). When the clouds of ignorance, the fog of egoism and the smoke of attachment hover in that inner sky, the Sun of Intelligence is hidden and things look murky and are mistaken.*

Uttarayana of the heart is when the inner sky is clear of all these, and when the Sun shines in full splendour… When a person passes away with this equipment of the effulgent Sun of wisdom in his clear heart, he can certainly escape re-birth.

[Geetha Vahini, P 190]

Q 90. What is *Dakshinayana*, and what is *Krishna-paksha?*

A. *Those who pass away in the other half of the year, the Dakshinayana, have the opposite destiny. Then the heart is beset with smoke and fog and cloud. The Sun is hidden and His effulgence has no splendour. And in the dark half of the month the moon wanes, symbolizing the waning of Godward thoughts. The new moon night is enveloped in complete darkness. All spiritual impulses suffer defeat. The thick smoke of Ajnana lies heavily on the mind. This* *is the meaning of the expression Krishna-paksha. Those who die at such an inauspicious time reap an inauspicious result.*

[Geetha Vahini, P 190]

Since the Uttarayana Marga is lit by the holy splendour of Jnana it is praised as the Sukla Marga or the White Path. The Dakshinayana Marga is dark, filled with tamas and Ajnana; so it is called the Dark Path or the Krishna Marga.

Those who discard the body and journey during Uttarayana move along the White Path and reach the stage of Liberation or Moksha, which is devoid of delusion, which is the seat and source of Brahmananda, from which there is no return to the world of name and Form. Those who leave the body during Dakshinayana and move along the Dark path, have to bear again the physical encasement called Deha, subject to birth and death.

[Geetha Vahini, P 190]

Q 91. **Do *Uttarayana* and *Dakshinayana* hold some other significance also?**

A. *Uttarayana is not so much a period of time; it is a state of mind. Those who discard the body with the Glory of Self-Knowledge move along Uttarayana Marga and those who die in ignorance of their Atmic reality move along the Pithryana, or Dakshinayana or the Dark Path.*

[Geetha Vahini, P 190]

***

2
MAN AND THE UNIVERSE

■ Man, Humanity

Q 92. What is the difference in character between *Manavas* and *Danavas*?

A. *Manavas are full of Prema or Love. Their hearts are springs of mercy. They are endowed with True speech. Peace is the characteristic of the mind of man...Desirous of acquiring these hidden treasures, if one drives and turns mental activities inward, then he becomes full of Prema or Love. Only those who have so filled themselves with love and who live in the light of that Love can be called Manavas (men). Those devoid of Prema or Love are Danavas, monsters, sub-humans.*

[Prema Vahini, P 77-78]

Q 93. In how how many categories human beings are classified?

A. *Based on their mental predisposition, human beings may be classified under four categories as follows: Deva-manava (Godly man), Manava-manava (The*

*human man), Manava-danava (Demonic man) and
Manava-pashu (The animal man).*

[SSS Vol. 26, P 222]

**Q 94. What are the traits of a *Deva-manava* (Godly
person)?**

A.   *About Deva-manava it is said: "Brahma Nishtha
Rato Devah". It means 'He is a Godly person who
enjoys communication with Brahman and is ever
established in Brahman, dedicating all actions to
God, looking upon all things as His manifestations
and joyfully experiencing all forms as reflections of
the Divine.*

[SSS Vol. 26, P 222]

**Q 95. What are the traits of a *Manava-manava* (the
human man)?**

A.   *It is said: "Sathya Dharma Ratho Marthyah" – 'He
alone is a man who takes delight in truth and
righteousness having faith in the spiritual
injunctions', and "Sathyam Vada Dharman Chara"
– 'speak the truth and practise righteousness'.* He
conducts his life according to the twin principles of truth
and righteousness. He considers duty and responsibility
as more important than rights and is endowed with
kindness, compassion, generosity, charity and forbearance.

[SSS Vol. 26, P 222]

Q 96. Who is a *Manava-danava* (demonic man)?

A.   **"*Madya-pana ratho danavah*" – "*He takes pleasure
in drinking intoxicating liquors. He spends his time
in such Tamasic activities as eating, drinking,
sleeping etc.*** *He is concerned solely with his own selfish
interests and enjoyments and never with the happiness*

of others. Kindness and compassion are alien to him. Not even a trace of discrimination and dispassion could be found in him. It is his nature to deride, abuse and hurt others. The very sight of a great and holy man will arouse in him feelings of jealousy and hatred. A person whose mind is filled with such evil thoughts and feelings is called a "demonic man".

[SSS Vol. 26, P 223]

Q 97. **And what about a** *Manava-pashu* **(the animal man)?**

A. *This type of man wastes his life in seeking only sensual pleasures from birth to death. He is worse than beasts.*

[SSS Vol. 26, P 223]

Q 98. **What does human stand for?**

A. *The word human is full of significance:*
'H' stands for **'high human values'.**
'U' stands for **'understanding of human sanctity'.**
'M' stands for being **'mindful of one's duty'.**
'A' stands for **'Anandam'.**
'N' stands for the **'Name of God'.**

[SSS Vol. 27, P 72]

Q 99. **What are the different facets of the personality of man?**

A. *All that you wish to acquire is within you. You are God. That is why I often tell you that you are not one person, but you are three persons. The one you think you are, the one others think you are and the one you really are. That is why we say that in the aspect of your body, in the aspect of your mind and in the aspect of your Atma, you have three different facets of your personality.*

[Summer Showers 1977, P 24]

Q 100. What is the true strength of man?

A.   *The true strength which one can have is the strength which comes from God and righteousness. One should have the two wheels of God and Dharma on a chariot for the journey of life in the world. We should experience these two, God and Dharma, as ideals in our life.*

[Summer Showers 1977, P 156]

Q 101. What is the purpose of human birth?

A.   **Resolve that the purpose of human birth is to reach the Lord through worship. All experience, all knowledge, all actions are towards that end.**

[Prasanthi V, P 32]

Q 102. How is one to attain the fulfilment of human life?

A.   *You can achieve anything with sense control. Today man has become weak because he lacks sense control. How can he expect to experience Divinity? Today, man is developing undue attachment. All the worldly relations are like passing clouds. They come and go, but morality comes and grows. Do your duty sincerely. Duty is God; work is worship.*

You have to recognise these three – first is that which once comes, then never goes; second, once goes, then never comes back; the third, neither comes nor goes. The first is jnana (wisdom), the second is Ajnana (ignorance) and the third is the principle of the Atma. The Atma is steady and eternal; it never changes. *The knowledge of the Atma originates from the heart. First of all, control your mind. Mind is like a mad monkey. The nature of a mind is determined by the nature of its thoughts. So, have pure thoughts and thence pure mind.*

[SSS Vol. 34, P 131-132]

Q 103. What is the primary duty of man?

A.   *The primary duty of man is to understand his innate nature and experience his divinity.*
[Sanathana Sarathi – Feb. 2003, P 47]

Q 104. How is one to foster humanness?

A.   *It is essential for man to foster humanity by practising human values. Human values are extremely precious. It is only when you practise human values will your life be redeemed.*

[Sanathana Sarathi – Feb. 2003, P 47]

Q 105. The body is called 'deha'. What does it mean?

A.   *The body is known as 'deha', which means 'that which is consumed by fire.' It is burnt on the pyre when life departs and consumed by the flames of desire when life persists. It burns on the fire of anxiety and fear, even when alive! There is another word, sareera, meaning 'that which withers away', which also means body.*

[SSS Vol. 14, P 249]

Q 106. What is the duty of man towards the body?

A.   *The body is a house given to you for rent. The owner is God. Live there as long as He wills, thanking Him and paying him the rent of faith and devotion.*

[SSS Vol. 6, P 145]

Q 107. What is it that grants special status to man?

A.   *Man is the crown jewel of all living beings that exist in this infinite cosmos. He is at the very apex of God's creation. Human life is most worthy, valuable and sublime. What is it that lends such great value to man? Is it the body or the form that is responsible for this? No, not at all. The body is ephemeral, consisting of foul smelling flesh. It is only a rented house for the Atma...But man who is unable to understand his humanness, is not capable of recognising the divinity within him.* **God is present in all beings as their indwelling spirit (Sarva Bhutantaratma).**

[SS – Aug. 2000, P 249]
[Summer Course Discourse on 16-5-2000]

Q 108. Which is the sanctified gift of God to man?

A.   *The true abode of God is the body, which God Himself has designed and created. The body is a living temple, a talking temple, a moving temple. It has been created by the pure Will of God. Hence, it is a sanctified gift of God. You must guard this sacred gift with utmost care. You must use the body in the right manner for the realisation of the Supreme Self.*

[Sanathana Sarathi – June 2000, P 181]
[Summer Course Discourse on 21-5-2000]

Q 109. Is humanness perishable?

A.   *The body, mind and intellect alone do not make a man? They are the vestures put on by man. The body is inert. The mind is negative. Man considers himself to be a combination of inert body and negative mind.* **But 'man' is eternal and changeless. 'Man' lives eternally at all times and in all states of existence. Whatever you hear, talk, think and act is the reflection of the inner being. ...Humanness is permanent and has no birth or death. This body is bound to change but the 'man' never dies. You take man to be the embodied being who is subject to birth and death. The permanent man lies in humanness and is imperishable.**

[SSS Vol. 33, P 321]

Q 110. **Where does the conscious effort by man for his transformation lead ?**

A. *From untruth to truth. It is a spiritual journey towards divinity. Where is such divinity? It is in every human being as the embodiment of truth.*

[SSS Vol. 35, P 318]

Q 111. **Where does divinity exist in man?**

A. *The divinity, which fills the entire cosmos, exists in man as 'Hridaya'. The Vedas name this 'Hridaya' (spiritual heart) as 'Atma'.*

[SS – Aug. 2000, P 249]
[Summer Course Discourse-II on 16-5-2000]

■ Life

Q 112. **What is the real nature of the life of man?**

A. *To a superficial observer, the life of man appears as a routine of eating and drinking, toiling and sleeping. But, verily life has a much greater meaning, a much deeper significance.* **Life is a sacrifice, a yajna. Each little act is an offering to the Lord.**

There are three lessons that can be learnt from life. These are:

(1) Impermance of created things (2) The role of man as a servant, and (3) God as the master.

This creation is the wherewithal of Puja; Man is the worshipper, and God, the worshipped. The game of life is played with these. Whatever is done from sunrise to sunset must be consecrated, as if it is the worship of the Lord.

Ceaseless efforts must be made to do the deeds that are pure and unsullied.

[Prema Vahini, P 9-11]

Q 113. Is life transient or permanent?

A.   *All life is so transient that it can disappear in one moment like a bubble. All that you see in this world is transient and not true.* What all we see during the daytime vanishes when we are asleep. All that we see in our dream during the sleep vanishes when we are awake. What we see and experience during the night is like a night dream. In the daydream what we see in the night dream is not present. Similarly, in the night dream, what we see during the day is not present. **You are present in the night dream; you are present in the daydream. You are present in both dreams, but the daydream is not present in the night dream and the night dream is not present in the day dream. You alone are present in both places and you should recognize this.**

[Summer Showers 1977, P 21]

Q 114. Are those leading family life eligible to follow the path of God?

A.   *In this context if you come to the conclusion that those who are in the family, living as a part thereof, do not have the right to follow the path of Brahman, it is not the right idea. The family life is like a chariot. Husband and wife are the horses. Dharma is the charioteer. Family or the bundle of worldly desires is the path and moksha is the goal. Thus the horses namely the husband and wife can lead the chariot of life to moksha if they follow the path of dharma. It is not right and it is a weakness to think that only yogis, jnanis* and rishis are entitled to moksha. The destination is available for everyone.

[Summer Showers 1974, P 64-65]

Q 115. What goal man should desire?

A. *The Vedas teach that man should have only one desire, namely, for Moksha (liberation). The human body, so filled with skills, is a gift from God to each of you. It has to be used as a raft, on which you can cross this never-calm sea of Samsara that lies between birth and death, bondage and liberation. Awaken to this primal duty even when your physical and mental faculties are keen; awake even while your power of discrimination is sharp. Do not postpone the launching of the raft, for it may become unserviceable soon. It may be burdened with illness, so that all your attention will have to be spent on its upkeep.*

[SSS Vol. 8, P 116]

Q 116. How should this goal of life be pursued?

A. *Ride safe on the raging waters of samsara (worldly life); be a witness, do not crave for the fruit of action, leave the consequences of all acts to God's Will. He is the doer; you are but the instrument. Pursue nobler ends; have grander ideals; sensory pleasures are trinkets, trivialities. The sages have discovered the disciplines that will keep you unaffected by the defeat or victory, loss or gain. Learn them, practise them and establish yourself in unruffled peace. Think of the incompatible joy that will surge within you, when you approach the shore of liberation.*

[SSS Vol. 8, P 116]

Q 117. How will the life be sanctified?

A.   *You have to be careful right from the beginning not to*
        commit sin. God is the eternal witness. You have to make
        every effort to earn divine grace and perform all actions
        as an offering to God. Only then will your life be sanctified.
        [SS – Jan. 2003, P 19 (Discourse on 19-11-Nov. 2003)]

Q 118. What has this life on the material plane to offer to
man and how is any one to live in the midst of
worldly activity?

A.   *Do not attach yourself too much to this body or to*
        the things that bring comfort to it.

        You earn three friends in this life.

        The first : The riches you accumulate, which refuse
        to come with you when you move out of this life.

        The second : Kith and kin, they accompany your
        body up to the burial ground or cremation-ghat.

        The third : The merit and demerit you have earned,
        they accompany you to the last.

        Sleep inside the mosquito curtain; the insects can
        do no harm; so also, do not allow the insects of
        kama, krodha, etc., to harm you. Get inside the
        curtain of sadhana while you are in the world. Be
        in the world, but do not let the world into you.
        [SSS Vol. 4, P 245]

■ Death

Q 119. What happens to the elements constituting the
body on death?

A.   *The human body is composed of cells, which draw strength*
        and life from food; food draws its nutrient value from the

soil. Soil – food – man—when the cycle is completed, man
returns to the soil. The soil is bhootha akasha—the food
grown out of the soil becomes consciousness, the chitta
akasha—and the chitta merges into the Atmic
consciousness or chidaakasha.

[SSS Vol. 14, P 229]

Q 120. How to take out the fear of death from the mind?

A. *Death stalks its prey everywhere, at all times with
relentless determination.* It pursues its victims into
hospitals, hill-stations, theatres, aeroplanes, submarines,
in fact, no one can escape it or take refuge from its grasp.
*God alone is the giver of life, the guardian of life
and the goal of life – God who is the Indweller in
this physical frame.* Be aware of Him all through life
and offer all your activity – breathing, talking, walking,
earning and spending – to Him, for it was by Him and
through Him that you were able to do all these things.

[SSS Vol. 8, P 187]

Q 121. What is the reality of life?

A. *You go to bed on a certain date and day; you awake
to find that the date and the day have changed! You
have grown a day older; death has come a step
nearer. Much water has flowed under the bridge.
Similarly, when you go into sleep (death), great
changes happen; you awake to a new date and a
new day, with old tendencies and traits still
affecting the new embodiment. Life is one long
ordeal; know this even when things seem to be quite
exhilarating. Any moment the road may turn into a
morass, the sky may darken, fortune may turn away.*

[SSS Vol. 8, P 189]

Q 122. Why is the thought of Yama – the Lord of death, so frightening?

A.   *Yama or the God of death is described as dragging his victims to his abode by means of the rope or Pasa. Well. He has no rope factory there, for supplying him with the rope he needs. You manufacture the rope yourself and have it ready round your neck; he has only to take hold of the rope and pull you along! It is a three-stranded rope, the strands being Ahamkara, vishaya-vasana and Kama, Egoism, Sense-attachment and Desires.*

[SSS Vol. 4, P 48]

Q 123. Does God of death come riding on a buffalo to take its victim? Why is there so much fear of death and how do we get over it?

A.   *Death is pictured by some as a terror-striking God who rides a monster-buffalo, and pounces on you with a noose. No, the noose is of your making. He does not pounce. He gives advance notice of his arrival to take you – notice in the form of intimations like grey hair, falling teeth, failing vision, decline of hearing, wrinkling of the skin etc. He does not ride any beast. He is only another name for Time. It is Time that creeps steadily towards you and shears the cord of life. So, utilise the capacity for Karma with which you are endowed to liberate yourself from the clutches of Time. The law of Karma holds out hope for you; as the Karma, so the consequences. Do not bind yourself further by seeking the fruit of Karma; offer the Karma at the Feet of God. Let it glorify Him. Let it further His splendour. Be unconcerned with the success or failure of the*

endeavour. Then, Death can have no noose to bind
you with. Death will come as a liberator, not a jailor.

[SSS. Vol. 6, P 55]

Q 124. How to end the cycle of birth and death?

A. *Man does not realise that the end of this cycle of birth and*
death is in his own hands. The tree came from the seed
and the seed from the tree and so on, from the beginning
of time. Yes, you may not know which came first, tree or
seed; but you can easily put an end to the cycle, by frying
the seed (desires). It won't sprout again.

[SSS Vol. 4, P 28]

Q 125. What *sadhana* is prescribed to end this cycle of birth and death?

A. *The very first lesson I gave when I declared My*
identity at Uravakonda was: "Manas bhajare Guru-
charanam, Dustara bhava sagara taranam." That
is to say, first know that you are in bhava-sagara,
this cycle of birth and death. Then resolve on 'taranam',
crossing it. Then fix on a Guru or the Name and Form
of God, which appeals to you; lastly, dwell on His
Glory, do bhajan, but do it with all your mind.

[SSS Vol. 4, P 11]

Q 126. What is the greatest truth that one must always remember?

A. *You must live in the constant thought of God as well as*
of another fact, death. The body is the car in which you
are riding to death. You may meet death any moment.
Remember death. Remember that time is running out
every moment; then, you will not be tempted to waste
time in idle talk or vain pursuits.

[SSS Vol. 3, P 192]

Q 127. How is one to avoid the fear of death?

A.   *Death is considered as something to be afraid of; as*
something that should not be spoken about in happy
circumstances! But, death is neither good nor bad. You
have no choice in the matter. You can't get it sooner if
you welcome it; nor can you avoid it if you condemn it as
bad. It is a consummation, which is inevitable; from the
moment of birth, the march to the cremation ground has
started. Some reach the place quicker than others, some
go by a round about route and arrive late. That is the
only difference, between man and man. But, yet, man
walks about as if death is but a distant calamity.

[SSS Vol. 3, P 174]

Q 128. What is the purpose of the time allotted to man
between life and death?

A.   *When man is about to leave the world, as leave he*
must, he is surrounded by his wife and children who
lament loudly, asking, "What is to happen to us
when you leave?" But the poor fellow is confronted
by a more urgent, a more personal problem: "What
is to happen to me?" And he has no more time to
discover the answer or to prepare for something good
to happen. In fact, if he had tried he could have
known the reality and gone with a smile, instead of
with a groan or a whine. Men are born with a
helpless lamenting cry; they should die with a smile
of happy joy. That is the purpose of the years between.

[SSS Vol. 6, P 146]

Q 129. Should one think of death?

A.   *Do not contemplate on death; it is just an incident in*
life. Contemplate on God, who is the master of all life.

[SSS Vol. 8, P 187]

Q 130. How does one enshrine *Kala* (the Lord of Time) in his heart to overcome the fear of death?

A. *The easiest means is chanting the name of the Lord. Community singing by an assemblage of devotees is to be preferred. This is known as Sankirtan (singing together glories of the Lord).*

[SSS Vol. 21, P 238]

■ Bondage

Q 131. What is the cause of bondage of man and how will he be liberated?

A. **No one can liberate you, for no one has bound you. You hold on to the nettle of worldly pleasure and you weep in pain.** *The kite is pursued by crows so long as it carries the fish in its beak and turns in the sky trying to dodge the crows who seek to snatch the fish. Tired at last, it drops the fish. That moment it is free. So give up the attachment to the senses, then, grief and worry can harass you no more.*

[SSS Vol. 5, P 64]

Q 132. What binds man to earth?

A. **There are three reasons for man to be born. One is sin, the second is unfulfilled desire or some experience, the third is lack of knowledge or ignorance.** *The feeling that he has not fulfilled a desire and his wanting to take birth again to fulfil such desire is one main reason. Man does bad things and commits a sin. He has to be reborn to experience the consequences. Ignorance makes you seek a rebirth under these circumstances. These three constitute the basis for our rebirth.*

[Summer Showers 1974, P 243]

Q 133. What are the seven types of ropes that bind man?

A.   *Man is bound by seven types of ropes. They are (1) Deham (body) (2) Kamam (desire) (3) Krodham (anger) (4) Ahamkaram (ego) (5) Karma (fate) (6) Ajnana (ignorance) (7) Aviveka or Avidya (lack of discrimination).*
                                                    [SSS Vol. 26, P 129]

Q 134. What is it that man has to get over for getting liberated?

A.   *Ignorance is the cause of ego, which breeds raga and dwesha (attachment and hatred). For getting liberation one has to get rid of the ego, ignorance and attachment. The ego gives rise to raga (desire), which plunges man in karma, which, in turn, causes janma (birth).*
                                                    [SSS Vol. 26, P 129]

■ Suffering

Q 135. How to escape sorrow?

A.   *Joy and peace do not inhere in the external objects; they are in you yourself.* But people in their foolishness search for those outside themselves in a world from which, today or tomorrow, they are bound to depart. *So long as one has worldly desires in view, he cannot escape sorrow.*
                                                    [Prema V, P 30]

Q 136. How will the suffering of man cease?

A.   *The removal of the recurring sorrow of Samsara can be affected only by the attainment of Brahman. It cannot be earned by means of desires. It can come only by experiencing the Atma.*
                                                    [Prasanthi V, P 64]

Q 137. Why is there no contentment in happiness?

A.   *You strain so much just to fill your small belly. You earn money in every possible way for this. Does this bring contentment to you? No. There can be no contentment in this. On this basis it is said: "Na Sukhat Labhyate Sukham" (you cannot derive happiness out of happiness). Happiness is the fructification of difficulties. If you want to have a taste of happiness and peace, then difficulties are necessary in life.*

   [SS – Sept. 2001, P 273 (Discourse on 22-8-2001)]

Q 138. What does *Klesha* mean?

A.   *Klesha is affliction in the mind or a mental complex.*

   [SSS Vol. 26, P 220]

Q 139. What are the 5 types of *Kleshas*?

A.   *They are: Avidya-klesha (Ignorance complex), Abhinivesha-klesha (Attachment complex), Astita-klesha (Vacillation complex), Lobha-klesha (Greed complex) and Dwesha-klesha (Hate complex). All these complexes are nothing but mental aberrations, which are injurious to man himself.*

   [SSS Vol. 26, P 220]

Q 140. Why does suffering invade man and how does one alleviate it?

A.   *You are bound to face the consequences of your actions. So, do good and you will certainly reap good results. Do not get disheartened if there is no immediate reward. Wait for a while, you will certainly be rewarded. Your suffering is nothing but the consequence of bad deeds in the past. Prayer alone can alleviate your suffering to some extent.*

   [SSS Vol. 33, P 163]

Q 141. How many types of ills does man suffer from and how are they caused and how is one to preserve good health?

A.   *Spiritual health is preserved and promoted by attention
to three gunas: Sathwa, Rajas and Tamas. Health is
preserved and promoted by attention to three humours:
Vatha (wind), Pittha (bile), and Kapha (phlegm). Tri-
dosha has to be avoided, that is to say, the three humours
must not get vitiated or unbalanced. A healthy body is
the best container for a healthy mind; illness makes the
mind agitated and anxious. The material and the spiritual
are the two pans in the balance; they have to be attended
to, in equal measure, at least until a certain stage of
progress is attained in spiritual development.*

[SSS Vol. 7, P 238]

Q 142. What are Rudras and how many are they in numbers?

A.   *Rudras are negative or destructive principles. They are
11 in numbers.*

[SSS Vol. 27, P 74]

Q 143. What are the functions of these *Rudras*?

A.   *The Rudras in association with Buddhi (the intellect) enter
the minds of the people and cause them various types of
difficulties and worries. Of these difficulties, three types
are predominant in the world. They are Adhibhoutika,
Adhyatmika and Adhi-daivika.*

[SSS Vol.27, P 74]

Q 144. What do *Adhibhoutika, Adhyatmika* and *Adhi-daivika* mean?

A.   *Adhibhoutika: refers to difficulties caused by the 5
elements (ether, air, fire, water and earth) and the 5 sheaths
(relating to food, life, mind, awareness and bliss –
Annamaya, Pranamaya, Manomaya, Vijnanamaya and
the Anandamaya sheaths). These sufferings are caused*

by human beings, animals, insects or other creatures to men.

Adhyatmika: *refers to the sufferings caused by Vata (wind), Pitta (bile) and Kapha (phlegm).*

Adhi-daivika: *refers to the calamities caused by man, by floods and droughts, storms and earthquakes and similar natural disasters.*

Of all the sufferings endured by human beings, those coming under these three categories are most prominent. All other calamities are encompassed by these three. For all these sufferings 11 Rudras are the cause. The whole world is permeated by the Rudras. Only Adhi-daivika has an element of security.

[SSS Vol.27, P 74]

Q 145. Do *Rudras* induce fear in the minds of the men?

A. *Whatever emanates from Rudras is fraught with fear. The name itself testifies to the dangerous power implicit in it. Rudram means that which induces fear.*

[SSS Vol.27, P 74]

Q 146. How can the effect of *Rudras* be contained?

A. *The Maha Shivaratri festival has been designed to subdue these 11 Rudras. This means that by the control of the senses the Rudras can be controlled. Indriya Nigraha (control of the senses) is not that easy...When the entire Shivaratri night is dedicated to the chanting of the Lord's name, one's mind, speech and senses all get centred on God. This is itself a form of sense control. At least on one day in a year all our thoughts and words should be centred on God. When this is done, people can realise the Supreme as described in the terms Satyam, Shivam, Sundaram.*

[SSS Vol. 27, P 75]

Q 147. Is there any example of this kind of total devotion to the Divine Will that leads to Moksha?

A. *Gargi devoted her entire life to the fulfilment of the Divine Will. People generally think that Narada loves to incite quarrel. He once asked Gargi, "Respected lady, what is your life's ambition?" "My only desire is to attain Divinity", she replied. "It is impossible", replied Narada. "Why?" asked Gargi. Narada replied, "Moksha and the attainment of Divinity are not ordained for unmarried women." Then Gargi said, "The only difference is in the body and the mind, and not in the Atma." Narada said, "That is impossible, for I have surrendered myself entirely to God already. Such being the case, do I have no possibility of attaining Moksha?" As this dispute was going on, Janaka intervened and said, "Mother, you can get married. What are you going to lose?" She thought for a while and considered the contents of all the Upanishads and Sastras. She then said, "All right then, I shall have a one-day marriage." Even Narada was perplexed as to what this one-day marriage meant. Gargi then said, "A marriage is a marriage, be it for a day or a hundred years. So, I shall have a one-day marriage; who is ready to accept this?" One of the sages named Sringi agreed. "Tadeva Lagnam, Sudinam Tadeva, Tarabalam Chandrabalam Tadeva, Vidyabalam Daivabalam Tadeva "-as the mantra was being chanted, and the sage tied the marital knot, Gargi immediately broke it and promptly attained liberation. Thus, Gargi attained her goal without transgressing her vows or any of the Sastric injunctions. Janaka said, "Gargi, your entire life is devoted to the fulfilment of the Divine Will. Then, how can Moksha elude you? You are destined for Moksha. You are indeed a great scholar. Today I shall get myself crowned by your hands."* Gargi *then explained the Dharma of the householder in the court of Janaka and said that such worldly relationships were temporary and not permanent.*

[SSS Vol. 32, Part II, P 81-82]

3
MAYA

■ Maya

Q 148. How is one to control ignorance or *Maya*?

A. *"As fog before the Sun, Ignorance melts away before* **Knowledge.***" Knowledge is acquired by uninterrupted inquiry. One should constantly be engaged in Inquiry on the nature of Brahman, the reality of 'I', the transformations that occur to the individual at birth and at death and such matters.* **As you remove the husk that covers rice, so too the Ignorance that adheres to the mind has to be removed by the frequent application of the abrasive Atmic Inquiry. It is only when full knowledge is won that one can get liberated, or in other words, attain Moksha.**

[Janana Vahini, P 1]

Q 149. Which is the basic truth on which *Maya* projects its play?

A. *The basic Truth upon which Maya (divine illusion) projects its kaleidoscope is described by seers as 'Sath-Chith-Ananda' (Being-Awareness-Bliss*

Absolute). This does not mean that Brahman has three attributes, namely: It exists beyond time and space; It knows and can be known; It is the source and acme of Bliss. They are not three distinct characteristics; they indicate the One, of which the three can be grasped by experience – not by words. Brahman cannot be defined by these three basic qualities. It cannot be described as performing any specific activity, for It is ever motionless. Nor can It be explained in terms of relationship with other entities for It is One, without a second.

[SSS Vol. 14, P 158]

Q 150. What is the truth of God, the objective world and man? What is their mutual relationship?

A. *Maya is the Will that causes all three. It is a clear flawless mirror. When the satwic nature is reflected in that mirror, God results; when the rajasic nature is reflected, the jeeva (individualised Self) results. It is ever anxious to grow, to grab, to survive and to be secure. When tamasic nature is reflected, matter (the objective world) is the result.*

All three are Paramatma, but they derive their reality as Its reflections. When undergoing reflections, they attain different forms and combinations and characteristics. The One becomes many; every one of the many is Real only because of the One in it. Maya too is a component of the One; by the emphasis on that component, the One transformed Itself into the many.

[SSS Vol. 14, P 159-160]

Q 151. So *Maya* is the mirror that reflects the One as three – God, Prakriti and Jeeva. What distorts the surface of this mirror, which changes the character of the reflection?

A.   *The mirror of Maya reflects within itself all that is before it. The convexity or concavity of the mirror, or the covering of dust that might have settled on it, will certainly blur the reflected image, but it cannot distort the objects themselves. Easwara (God), Prakrithi and Jeeva (the Almighty God, objective world and individualised self), all three are images of Paramatma (Supreme Soul) reflected in the mirror of Maya and warped by the gunas (qualities) that tarnish the surface of the mirror. It is the mirror that pictures the One as many. But the One is ever One.*

[SSS Vol. 14, P 160]

Q 152. Is it possible to discover the beginning or the end of *Maya*? Can one know when *Maya* will end?

A.   *None can discover the beginning of Maya. Neither the personalised God (Easwara), nor the individual self (soul), nor the objective world can ever succeed in discovering the beginning of the Maya, which brought them into existence and started the chain of 'act-consequence-act.' Nevertheless, one can succeed in discovering when Maya will end! When will it end? When the objective world is ignored, set aside, denied or discovered to be immanent in the Divine, the jeeva (individualized being) is no more. When the jeeva is no more, the Easwara (Cosmic Being or personalised God) is also superfluous and disappears. And when the Easwara has faded out, the Brahman (Absolute Reality) alone Is. When a personalised God, a personality separate from the rest, called jeeva, and the mental creation of that jeeva, called prakrithi (the objective world), are non-existent in the developed consciousness of man, Maya, the progenitor of all three, cannot persist.*

[SSS Vol. 14, P 161]

Q 153. What is the main obstacle on the path and how to get past it?

A. *For Maya-constituted beings, there are two Maya-gates; the appetite for sex and the appetite of the tongue. These two have to be conquered by every man; so long as they persist, they cause sorrow. All worldly desires are comprehended by these two; so, only those who have mastered these two can be said to have successfully waded through the world. These are the causes of all sins; and, sin is the nature on which Maya thrives. Really speaking, this Maya-prapancha or world has to serve only the purpose of just sustaining the body. Those aspiring for Liberation have to subdue the senses.*

[Prema V, P 97]

■ Gunas

Q 154. How do the three qualities of *Tamas, Rajas* and *Satwa* affect man?

A. *Tamas is ignorance. Its removal makes discrimination possible and allows Rajas to surface. Rajas binds by alluring the mind into a continuous chain of desires. When Rajas is also surpassed Satwa reigns and brings enlightenment.*

[Summer Showers 1991, P 20]

Q 155. The Upanishads say that God has no attributes or *gunas* at all and, therefore, is present everywhere? How is this explained?

A. *God has no attributes or gunas at all and, therefore, is able to be present everywhere. If space or akasha, which*

*has only one quality, namely sound, is present everywhere,
then God who has no quality or no attribute at all, can be
present everywhere.*

[Summer Showers 1977, P 74]

**Q 156. If God is omnipresent and is above *gunas*, how is
it that the *gunas* are not in Him but He is in the
gunas?**

A.   *The moment we say that He is everywhere, it follows that
He is present in the gunas also. **He is in the gunas but
gunas are not in Him.***

[Summer Showers 1977, P 74]

**Q 157. How is it possible that He (God) is in the *gunas*
but the *gunas* are not in Him?**

A.   *It is like this. The mud is present in the pot but the pot is
not present in the mud. The pot is created. The pot has a
form. The form has been given in an artificial way.
However, if God is in His formless aspect, it is not possible
for people to easily recognise the formless aspect. So, he
takes a human form, and comes to the world. In this way,
He wants to demonstrate to the people the ideal path they
should follow.*

[Summer Showers 1977, P 74]

**Q 158. If it is through performance of *karmas* that *tamasic*
and *rajasic gunas* are transcended and *satwic* is
gained, how would one know which *karmas*
promote *satwa*?**

A.   *Many are content with their dealings with the objective,
tamasic world. Their ideal is only to amass material wealth
and satisfy material needs. Examine yourselves and
discover at what level you are by analysing your desires
and activities. In this way you can yourself sublimate your*

thoughts and urges. It is through activity (karma) that gunas are given up or gained. Activity (karma) causes birth and death and fills up the years of one's life. It supports good and evil, joy and grief. **It is the Atma that illumines all, but man is in the dark about its existence. All things are cognised because the Atma is behind the cognition. It is the Universal Witness. You must establish yourself in the position of a witness.**

[SSS Vol. 14, P 167]

■ Ignorance (Ajnana, Delusion)

Q 159. What is *Bhraanthi* (ignorance, delusion)?

A. *Bhraanthi refers to the deluded state of mind in which a person mistakes, for instance, a rope for a snake and vice versa. This is regarding unreal as real and the real as unreal, the temporary as permanent and the permanent as temporary.*

[Summer Showers 1990, P 83]

Q 160. What is *Pramaadam?*

A. *Such delusions (the Bhraanthi) invariably lead to accidents or dangerous situations – Pramaadam (Pramaad). If you hold a snake thinking it is a rope, you are certainly in for trouble. Man today regards the body real, not knowing that it is as unreal as a water bubble, which may burst at any time.*

[Summer Showers 1990, P 83]

Q 161. How to become delusion-free for attaining *Moksha*?

A. *The difficulty is all about purifying the mental behaviour, which is spoiled by the delusions of the world. Delusion-*

*less behaviour is necessarily pure. It is without any trace
of defect and doubt. Therefore, if men first control and
conquer the external delusion, as much as possible, the
internal tendencies will easily move in the direction of
Atmananda.* **Yoga and Tapas is only another name
for the path of control and conquest of these external
tendencies and delusions. When man subdues
delusion of all types, the journey ends in Moksha.**

[Prema Vahini, P 93]

Q 162. What is the sign of animal nature in man?

A.   *The manner of living in which deha-bhraanthi (delusion
regarding the body) is prevalent is Pashutva (animal
existence).*

[SSS Vol. 25, P 166]

**Q 163. How to get over the identification of the Self with
the body?**

A.   **The craving for objective pleasure which is based
on body-consciousness has to be removed by dhyana
and tapas.**

[Geetha Vahini, P 223]

Q 164. How can *Ajnana* or false knowledge be expelled?

A.   **Ajnana can be destroyed only when one knows the
Atma Principle (Knowledge of the Self).**

[Sutra Vahini, P 4]

**Q 165. What happens when Ajnana or the false
knowledge disappears?**

A.   *When the false knowledge disappears, the sorrow produced
by one's involvement in the ups and downs of samsara or
the world of change, also gets destroyed.*

[Sutra Vahini, P 4]

■ Body Consciousness, Attachment

Q 166. How best can we get rid of the body consciousness?

A. *The body should be considered as an instrument. Only then, gradually the identification with the body can be got rid of. Man is perpetually enhancing the attachments relating to the body. Because of these attachments and infatuations, the Ego principle gets inflated. As the ego sense grows, the spiritual aspiration becomes weaker.*

[SSS Vol. 25, P 205]

Q 167. Are mere purity of heart and steady faith enough to find God?

A. *There should not be an iota of 'identification of the Self with the body' (Deha-bhraanti).*

[Geetha Vahini, P 222]

Q 168. What is *Vyamoha*?

A. *Vyamoha is the dust that settles upon the glass of the chimney of the lantern and dims the light. The attachment to sensual objects and to the pleasure they give is the soot that sticks to the inside of the chimney; that too dims the light. Clean the chimney by Namasmarana every day and the flame will shine for you and others. Also have good activities and good companionship. That will help very much in spiritual sadhana.*

[SSS Vol. 1, P 87-88]

169. Why is it necessary that intellect must be cleansed of all deluding attachments for gaining progress on the Godward journey?

A. *The term virtue is only another name for the 'intelligence' that follows the promptings of the Atma, the Self, which is our Reality. Only he who has such virtue can win the awareness of the Atma, the Truth. A man of Virtue has a place in the region of the liberated.*

[Sutra Vahini, P 21]

Q 170. The body is called a chariot. What does it mean?

A.   *The deha (body) is a vehicle that even gods aspire to possess. You know that gods seek to come into human form so that they could utilise the intelligence, discrimination, detachment, etc., that the human body alone is capable of exercising, to realise the Ultimate Reality, which when known makes everything else known. The body is the ratha (the chariot) of the individual or the jeevi, the dehi, the resident, the master. It is the castle from which one can fight against the foes of attachment and egoism; it is the boat by which one can cross the sea of change and chance.*

[SSS. Vol. 6, P 145]

Q 171. What is the duty of man towards the body?

A.   *Body is known as sareera, meaning ' that which withers away'. While living, it is afflicted by wants and wishes that rob it of peace. When dead, it becomes dust. Starting its career as a ball of dust, it soon appears as a tender charming baby and an active child; it transforms itself into a straight, strong, attractive youth and is reduced later to the pathetic shape of old age. Hence, it is named sareera; and 'person' who lives in it, is known as sareeri. It is our duty to keep the body in good trim.*

[SSS Vol. 14, P 250]

The body is a house given to you on rent. The owner is God. Live there as long as He wills, thanking Him and paying Him the rent of faith and devotion.

[SSS. Vol. 6, P 148]

Q 172. What is true wisdom?

A. *Purity of thought, word and deed is true wisdom. Your body, mind and actions must be pure.*

[SSS Vol. 35, P 345]

Q 173. How can we experience the Truth?

A. *'Sathyannasti Paro Dharma' (there is no greater Dharma than adherence to Truth). The fundamental Truth is God. Likewise, Love is God. So, live in love.* **True love is related to the heart, not to the body. Divine Love is "heart to heart, not body to body." Body is like water bubble, mind is like a mad monkey. Don't follow the body, don't follow the mind. Follow the conscience. Only then can you experience the Truth.**

[SSS Vol. 32 Part-2, P 127-128]

Q 174. What is the first step in the long road of *sadhana*?

A. *All Avatars teach, as the first step in the long road of sadhana, the giving up of attachment. In the Trethaayuga, the Yoga Vasishtha taught the same rule. In the Dwaparayuga, Krishna taught Arjuna to give up vishaya-vasana (attachment to the objective world).*

[SSS Vol. 7, P 142]

Q 175. Should not one aspire for worldly achievements?

A. *Do not aspire for wealth, position and power. God will give you whatever you deserve. Develop love for God. That is the highest sadhana.*

[SSS Vol. 32 Part 2, P139]

Q 176. What is to be discarded and what is to be earned?

A. *What has to be discarded is the Deha, this physical case; what has to be earned is Parabrahmam, the Universal Absolute. The Deha has your Reality,* *your Swarupam, the un-discardable, indestructible, undying Sathyam and Nithyam. That Reality is the entity called Atma, or what is the same thing, Paramatma. Since you are that, you cannot cast it off. Casting off the body is like shifting from a house occupied for some years, and birth is your entry into a new one. Both these are physical acts, not affecting the Atma. Those who are toiling in the falsehood of Deha-tathwa cannot have the Atma revealed to them.*

[Geetha Vahini, P 163]

4
HUMAN TRAITS AND VALUES

■ Nature, Characteristics And Traits

Q 177. **What are the characteristics of the objective world and how should man lead his worldly life in the midst of transient nature of all objects and relations?**

A. *Man is prone to three kinds of mistaken ideas. One is to consider what does not belong to him as his own. Another is to regard persons who do not belong to him as his own. The third is to regard the evanescent as the eternal.* **Man considers the body as his real self...This is the first mistake.**

Secondly in worldly affairs man is misled by the belief that he is the owner of the properties of various kinds – houses, vehicles, etc. You build a house and call it yours. You sell it and it is no longer yours. It is yours as long as you use it. Forgetting that these possessions are temporary, you develop attachments for them. Nothing is yours. How can those things which belong to the body be yours? All these are caused by Maya (delusion), the sense of possessiveness and the aberrations of the mind. All of them are passing clouds. Before marriage, no one can say who is the husband and who is the wife. Before birth, no one can say who is the mother and who is the child...

Thirdly, all these are related to the changing body. It is wrong to regard the body as permanent. While discharging your duties, you have to keep the Supreme always in mind. The worldly life has to be led, with spiritual relation as the goal. The ideal must be based on the recognition that nothing belongs to you. As God is the basis of everything, you have to develop faith in God.

[SSS Vol. 23, P 74-76]

Q 178. How have evil traits come into our system?

A.   *Man has passed through many animal lives before he has come to earth in human form. Strains of animal nature such as cruelty, anger, greed and hatred still persist in him. Man is many animals in one. He must cast off these traits from his composition.*

[SSS Vol. 13, P 243]

Q 179. How are we to put out these awful flames?

A.   *Well, Sanathana Dharma (the ancient spiritual code) has certain extinguishers tested by experience and guaranteed by sages. They are Sathya, Dharma, Shanthi and Prema. Saturate your heart with these and you are rendered fire proof.*

[SSS Vol. 5, P 51]

Q 180. Do the evil qualities affect the life span of a man?

A.   *Desire, anger and hatred are not human qualities; they are bestial tendencies. Man is supposed to live for a hundred years but his life span is cut short by these evil qualities. When these evil traits are totally subdued, man can enjoy a long and happy life. He should constantly remind himself that he is a human being and not a beast. In this manner, he can keep a check over his bestial tendencies.*

[SSS Vol. 35, P 244]

Q 181. How are we to avoid the forces of evil?

A. *Human being does not merely mean the physical body consisting of five senses. True human being is one who makes proper use of the five senses without giving scope to evil quantities like lust, anger, greed, infatuation, pride and jealousy. One should not fall prey to them.* **Foster the noble qualities that originate from the heart. Wherefrom do the evil qualities like lust, greed etc., arise? They arise out of the food you consume. So, keep control over your food habits. Take only sathwic food. Then you will get only sacred thoughts. God has gifted you with many noble qualities. They are innate in you. But you are neglecting them.** *Reading, writing, taking up jobs, earning money, building mansions, etc., originate from the head and are related to the Pravritti marga (outward path). These are all acquired by you with some effort. But you do not need to make any special effort to acquire the noble qualities like compassion, love, forbearance, etc., as they are latent in you.* **Head is the source of bad thoughts and heart of noble thoughts.**

[SSS Vol. 33, P 114]

Q 182. What is the sign of animal nature in man?

A. *It is the delusion regarding the body. It is identification of the body with the Self (the "I"). This is the mark of the animal nature in man.*

[SSS Vol. 25, P 167]

Q 183. **In the olden days animals were sacrificed during** *Yajnas* **and** *Yagas* **(sacrificial rites). Is killing of animals justified even as a religious act?**

A. *Some may try to argue animals were sacrificed. But they are not correct. Only a few ignorant Pandits and misguided elders used to indulge in animal sacrifice. But those who recognised the inner meaning of this ritual used to give prime importance to the sacrifice of beastly qualities in man while performing such religious ceremonies. The sum and substance of the various religious practices is to destroy animality in man.*

[SSS Vol. 25, P 168]

■ Human Values

Q 184. **Which is the foremost among the human values?**

A. *In my view, among the human values, Truth is primary. There is no greater Dharma than Truth. Truth is the life-breath of man. When truth goes, life goes. Holding fast to Truth (Sathya), you should make Righteousness, Peace, Love and Non-Violence (Dharma, Shanti, Prema and Ahimsa) the guideposts for your life.*

[SSS Vol. 19, P 53]

Q 185. **How will the human body acquire value?**

A. *From head to foot, man is filled with anger today. He has become like an animal. Even an animal is better than man. An animal has a reason and season. Today, man has no reason and no season. If you behave in this manner, how can you call yourself a human? To call yourself a human, first and foremost show humanness in action. Just because you have a human body, you cannot call yourself a human.*

> *The human body will have value only when you cultivate human values, namely, Sathya (truth), Dharma (righteousness), Santhi (peace), Prema (love) and Ahimsa (non-violence).*
>
> [SSS Vol. 34, P 141]

■ Sathya (Truth)

Q 186. Of all the qualities, which one is the greatest?

A. *The whole world is permeated with Truth. Truth is all-pervasive. Truth can neither be hidden nor changed.* **Trikala Badhyam Sathyam** *(Truth is that which remains the same in the past, present and future).* **Sathyannasthi Paro Dharma** *(there is no Dharma greater than adherence to Truth). Truth is the noblest of all vitues.*

> **"The creation emerges from Truth**
> **and merges into Truth,**
> **Is there a place where Truth does not exist?**
> **Visualise such pure and unsullied Truth."**
>
> **(Telgu Poem)**
>
> [SSS Vol.34, P 248]

Q 187. What could be the definition of the ultimate Sathya which is the pole star guiding our journey of life?

A. *Truth is something that is not modified by time or space or guna (attribute). It must be the same forever, unaffected and unchanged; then alone is it truth. It should not be proved false by some subsequent event or knowledge.*

> [SSS Vol. 3, P 210]

Q 188. Does truth protect and promote the welfare of its adherents?

A.   *Have faith that truth will save you in the long run; stick to it regardless of what might befall.*

[SSS Vol. 1, P 43]

Q 189. Truth is sometimes bitter. How should the bitter truth be uttered?

A.   *The power of truth surpasses the power of the atom bomb and the hydrogen bomb. There is no greater weapon than truth. But you should know how truth should be uttered.* **Anudevgakaram Vakyam Sathyam Priya-hitam Cha Yat (speak truth in such a way that it is pleasing and does not annoy others). You should not utter harsh words.**

[SS – Aug. 2000, P 236 (Dasara Discourse V, on 18-10-99)]

Q 190. What care should be taken in speaking the truth in daily life? Should one avoid speaking an unpleasant truth so as not to hurt others?

A.   *The Shastras say,* **"Sathyam bruyaath, Priyam bruyaath, na bruyaath Sathyam apriyam"** *- Speak the truth, but speak pleasantly. Simply because a statement will be welcome to the hearer, don't speak it out to win his approval; if speaking truth will cause grief or pain, keep silent. That is the vow of truth in ordinary daily life. Both unpleasant truth and pleasant untruth have to be avoided.*

[SSS Vol. 7, P 233]

Q 191. How are truth and love related to each other?

A.   *The experience of truth alone can foster love. Truth is the current and love is the bulb it has to illumine. Through truth you can experience love; through love you can visualise truth.*

[SSS Vol. 8, P 77]

◼ Dharma

Q 192. What is Dharma?

A. *God created this Jagat on His own initiative and He ordained various codes for its upkeep and smooth running. There are rules of correct conduct for every being. These form Dharma.*

[Geetha Vahini, P 65]

Q 193. When is it necessary to follow the code of *Dharma*?

A. *It is only when there is Prakriti or world around you that you require a code of dharma to follow.*

[Summer Showers 1974, P 64]

Q 194. What is the real *dharma* of a devotee?

A. *The Gita declares that though a person may have deep devotion to the Lord, **he cannot be called a Bhakta if he lives without regard to the commands of the Lord**, that is, the dharma laid down in the shastras, which embody His orders, revealed to saints and seers.*

[Geetha Vahini, P 226]

Q 195. Is Dharma the same for all?

A. ***Every single thing in the world has its own special Dharma or uniqueness of duty, and nature. Take the five elements, the components of Prapancha. Of these, water has movement and cold as its Dharma; combustion and light are the Dharma of fire. Each of the five has its unique Dharma.*** *Humanity for man, animality for animals, these guard them from decline. How can fire be fire, if it has no power of combustion and light? It must manifest the Dharma to be itself.*

[Geetha Vahini, P 66]

Q 196. Is Dharma imposed from outside?

A.   *Dharma is not imported from somewhere outside, nor can it be removed. It is your own genuine nature, your uniqueness.*

[Geetha Vahini, P 66]

Q 197. How to observe Dharma?

A.   *By being 'yourself'. If a thing breaks loose from its Dharma and behaves as the whim dictates, then it is doing A-dharma.*

[Geetha Vahini, P 67]

Q 198. Can Dharma be destroyed?

A.   *The Sahaj-dharma of man was overpowered in course of time and it declined. So it was said to have been 'destroyed', though it is something that cannot be destroyed.*

[Geetha Vahini, P 67]

Q 199. How is Dharma resurrected if it declines?

A.   *"When decline descends on the Dharma which has been laid down, I incarnate as the Naraakara from the state of Niraakara, in order to revive it and protect it and save the good from fear", said Krishna.*

[Geetha Vahini, P 65]

Q 200. What is the meaning of 'establishment of Dharma'?

A.   *Establishment of Dharma is only weeding the field. In this Kaliyuga, Dharma has become a mere matter of words. Dharma is not just the magical manipulation of words. This must be clearly understood.* **What has to be spoken is Truth, what has to be acted is Dharma.**

        "Satyam Vada, Dharmam Chara" – has been the clarion call of the Upanishads, the repositories of the Indian culture.

[Geetha Vahini, P 67]

Q 201. Is any special effort needed for throwing *A-dharma* out of action?

A.   *No special exertion is needed for putting it out of action. When Dharma is practised, A-dharma will decline by itself. The valuable crop of Sahaj-dharma has to be cultivated with care and attention.*

[Geetha Vahini, P 68]

Q 202. What is *Dharma-sthaapana*?

A.   *Dharma, since it is associated with Sathya, is indestructible. To make Dharma that has become hidden, visible once again, that is 'Dharma-sthaapana'.*

[Geetha Vahini, P 69]

Q 203. What is the principle of Dharma?

A.   *Burning is the dharma of fire; coolness is the dharma of ice. Fire is no fire without burning; ice is no ice without coolness. Similarly, the dharma of man lies in performing actions with the body and following the commands of the heart. Every act performed with thought, word and deed in harmony is an act of Dharma. Thus, a dharmic life is a divine life.*

[Summer Showers 1996, P 17]

Q 204. Is Dharma the same for all people?

A.   *Dharma is of various kinds: Dharma of a householder, a celibate, a recluse and a renunciate. But the dharma of the heart is the supreme dharma. The dharma of the heart is verily the dharma of life as well. The unity of thought, word and deed has to be achieved at any cost. **The synthesis of humanity in Divinity and Divinity in humanity leads to Totality (Poornatva). It is said: "Poornamadah Poornamidam, Poornaat Poornam Udachyate". This totality is present fully in human beings.***

[Summer Showers 1996, P 17]

Q 205. **Which Dharma is related to the awareness of the "I"?**

A.   *The Dharma concerning the awareness of the "I" – Prajna Dharma. It is the Dharma which pervades equally the body, the mind, the Will and the Antahkaranas (inner instruments).* **It has been defined as "Constant integrated Awareness".** *It expresses itself as "I" and* **shines forth in its fullness. It manifests itself throughout the world.**

[SSS Vol. 25, P 211]

Q 206. **What is meant by the Vedic declaration: "Sathyannasthi Paro Dharma"?**

A.   *Anger, hatred and jealousy are demonic qualities. These qualities should be annihilated and human values should be cultivated. Sathya and Dharma are chief human values. That is why the Vedas proclaim:* **"Sathyannasti Paro Dharma"** *(there is no Dharma greater than truth) and Sathyam Vada, Dharmam Chara (speak the truth and adhere to righteousness). You should follow this command of the Vedas.*

[Sanathana Sarathi Aug. 2000, P 236]
[Dasara Discourse on 18-10-95]

Q 207. **Is it true that Dharma stood on 4 legs in Kritayuga, on 3 legs in Treta, on 2 legs in Dwapara and now in Kaliyuga it has only one leg?**

A.   *Some Pandits explain the Gita verse, which declares that God incarnates when Dharma (virtue) declines in this way. They also say in the same breath that God incarnated as Rama in the Treta Age, and as Krishna in the Dwapara Age, with the avowed purpose of restoring Dharma! According to them, when Krishna incarnated Dharma*

had 2 legs, but when His human career was closed, Dharma
lost one more leg and had to survive in agony, having only
one solitary leg! Can such absurdity be ever believed? No.
The incarnations of God have always fulfilled their tasks.
Dharma has always been restored, in full.

[SSS Vol. 9, P 72]

■ Santhi

Q 208. What is the meaning of *Prasanthi*?

A.   *It is as the backbone to each individual, and for the sadhaka
it is as the very breath. Many feel that they have peace
when some worldly desire that was vexing them is
satisfied! But, that is not Real Peace; it is but a temporary
short-lived interval between one worry and another.*

*Pra-santhi means the absence of desire and anger, greed
and hatred. Prasanthi means success in the elimination
of these qualities, grouped under Kama and Krodha...This
Santhi is the innate nature of man. Santhi is the force,
which comes to the aid of those who try to develop Viveka,
Vairagya, Vichakshana, discrimination, renunciation and
keenness of intellect. It is but a phase of the Atma itself.
No blemish can mar it. Santhi must be manifested in
feeling, word, posture and deed. Then Santhi becomes
Prasanthi, the Real Santhi.*

[Prasanthi V, P 1-2]

Q 209. Where does *santhi* lead?

A.   *Santhi is a shoreless ocean; it is the Light that illumines
the world. Having it is having all. It confers knowledge
of both this world and that. It leads to understanding of
Brahman, the very fulfilment of human life. **Pure love***

can emanate only from a heart immersed in santhi,
for it is an atmosphere that pervades and purifies.

[Prasanthi V, P 6]

Q 210. How is *Prasanthi* achieved?

A.   *Genuine santhi is won by the control of the senses only.*
Then it can be called Prasanthi. Calming the mental
agitation that surges like waves, levelling the swirls and
whirls of likes and dislikes, love and hate, sorrow and joy,
hope and despair, santhi is earned and maintained without
disturbance. Knowledge of Atma destroys illusion, doubt
and sorrow. Hence, Atma-jnana confers the steadiest
santhi and with it Holiness and Happiness.

[Prasanthi V, P 4]

Q 211. What is the cause of *A-santhi* in man?

A.   *Ahamkara causes A-santhi. Man creates and develops in*
himself an abounding variety of selfish habits and attitudes
and so, he causes great discontent for himself. The impulse
for all this comes from the greed for accumulating
authority, domination and power, the greed for things
which can never be eternal and full. The effulgence of Atma
is obscured by Ahamkara. Therefore, when Ahamkara is
destroyed, all troubles end, all discontents vanish and Bliss
is attained.

[Prema V, P 23]

Q 212. What is the secret of attaining the supreme state of
equanimity?

A.   *One may master all forms of knowledge,*
One may vanquish one's adversaries in debate,
One may fight with valour and courage over vast
kingdoms,
One may offer cows and gold as an act of charity,

One may count the countless stars in the sky,
One may tell the names of different living creatures on
the earth,
One may be an expert in the eight limbed Yoga,
One may reach even the moon,
But, is there anyone who can control the body, mind and
senses?

Turn the vision inward and achieve the supreme state of equanimity of the mind.

[SS – Feb. 2003, P 45 (Discourse on 1-1-2003)]

Q 213. How is Santhi related to our actions (*karmas*)?

A.   *Asanthi comes only when fruit of action is desired. If the fruit is discarded and joy is derived from the very karma itself, then one gets Prasanthi.*

[Prasanthi V, P 57]

Q 214. How does *Santhi* become complete and the stage designated as Yoga (oneness) is reached?

A.   *The mind is the Kurukshetra where good and bad, rights and wrong contest for supremacy. Iron has to be beaten flat by iron alone. So too, the inferior low mind has to be shaped better by the superior mind itself.*

What Sadhakas have to do is this: "First Viveka is to be developed: that is to say, the capacity to distinguish the eternal from the transitory and to decide which is worthy. Second, a sincere attempt has to be made to experience what is so chosen as worthy and true. Third, that attempt should not be given up whatever comes in the way. These three can be called the genuine tapas. From this tapas alone is born real santhi and joy."

[Prasanthi V, P 8]

Q 215. What helps in the cultivation of *Santhi*?

A.   *Neither Santhi, nor the Bhakthi that gives it, can be got through another; it has to be created and developed, each one for himself. Still one should have also the Grace of the Lord; which is fundamental. With His grace one can experience even unattainable Ananda. Do not doubt the usefulness of sadhana. It can never be fruitless for anyone. Hold firm to that conviction.*

[Prasanthi V, P 10]

Q 216. Is there any relation between *Santhi* and *Jnana*?

A.   ***Through Santhi alone can Bhakthi expand and Jnana strike root.*** *Jnana, born of Santhi is the one and only means of living the full life or the life that knows no death, because the enquiry 'Who am I' clears the path for Realisation. Santhi embellishes every act; it softens the hardest core of man; it takes you to the footstool of the Lord and wins for you the vision of God.*

[Prasanthi V, P 11]

Q 217. What is the main hurdle in the way of attaining *Santhi*?

A.   ***To earn Santhi, its inveterate enemy anger must be laid low.*** *Anger is the harvest of the tantalizing mind; it enslaves man and fogs his understanding. Understanding becomes easy when you are full of Bhakthi; and your devotion is deep-rooted. The form of Bhakthi called Santha-bhakthi is the best path for attaining eternal, everlasting Ananda.*

[Prasanthi V, P 11]

Q 218. How is one to control anger?

A.   *As soon as you get angry, you should immediately leave that place and go out into the open and quietly* *walk a furlong. Then your anger will disappear. An easier method is to stand before a mirror and look into your own angry face. You will dislike your own face and look upon it with disgust or aversion.*

[SSS Vol. 25, P 176]

Q 219. How to check bad temper?

A. *Learn to speak little and to speak softly. That will reduce the chances of getting angry. Search out the good in others and evil in yourself.*

[SSS Vol. 4, P 184]

■ Prema (Love)

Q 220. How is *Prema* cultivated?

A. *It can be done through two methods:*

Consider the faults of others, however big, to be insignificant and negligible. Consider always your own faults, however insignificant and negligible to be big and feel sad and repentant. By these means, you avoid developing bigger faults and defects and you acquire the qualities of brotherliness and forbearance.

Whatever you do with yourself or with others, do it remembering that God is omnipresent. He sees and hears and knows everything. Whatever you speak, remember that God hears every word; discriminate between the true and the false and speak only the truth; whatever you do, discriminate between the right and the wrong and do only the right. Endeavour every moment to be aware of the omnipotence of God.

[Prema V, P 29]

Q 221. When does man qualify to receive Love of God?

A.   *Divinity is embodied in all creatures and the fundamental truth should be exemplified in practice by man. He must extend the field of his love until it encompasses the entire creation. It is only then that he will deserve to be worthy of God's Love.*

[SS 1979, P 107]

Q 222. How is love of God generated in the heart?

A.   *Only after all the evil thoughts in you are out, it is filled with pure love. Undesirable qualities such as hatred, negative criticism, the habit of blaming others and finding fault with them have to be given up...**It is only when the heart is purged of all vices that it can overflow with Love. The plant of Prema can be nurtured only in the field of pure, immaculate heart.***

[SS 1979, P 106]

Q 223. Is this Love Principle present in all?

A.   *The Love is present in all. It is the form of the Divine. Because the Divine is present in all, whomever you love, you are loving the Divine...It is the Atmic Principle that is always with you at all times.*

[SSS Vol. 25, P 233, 234]

Q 224. Which is the purest form of Love?

A.   *Love is one but is expressed in many ways. It is the same Love Principle assuming different forms and exhibiting in different relationships. Experiences are varied, but the goal is one. The forms of love keep changing according to one's relationships. The love between husband and wife is termed moha (infatuation). The love between a mother and child is called vaatsalya (maternal love). The love between kith and kin is called anuraag (attachment),*

The love towards God is termed as Bhakthi (devotion). This is Pure Love.

[SSS Vol. 25, P 234]

Q 225. What is the principle of love?

A.   The whole world is permeated with love. In this world, there is nobody without love. There are however, two types of love in this world – one is worldly, while the other is spiritual or divine. **Divine love is totally selfless. It is love for love's sake; there is no other consideration. But worldly love is tainted with selfishness. Love is selflessness; self is lovelessness. Love is God; live in Love.** Divine love is Nirguna, Niranjana, Sanathana, Nikethana, Nitya, Shuddha, Buddha, Mukta, Nirmala Swarupi (attributeless, pure, final abode, eternal, unsullied, enlightened, free and embodiment of sacredness). Such divine love is all-pervasive.

[SSS Vol. 34, P 193-194]

Q 226. How to cement the bond of love with God?

A.   *While struggling in the spiritual field, you should take Parameswara Himself as your protector... Easwara has His eyes fixed on the Jivi. He has in His hand the string of the kite which is man...the string is the bond of love and grace. You must do and earn auspicious Samskaras in order that bond of Love and Grace may exist and get tightened.*

[Prema V, P 49]

Q 227. How will the love to God sprout in the heart?

A.   *If you have no spring of Love in you, dig into your heart with external instruments like puja, stotras, etc., and it will start flowing.*

[SSS Vol. 5, P 70]

Q 228. What is the best way to love God?

A.   *The best way to love God is to love all and serve all.* Your acts of service should be suffused with the spirit of love. Without the positive aspect of love, all service you render becomes negative in nature.

[SS – Feb. 2003, P 51 (Discourse on 1-1-2003)]

Q 229. At what stage in life do the desires crop up and how should love for God be inculcated to banish desires?

A.   *At the time of birth, man has no desires. But as he grows up, he acquires many desires, which lead to bondage. Man should fill his mind with love for God.* He should forget all his worries and contemplate on Him. This is possible only through practice. Reading, writing, walking, talking, all these are learnt only through practice. Likewise, even in the path of spirituality, practice is very essential. Start practising love. That is the correct spiritual practice.

[SSS Vol. 33, P 308]

Q 230. Can we count on the Love of Sai?

A.   *"Cultivate nearness to Me in the heart and you will be rewarded. This is a great chance. This chance will not come your way again, beware of that. If you cannot, if you do not cross the sea of grief now taking hold of this chance, when again can you get such a chance?* Really you are the fortunate few out of millions and millions of people who have come (at Prasanthi Nilayam), though no one specially invited you to be present here. That is what I call the mark of destiny.

[SSS Vol. 4, P 183]

■ Ahimsa (Non-Violence)

Q 231. What is the essence of non-violence doctrine?

A. *The meaning of Ahimsa is that either in thought, word or deed, you should not cause harm to anybody.*

[SS 1977, P 235]

Q 232. How are Ahimsa and Sathya related to each other?

A. *Ahimsa is another phase of Sathya. When you are aware of the kinship, the oneness in God, the fundamental Atmic unity, no one will knowingly cause pain or distress to another.*

[SSS Vol. 7, P 234]

Q 233. How to get established in Ahimsa?

A. *Ahimsa does not mean merely not injuring a living being. You should not cause hurt even by word, look or a gesture. Tolerance, fortitude, equanimity – these help you to be steady in Ahimsa.*

[SSS Vol. 14, P 298]

Q 234. Do acts of physical damage or injury necessitated for saving one's own or other's life, also fall in the category of Himsa or violence?

A. *If a dacoit cuts off your hand, it is Himsa (violence); if the doctor amputates it, he saves life and so it is Ahimsa.*

[SSS Vol. 3, P 211]

Q 235. How do we view in the context of the doctrine of non-violence, the battle of Kurukshetra fought with the approval of the Lord Himself, resulting in the loss of millions of human lives?

A. *Krishna wanted the peace and yet he encouraged the big battle in which forty lakhs of people were killed. Krishna* *gave an appropriate answer to this. He said: "Arjuna! Let us take the case of a cancerous growth on the body, and this cancerous growth gives pain to the whole human body, although the growth itself is confined to a localised area. In that cancer you have so many small germs present in the wound. When the doctor performs an operation on this cancerous growth, he will not think that he is going to kill a million germs and therefore stop the operation. He will surely kill the disease causing germs and save the patient… In this battle or the operation, forty lakhs of disease causing germs will be killed for the benefit of the world. Is this bad or is this good for the good of the world?"*

[Summer Roses on the Blue Mountains 1976, P 34-35]

Q 236. How should we view in the context of non-violence the burning down of Lanka by Hanuman?

A.   *Hanuman burnt down the whole of Lanka, which was as prosperous as heaven itself, but we still regard him as a sacred person. The reason for this is that what Hanuman burnt down was the sin itself…he caused injury to the demons and the Rakshasas. In order to remove the demoniac qualities in us we have the complete right and power.*

[Summer Roses on the Blue Mountains 1976, P 37]

■ Seva

Q 237. Does Seva win the grace of God?

A.   *Seva is the highest of path of devotion, which wins the grace of God. It promotes mental purity, diminishes egoism and enables one to experience the unity of mankind.*

[SSS Vol. 19, P 203]

Q 238. What should be the faith of a devotee engaged in Seva?

A. *Seva activity must be free from all attachment to the self and based on firm faith in the Divine resident in every being. Seva has to be considered as worshipping the form that God has given you the chance to worship.*

[SSS Vol. 19, P 201]

Q 239. What is *Narayan Seva*?

A. *When a hungry Nara (man) is served a hearty meal, what is being done is Narayan Seva, for, Nara (man) is only "a form and name" projected by Maya (human ignorance) on Narayana (God).*

[SSS Vol. 19, P 201]

Q 240. What is the essence of real *Seva*?

A. *All men, all living beings, are cells in the Body of God. Their origin, continued existence and progress, are all in God, by God, for God. The individual is a unit in this unity. Faith in the truth is the basic qualification the Sevak must acquire.*

[SSS Vol. 19, P 201]

Q 241. How does *Seva sadhana* lead to realisation?

A. *Among the nine steps of devotional progress, the fourth and the fifth highlight the attitude of seva. It is referred to as **Pada-sevanam and Dasyam** (serving the Feet of the Lord; acts offered at the Feet of the Lord; feeling oneself as the servant of the Lord). Service is basically activity arising out of the yearning to win the Grace of God. Through seva alone can man attain mastery of the senses and through such mastery of the passions and predilections, man can attain Divinity itself.*

[SSS Vol. 9, P 60]

Q 242. What is the basic instrument of a *sevak*?

A.   *The spirit of sacrifice is the basic equipment of the sevak. Without the inspiration of the sense of sacrifice, your seva will be hypocrisy, a hollow ritual.*

[SSS Vol. 9, P 61]

Q 243. How can one attain the Grace of God through *Seva*?

A.   *God is Love and can be won only through the cultivation and exercise of Love. He cannot be trapped by any trick. He yields Grace only when His commands are followed – commands to love all, to serve all.*

[SSS Vol. 9, P 62]

■ Conduct

Q 244. What code of conduct should be followed in life?

A.   *My life is My Message, as I often declare. I have been re-emphasising the Upanishadic exhortation, "Speak Truth; act righteously; revere the mother as Divine, revere the father as Divine, revere the preceptor as Divine."*

[SSS Vol. 11, P 283]

Q 245. What kind of thoughts and conduct bring one close to God?

A.   *"See no evil, see only what is good;*
        Hear no evil, hear only what is good;
        Think no evil, think only what is good;
        Talk no evil, talk only what is good;
        Do no evil, do only what is good;
        THIS IS THE WAY TO GOD."

[Summer Showers 1991, P 61]

Q 246. What should be our ideal behaviour towards others who harm us?

A.   *Forgive those who have harmed you and criticized you. Have faith that whatever happens is for your own good. If someone hurls abuses on you, do not retaliate. Enquire within yourself whether he has criticised the body or the Atma. If he has criticized the body, indirectly he has done a favour to you because the body is nothing but a heap of flesh, blood and bones. On the other hand, if he has criticised the Atma, it amounts to criticising his own self, because the same Atma exists in both of you. One should cultivate this kind of forgiveness and broad-mindedness.*

[SSS Vol. 33, P 164]

Q 247. How is one to conduct oneself for accomplishing the journey of life?

A.   *There are three lines along which endeavour has to be directed.*

1. Spiritual exercise and discipline.

2. The cultivation of detachment and

3.The development of confidence in one's Self.

Without these three, life is a wearisome and wasteful journey through the sands.

[SSS Vol. 8, P 241-242]

Q 248. What should man avoid doing in life?

A.   *Do not sow fear in others' hearts; do not inflict pain on others; do not promote anxiety or grief. If you take pleasure in the pain of others, you only scotch the divinity in you.*

[SSS Vol. 5, P 161]

Q 249. The golden rule of conduct?

A.   *Live up to the moto:* **HELP EVER, HURT NEVER.**

[SSS Vol. 26, P 22]

Q 250. What principle of gratitude should be followed?

A.   *I must condemn the absence of gratitude. Ingratitude is the hallmark of wild beasts, not of man. Man today is all humility, all obedience until his wish is fulfilled. Once it is satisfied, he tries even to ruin the person who helped him realise it. This does not befit man. He must be conscious of benefits derived and eager to repay the debt.*

[SSS Vol. 5, P 161]

Q 251. What is sacred about the quality of *Kshama* (forbearance)?

A.   ***Forbearance is truth,***
forbearance is righteousness,
forbearance is non-violence,
forbearance is the teaching of the Vedas,
forbearance confers happiness and heavenly bliss.

[SSS Vol. 33, P 164]

Q 252. What is the significance of "*Kritaghnaghnaya Namah*"?

A.   *Do not be a Kritaghna (ungrateful). Ingratitude is utter cruelty.* **There is a mantra in Suryanamaskara, "Kritaghnaghnaya Namah" (salutations to the sun who punishes the ungrateful). It emphasises the fact that any help received should be reciprocated to the extent possible. Hurting someone who has helped you will result in losing your eyesight.** *It is the radiance of the sun that is reflected in your eyesight. All that you see is through the reflection of the sun's radiance. The sun withdraws its radiance from the eyes of those persons who commit the sin of ingratitude.*

[SSS Vol. 35, P 138]

■ Human Effort

Q 253. How are human effort and Divine grace inter-related and how do they help the seeker achieve oneness with the Divinity?

A.   *Even if you sow seeds, you cannot expect the crop if there is no rain. Even when there is rain, you cannot expect the crop if you do not sow seeds. Likewise, both human effort and Divine grace are needed to achieve success in any endeavour. Though butter is present in the milk, one cannot see it, unless one makes it into curd and churns it. Likewise, though Divinity is all-pervasive, one cannot experience it unless one makes appropriate efforts. Human effort can be compared to the process of churning. Once the butter is separated from the curd by churning, it will not get mixed with it again. If you partake of the churned butter, your entire being experiences it. Likewise, you will become one with Divinity once you experience it.*

[SSS Vol. 32 Part-2, P 189]

Q 254. Why do man's efforts not always yield the desired results?

A.   *Man's activities yield the desired result only when the Kala, Karma, Karana and Kartavya (time, action, cause and duty) are in harmony with each other. Hence, man should make sincere efforts and wait for the right time. When the action fructifies, he should utilise it in accordance with the time and circumstances.*

[SS – Feb. 2003, P 48   (discourse on 1-1-2003)]

Q 255. What are the four *Purusharthas* prescribed for the fulfilment of human life?

A. *The four Purusharthas are Dharma, Artha, Kama and Moksha. For Kama and Artha (Kama is desire, lust; Artha is wealth) we have Dharma and Moksha on either side. We should regroup the four into two groups. If we take these four and treat them as four separate entities, we will not get any benefit out of our actions. If we can combine Dharma with Artha and Kama with Moksha, then we realise that we will have to acquire wealth for the sake of Dharma and we must turn all our desires to acquire Moksha. Wealth (artha) and Desire (kama) are things which are impermanent and such things cannot give happiness to man. When these impermanent things — Artha (wealth) and Kama (desire), are combined with permanent things like Dharma and Moksha, they also acquire such sacredness and become somewhat true and permanent. Our purpose should be to combine the impermanent things with the permanent things of life.*

[Summer Showers 1974, P 63]

Q 256. The scriptures say that it is necessary to direct the mind towards *Nivrithi* and not toward *Pravrithi*. What is the *Nivrithi Marga*?

A. *What arises from the head is 'Pravrithi' (materialistic) and what springs from the heart is 'Nivrithi' (spiritual). Human life is interwoven with 'Pravrithi' and 'Nivrithi'. The six vices—desire, anger, greed, pride, infatuation, and jealousy lead us on 'Pravrithi' marga whereas Love, Truth, Patience, Sacrifice and Compassion lead us on 'Nivrithi' marga.*

[Summer Showers 1993, P 64]

■ Character, Morality

Q 257. How is character an essential part of religion?

A. *Religion is three-fourths character. No person can claim to be religious if he merely observes the sacraments and rules, and fails to be upright and compassionate. Character alone can harden one to the blows of pain and pleasure.*

[SSS Vol. 9, P 59]

Q 258. Which is the most powerful facet of human personality?

A. *Man feels that riches are paramount, but what he fancies as wealth are but material, momentary, trivial things. Character, virtue, brotherhood, charity – these are the real riches. The company of the good and godly is wealth, most worthy. Wisdom is the most precious wealth.*

[SSS Vol. 15, P 322]

Q 259. What is the cause of misery in this *Kaliyuga* age despite so many paths being available to man for acquiring happiness as compared to previous *Yugas*?

A. *The reason lies in human behaviour, in man's way of living itself. Human life is undoubtedly the highest in evolution and to give it meaning, spiritual endeavour is essential. For this way of life, character is all-important.* **Some say knowledge is power, but it is not true. Character is power.** *Even the acquisition of knowledge demands a good character. So, everyone must yearn to attain a flawless character without any trace of evil*

[Prema Vahini, P 1]

Q 260. What are the qualities that make up a flawless character?

A.   *Love, Patience, Forbearance, Steadfastness and Charity
– these are the qualities that have to be revered.*

[Prema Vahini, P 3]

Q 261. What are the means to cultivate moral strength?

A.   *Give up all that drags you down into evil; strengthen
all that lifts you and takes you nearer me.*

[SSS Vol. 8, P 193]

■ Self Confidence, Faith, Will Power

Q 262. What is the pre-requisite to achievement in life?

A.   *Without self-confidence, no achievement is possible. If you
have confidence in your strength and skill, you can draw
upon the inner springs of courage and raise yourselves to
a higher level of joy and peace, for confidence in yourselves
arises through the Atma, which is your inner reality.*

[SSS Vol.7, P 187]

Q 263. How is one to recognise the Divine power?

A.   *Develop faith in yourself and faith in God. Only then
will you be able to experience Divinity.*

[SSS Vol. 30, P 354]

Q 264. What do we need to manifest the divine vision?

A.   *Have faith in yourself, your own capacity to adhere to a
strict timetable of sadhana (spiritual discipline), your own
ability to reach the goal of realisation. When you have no
faith in the wave, how can you get faith in the ocean?*

[SSS Vol. 6, P 121]

**Q 265. What innate divine powers do the humans have in
them?**

A.   **The whole world is a combination of Ichcha Sakthi**

(will power), Kriya Sakthi (power of action) and Jnana Sakthi (power of wisdom). Ichcha Sakthi is related to the mind, Kriya Sakthi to the body and Jnana Sakthi to the Atma. That is why it is said, you are not one person, but three – the one you think you are (physical body), the one others think you are (mental body) and the one you really are (principle of the Atma).

[SSS Vol. 32 Part 2, P 138]

Q 266. How do desires affect will power and the state of mind?

A.   *You can have a comfortable journey of life only when you reduce the luggage of your desires. The lesser the desires, the greater will be the will power. The body has death but not the mind. The mind is responsible for everything. So, fill your mind with pure and selfless thoughts. Then you will attain the state of Illumination Mind. Gradually you will cross Illumination Mind and attain Over Mind. This is known as Amanaska (non-existence of mind). Once the mind is withdrawn, only the principle of the Atma, i.e., the Super consciousness exists.*

[SSS Vol. 33, P 309]

Q 267. What strengthens *Ichcha Sakthi* (will power)?

A.   *Developing good thoughts fosters the Ichcha Sakthi (will power). The will power increases as and when one reduces desires. When excessive desires are entertained, the will power declines.*

[SSS Vol. 26, P 128,129]

Q 268. How *Ichcha Sakthi* (will power) affects our *sadhana*?

A.   *Ichcha Sakthi fosters Prana Sakthi (Life Principle), Medha Sakthi (Intellectual power), Grahana Sakthi (power of understanding), Nirnaya Sakthi (power of determination) and Vaak Sakthi (power of speech). One who uses one's will power in the right manner, shines as a virtuous person. By reducing just one of your several habits like smoking or coffee addiction, you can experience an increase in your will power and intellectual ability. When the will power is weak, one cannot steady his mind in meditation, and it will only be a waste of time. One should reduce desires to progress in spiritual sadhana.*

[SSS Vol. 26, P 128-129]

■ Discipline

Q 269. What are the two most important guideposts for man in life?

A. *Discipline and restraint. Na sreyo Niyamam Vinaa (there can be no credit or fame without discipline). Without discipline and restraint man will ruin himself. The sun and the moon, the stars and the planets, wind and weather are all subject to certain laws. All things in Nature obey their respective rules of conduct including birds and beasts. Man endowed with a sacred birth and having intelligence and reason fails to observe restraint. What accompanies man in his final destiny is not samsara (worldly achievements) but samskara (the good acts).*

[SSS Vol. 20, P 154]

Q 270. How is discipline most important for reaching self-fulfilment?

A. *The real you is Atma. This can be learnt only by constant meditation, by moving in good company, by listening to the* *talks of realised men, by following some prescribed course of discipline. That is why I lay so much emphasis on discipline.*

[SSS Vol. 4, P 230]

Q 271. How are devotion and duty without discipline?

A. *Discipline is essential for the success of every endeavour of man. whatever the field, whether it be economic, social, educational, or merely material and worldly. It is even more essential for success in spiritual effort.*

[SSS Vol. 10, P 193]

Q 272. Is discipline needed to be enforced even after Self-realisation?

A. *You should never give up the habit of discipline. When you reach the state of perfection, you do not have to think of regulations or discipline.*

[Summer Showers 1972, P 247]

■ Surrender

Q 273. What does surrender really mean?

A. *It is not a question of surrendering or giving to some other one. One surrenders to oneself. Recognition that Atma is oneself is surrender. Surrender really means the realisation that all is God, that there is nobody who surrenders, that there is nothing to be surrendered, nor is there anyone to accept a surrender. All is God. There is only God.*

[Conversations, P 102]

Q 274. What is the need for surrender?

A. *The discontented man is as bad as lost. Rely on the Lord and accept whatever is your lot. He is in you, with you. He knows best what to give you and when.*

[SSS Vol. 6, P 176]

Q 275. Is surrender to God's will the safest path for the devotee?

A.   *When you travel by train, you have only to purchase the ticket, enter the proper train, and take a seat, leaving the rest to the engine. Why should you carry the bed and trunk on your head? So, too, put your trust in the Lord and carry on to the best of your ability.*

[SSS Vol. 1, P 174]

■ Culture

Q 276. Which are the three strong convictions of the ancient Indian culture?

A.   *1. **Karma Theory** – results of karmas are inescapable.*

*2. **Avatarhood** – God incarnates in human form as an Avatar.*

*3. **Permanence of God** – Everything in the world is a form of God and is naturally sacred.*

[Summer Showers 1991, P 49]

Q 277. How does culture help in the transformation of man?

A.   *Culture is the conscious effort put in by man to achieve transformation in his daily life from untruth to truth, from unrighteousness to righteousness and from mortality to immortality. It is a spiritual journey towards divinity.*

[SSS Vol. 35, P 318]

Q 278. Why are the traits of wickedness and crookedness found in man? How can man become cultured?

A.   *Man's present is but the result of his past and the habit formed during that long period. Whatever be the nature* of the character that he has come by, it can certainly be modified by modifying the accustomed process of thought and imagination. The wickedness of no man is incorrigible. Was not Angulimala, the dacoit, turned into a kind-hearted person by the Buddha? Did not the thief Ratnakara become Valmiki, the sage? By conscious effort, habits can be changed and character refined.

[Prema V, P 3]

■ Punya And Paapa

Q 279. How sinful is meat eating?

A. *Meat eating promotes only animal qualities. By eating the flesh of various animals, the qualities of these animals are imbibed. How sinful is it to feed on animals, which are sustained by the same five elements as human beings! This leads to demonic tendencies, besides committing the sin of inflicting cruelty on animals. Hence, those who genuinely seek to become devotees of God have to give up non-vegetarian food. Calling themselves Sai devotees or devotees of Rama and Krishna, they fatten on chicken. How can they be deemed Sai devotees?*

[SSS Vol. 27, P 277]

Q 280. With reference to the slogan "Help ever hurt never", how helping or hurting others is viewed in spirituality?

A. *When you help others, that itself is your reward. The scriptures declare: "Praopakarah Punyaya, Papaya Parapeedanam" (you earn merit by helping others and commit sin by hurting them). Hence, always be helpful. Do not commit the sin of hurting others.*

[SSS Vol. 35, P 140]

Q 281. How has one to undergo punishment for sin?

A.   *Man does bad things and commits sin. He has to be reborn to experience the consequences.*

> [Summer Showers 1974, P 243]

Q 282. According to *Sastras* what is *Punya* (merit) and what is *Paapa* (sin)?

A.   *"Ashtaadasa Puraanesu Vyasasya Vachanadwayam Paropakaarah Punyaaya Paapaaya Parapeedanam"*
"The eighteen Puranas of Vyasa teach two instructions:
To help is merit, to harm others is sin".

> [SS 1991, P 150]

Q 283. Has the soul to suffer for the sins committed by the body and the mind?

A.   *"No sin can affect you, for you are not the doer...Like oil on the tongue, Collyrium on the eye, lotus leaf on water, the deed is with you, but of you. Whatever you do or hear or see, you remain unaffected...you are eternal, the very source of Bliss, above and beyond all this, the Atma swarupa itself. That is your genuine nature. You are unrelated to these activities that are called deeds and these consequences. You are not the doer; you are just the Witness, the See-er! All yor perplexity has arisen from the delusion that you are the doer, from your ego and the sense of 'mine'.*

> [Geetha Vahini, P 112]

***

5
BODY - MIND COMPLEX

■ Four Tyres Of Bodies

Q 284. How many *Tattvas* (principles) constitute the human body?

A. *The body is composed of 25 Tattvas (principles):* 5 *organs of action (karamendriyas),* 5 *organs of perception (Jnanendriyas),* 5 *vital airs (Pancha Pranas),* 5 *sensations (Pancha Tanmatras),* 4 *internal instruments (Antahkarana) i.e. manas, buddhi, chitta, ahamkara and the life source — Atma.*
[Summer Showers 1993, P 41]

Q 285. How many *Tattvas* (principles) make the subtle body (sukshma sarira)?

A. *The subtle body contained in the physical body consists of 17 principles suffused with Tejas (effulgence).* These are 5 sensations, 5 organs of perception, 5 pranas, mind and intellect.
[Summer Showers 1993, P 41]

Q 286. Which body experiences the trials and tribulations, joys and sorrows of the world?

A.   *It is he subtle body, which experiences the trials and
           tribulations, joys and sorrows of the world. Hence, the subtle
           body is also known as* **'Yaatana Deha'** *(the suffering body).*
                                              [Summer Showers 1993, P 41]

Q 287. What constitute the causal body?

A.   *The Causal Body (Karana Deha is made up of two
           principles of Chitta (reflective mind) and 'Pragya'
           (constant integrated awareness).*
                                              [Summer Showers 1993, P 41]

Q 288. What constitutes the super-causal body?

A.   *The Super Causal Body (Mahakarana Sareera)
           which is also known as the Over mind. It is self-
           resplendent, self-luminous and self-radiant. The
           Super Causal body is also known as 'Uniki'
           (existence). 'Uniki' is nothing but the knowledge of
           oneself.*
                                                         [SS 1993, P 41]

**Q 289. What other name is there for the super-causal
        body?**

A.   *The Super Causal body is also known as 'Uniki'
           (existence). 'Uniki' is nothing but the knowledge of
           oneself. Since 'Uniki' is synonymous with awareness, this
           is known as 'Eruka'. The non-awareness of this is known
           as 'Marupu' (forgetfulness). The gross, the subtle and the
           causal bodies are stamped by this 'Marupu'.*
                                              [Summer Showers 1993, P 41]

**Q 290. Which are the three states of consciousness relating
        to the three bodies?**

A.   *The three states of waking, dreaming and sleeping (waking
           state – physical body, dreaming state – subtle body,*

sleeping state – causal body) are also enveloped by the forgetfulness.

[Summer Showers 1993, P 41]

Q 291. Which is the fourth one, the fourth state?

A. *It is the Divinity that pervades the spheres of awareness as well as non-awareness and is known as 'Tarakam'; it shines with equal splendour running as an undercurrent in all these states.*

[Summer Showers 1993, P 41]

Q 292. How does the universe get activated and energised?

A. *It is by the five attributes of Feeling, Form, Quantity, Colour and Energy that the mind pulsates, activates and energises the universe. Since the universe is suffused with the mind, these five attributes too suffuse the universe.*

[Summer Showers 1993, P 40]

Q 293. What is meant by *Kshara* and *Akshara*?

A. **'Kshara' and 'Akshara' mean perishable and imperishable. Whereas the body is 'Kshara', the Atma is 'Akshara'.** *The life is marked by the existence of the perishable body and the imperishable self. The perishable body envelops the imperishable Self. The imperishable Self is enveloped by the perishable body. These two exist together intertwined and interconnected. Life is a harmonious blend of Prakriti and Paramatma.*

[Summer Showers 1993, P 42]

Karana (Causal) and Mahakarana (Supercausal) bodies

Q 294. What constitutes the *Karana Sareera* (Causal body)?

A. *It is made up of only two constituents. Chitta (Will power) and Prajna (Constant Integrated Awareness). Because of*

its association with Prajna, this body is called Prajnanam
or Prajna.

[SSS Vol. 26, P 209]

Q 295. What constitutes the *Maha-karana* (the Over Mind)?

A.   *This is the fourth one. This is self-luminous and effulgent
in its original form. This is called 'Uniki' (a Being that is
self-knowing). Because of its capacity for self-knowing, it
is also called "Eruka" (Awareness).*

[SSS Vol. 26, P 209]

Q 296. Which bodies are associated with "Forgetfulness"?

A.   *As against Awareness, there is its opposite, Forgetfulness.
The physical, subtle and causal bodies belong to the latter.*

[SSS Vol. 26, P 209]

Q 297. What is "Forgetfulness"?

A.   *It is non-awareness of the true Self.*

[SSS Vol. 26, P 210]

Q 298. To what state the three *Jagrat*, *Swapna* and *Sushupti* belong?

A.   *They also belong top the state of Forgetfulness of the
Consciousness.*

[SSS Vol. 26, P 210]

Q 299. Are 'Awareness' and 'Forgetfulness' states interrelated too in some respect?

A.   *True form is Awareness. Awareness is the stable base.
Forgetfulness is gross. But in both the subtle awareness
and the gross Forgetfulness there is a Divinity that is
present equally. The jivatma is present always in all the
three states of Consciousness and in Awareness as well
as Forgetfulness as the Inner Being.*

[SSS Vol. 26, P 210]

Characteristics of Bodies

Q 300. What do *Akshara* and *Kshara* mean?

A.   *Akshara means that which is indestructible. Kshara means that which is liable to change. The body is Kshara. The Atma is Akshara. Paramatma is Akshara. Prakriti is Kshara.*

[SSS Vol. 26, P 21]

Q 301. What constitutes the gross body?

A.   *The gross body is made of food.*

[SSS Vol. 33, P 307]

Q 302. What are the constituents of the subtle body?

A.   *The mind, the intellect, the Chitta and the Ahamkara constitute the subtle body.*

[SSS Vol. 33, P 307]

Q 303. Which body experiences pleasure and pain?

A.   *It is the subtle body that experiences pain and pleasure.*

[SSS Vol. 33, P 307]

■ Koshas And Chakras

Q 304. Which are the 5 *Koshas* in man?

A.   *While man's physical body is composed of five basic elements (earth, water, fire, air and space), his subtle body has Pancha Koshas (five sheaths) one within the other. The first of them is the Annamaya Kosha (the food or material sheath). Within it is the Pranamaya Kosha (the sheath of life or breath). Within it is the Manomaya Kosha (the mental sheath. Within it is the Vijnanamaya kosha (the*

sheath of higher wisdom). The last sheath is the Anandamaya Kosha (the sheath of bliss). Starting with food, man must reach the destination of Bliss. The spiritual journey is from "I" to "We". Therein lies fulfilment – the realisation of the One in the many.
[SSS Vol. 20, P 61]

Q 305. What keeps the three subtle bodies – the *Pranamaya*, the *Manomaya* and the *Vijnanamaya* under control?

A. *All the four superficial Koshas, the Annamaya kosha, the Pranamaya Kosha, the Manomaya kosha and the Vijnanamaya Kosha, are all arising from the base Anandamaya Kosha. The spirit of Atma, which is the base for all these things, is the ananda, which is at the bottom of all these other Koshas.*
[Summer Showers 1977, P 127]

Q 306. What are the characteristics of the different bodies and koshas? How are they inter-related?

A. *The word **Annamaya Kosha** refers to the material human body. This material human body builds itself on food material, grows out of food and decays when there is no food.*

*The next layer that gives strength and protects the external human body is the **Pranamaya Kosha**, or an inner layer. This part of the body is called the Maya-deha. The Pranamaya Kosha is dependent upon the heat created in the body and enables heat to flow in the body and thereafter blood starts flowing into the blood vessels.*

*The next layer **Manomaya Kosha** is related to the mind. If Manomaya Kosha is not there, then the Pranamaya and Anandamaya Koshas cannot exist. The Manomaya Kosha is responsible for all kinds of thoughts and desires. To* *some extent, this mind or the Manomaya Kosha helps and becomes a support to the Pranamaya Kosha.*

*The next layer is **Vijnanamaya Kosha.** It has the function of enabling man to get the discriminatory power by which he distinguishes between good and bad. If there is no Vijnanamaya Kosha, the other layers Manomaya, Pranamaya and Annamaya will be lifeless and will not be able to function. This Vijnanamaya Kosha enables us to learn the nature of matter and how matter functions. It enables us to recognise whatever reactions and resounds exist in the entire material world.*

*All these Koshas are all arising from the base **Anandamaya Kosha**. The spirit of Atma which is the base for all these things is the Ananda which is at the bottom of all these other Koshas.*

[Summer Showers 1977, P 125-127]

Q 307. Which are the important *Chakras* (energy plexus) among the *Shat-chakras* (the 6 centres of life energy)?

A. Two are important. One is the *Hridya Chakra* – the *Chakra* relating to the heart. The other is the *Sahasrara Chakra* – the *Chakra* relating to the head.

[SSS Vol. 26, P 287]

Q 308. What is the importance of the *Hridya Chakra* or *Anahat Chakra*?

A. *This Chakra is Lotus of the Heart. This "Lotus" has 8 petals. Every petal is called Prakriti (Nature). All the 8 petals are under the sway of the Lord. This means that God is the Adhipati (master) of the 8 petals. Because Lord Krishna is the Pati (husband) of these 8 petals, He is said to have 8 'queens', according to spiritual texts. Those who*

*did not understand the esoteric meaning of all this,
described Lord Krishna as having 8 queens and as having
sported with 16,000 Gopikas. The real meaning of the
reference to Krishna's '8 queens' is that He is the Lord of
the Lotus of human heart. As such, He holds sway over
the heart. When this is rightly understood, the supreme
greatness of the Divine will be apparent.*

[SSS Vol. 26, P 287]

Q 309. What is the importance of *Sahasrara Chakra*?

A.   *It is a 1000 petalled lotus, each petal having 16 Kalas
(phases). There are thus 16,000 kalas in the sahasrara.
These phases are symbolically described as the wives of
the Lord. The inner meanings of these expressions should
be properly understood by the devotees. Going by this
superficial and literal meaning of these terms, the nature
of the Divine is misconstrued and misinterpreted.*

[SSS Vol. 26, P 288]

Q 310. How are the five values of *Sathya, Dharma, Santhi, Prema* and *Ahimsa* related to our different inner instruments?

A.   *Santhi* comes from *Manomaya kosha*
Sathya comes from *Vijnanamaya kosha*
Dharma comes from *Annamaya kosha*
Prema comes from *Pranamaya kosha* and *Manomaya kosha*
Ahimsa comes from *Anandamaya kosha.*

[SSS Vol. 26, P 137]

Q 311. How to experience Divinity in the Bliss sheath?

A.   *The heart of the human being is like the sky in which the
'Self' is the sun shining constantly. Just as passing clouds
obstruct the vision of the sun temporarily, attachment to
world and worries and troubles will obstruct the vision*

*of the Inner Self. But, once the clouds clear, you can have
the vision of the inner Self which is resplendent within.
By means of Dhyana Sakthi and Prana Sakthi, you can
experience Divinity in the Bliss sheath, which fosters the
five human values.*

[SSS Vol. 26, P 137]

■ Antahkarana

Antahkarana – The Inner Instrument

Q 312. What is *Prajnana?*

A.	*Man is not just a combination of body and mind. He
possesses* **prajnana (pragyan)– constant integrated
awareness.** *Prajnana is the permanent witness or
awareness pervading the Antahkarana.*

[Summer Showers 1991, P 46]

Q 313. What is *Antahkarana?*

A.	*Man's thinking faculty is categorized into four entities
based on function –* **manas (mind), buddhi (intellect),
chitta (memory or subconscious mind stuff) and
ahamkara (ego). This constitutes Antahkarana,** *the
inner instrument of the soul.*

[Summer Showers 1991, P 46]

Q 314. What is mind?

A.	***The mind is a bundle of thoughts.*** *"Sankalpa
Vikalpaatmanam Manah" –The mind continuously
decides for and against issues…Repetition strengthens
thoughts. We strengthen our mind by repeatedly
remembering unnecessary matters.*

[Summer Showers 1991, P 46]

Q 315. What is *chitta*?

A.   *Chitta – memory. This is just a repository of past impressions. (This is also called the Sub-conscious mind stuff).*

[Summer Showers 1991, P 46]

Q 316. What is the role of the intellect?

A.   *The intellect is the link to the Divine, discriminating between the temporary and the permanent.*

[Summer Showers 1991, P 46]

Q 317. What is ego?

A.   *The ego identifies with the body. Aham ('I') + aakaaram (form) is Aham-kaaram, - Ego. Ego merges the sense of individuality with the physical form.*

[Summer Showers 1991, P 46]

Q 318. How to attain purification of this inner instrument – the *Antahkarana*?

A.   *All four – mind, intellect, memory and ego – are aberrations of the true mind. The one mind has four names...***First purify the inner instrument. To this end, it is compulsory to engage in action (karma). Without activities, the mind cannot be purified. The Vedas say – "Chittasya Suddhaye Karmaha" – The mind is refined with action. Every man must undertake good deeds to purify the mind.**

[Summer Showers 1991, P 47]

Q 319. Has the '*Antahkarana*' consisting of mind, intellect, *chitta* (memory) and ego any forms?

A.   *The mind, the intellect, the memory and ego which together constitute Antahkarana are formless but the external instruments, the sense organs, which are the media through which the Antahkarana perceives the phenomenal world, have forms.*

[Summer Showers 1990, P 83]

Q 320. What are the defects or impurities that render the *Antahkarana* impure?

A. *The Antahkarana is subject to four kinds of defects, viz, Bhranthi (delusion), Pramad – Hazard or Danger, Karanaapaatavam – weakness of the instruments, and Vipralipsa – Jealousy. These four defects result in the malfunctioning of the Antahkarana.*

[Summer Showers 1990, P 83]

Q 321. How does '*Karana apatavam*' or weakness of the *Antahkarana* affect it?

A. *This weakness affects both the inner instrument – Antahkarana and the external instrument – the sense organs.*

[Summer Showers 1990, P 84]

■ Mind

Q 322. Has the mind its own intrinsic power to directly experience the sense objects?

A. *The mind is like a mirror. It has no intrinsic power to directly experience sense objects except through the concerned sense organs.*

[Summer Showers 1990, P 76]

Q 323. How many kinds of pollutions or impurities afflict the mind?

A. *The mind is subject to three kinds of pollution: Mala, Vikshepa and Avarna.*

[SS 1990, P 76]

Q 324. What is *Mala* and how to get rid of this impurity?

A.   *Man commits many offences, knowingly or unknowingly not only in this life but also in previous lives. The imprint of these actions is carried by the Chitta – memory, life after life, like the dust accumulating on the surface of a mirror day after day. Thus the mirror of man's mind gets covered up by such dirt, which is technically named as "Mala".* On account of this Mala, man is unable to see clearly the reflection of his real identity in the mirror of his mind. Hence, it is necessary to cleanse the mirror of the impurities covering it.

This cleansing is done by regulating one's food and living habits including recreation. Purity should be ensured with regard to Patra shuddhi (vessel used for cooking), Padaartha shuddhi (cooking materials) and Paaka shuddhi (Process of cooking). Many of the ills that people suffer today are due to consuming things obtained through unfair means as well polluted by the vibrations from cooks of questionable character. The way out suggested by the scriptures is to offer the food to God before consuming it, duly regarding it as God's gift (Prasad).

[Summer Showers 1990, P 78-79]

Q 325. What is *Vikshepa* and how to check it?

A.   *The second distortion of the mind is Vikshepa. This is due to constant wavering of the mind, like the movements of the reflected image in a mirror that is kept moving or shaking frequently. To control this waywardness of the mind, one should undertake various spiritual practices like meditation, prayer and the nine modes of devotion mentioned in the Scriptures.*

[Summer Showers 1990, P 80]

Q 326. How to acquire the steadiness of mind?

A.   *Steadiness of mind is pre-requisite for concentration. For this, you should bend the body, mend the senses and end the mind. This is the process of attaining immortality. You should keep your body, senses and mind under your control.*

[Summer Showers 1990, P 80]

Q 327. What is *Avarana* – the third distortion of the mind?

A.   *This may be likened to a thick cloth covering the mirror of man's mind, which does not at all permit of any reflection whatsoever of the image of the Self.*

[Summer Showers 1990, P 81]

Q 328. What is the effect of these distortions of the mind on man?

A.   *While Mala does not enable us to have a clear and correct image of the Self, Vikshepa results in seeing the self as wavering, Avarana altogether hides the Reality – the Self, and makes one identify wrongly with the body.*

[Summer Showers 1990, P 81]

Q 329. Are we not experiencing the real world through the impure mind – *Antahkarana*?

A.   *That which you are experiencing as the real world is only the 'Reaction', 'Resound' and 'Reflection' of your 'Real Self'.*

[Summer Showers 1990, P 81]

Q 330. What exactly is the thick cloth that covers the mirror of one's mind?

A.   *The cloth is made up of the gang of six inner enemies of man – viz. **Kama** (desire), **Krodha** (anger), **Lobha** (greed), **Moha** (attachment), **Mada** (pride) and **Matsarya** (jealousy).*

[Summer Showers 1990, P 82]

Q 331. **Which is the best means of removing this thick envelope of *Avarana*?**

A.   *Developing love for all. Love is God. Live in love.* Love is the only bond that can unite all and make us realise the One reality behind all seeming diversity.

[Summer Showers 1990, P 82]

Q 332. **How to cleanse the mind?**

A.   *To cleanse the mind, prayer is the water and repentance is the soap. In addition, have a resolute determination not to repeat mistakes.*

[SSS Vol. 5, P 28]

Q 333. **What helps to purify the nature of the mind?**

A.   *Science would testify that the nature of the mind depends upon the food we consume. The gross material of food we excrete, but the subtlest part is used by our system to feed the intelligence and the subtlest part becomes the mind.*

[SSS Vol. 10, P 187]

Q 334. **What is that man must control to win the battle of life against mind?**

A.   *The ego – the ego brings wave after wave of wants and wishes before your attention and tempts you to attempt to gain them. It is a never-ending circle. So try to reduce your wants and expand the range of your love in order to be free from the coils of your ego.*

[SSS Vol. 14, P 86]

Q 335. **How to make the mind ego-free?**

A.   *When man is aware that the same Divine Consciousness that motivates him is equally motivating all others, then love ousts the ego into the background and takes charge of man's activities, words and thoughts.*

[SSS Vol. 14, P 83]

Q 336. How will the unsteadiness and waywardness of mind go?

A. *Though born as a human, man is burdened by animal instincts and impulses that have attached themselves to him during his previous lives as an animal...Some are endowed with profuse unsteadiness and waywardness, an inheritance of their monkey existence. Man is known in Sanskrit as 'nara' and the monkey as 'vanara'. When 'va' (valam, tail) is subtracted, 'vanara' is reduced to 'nara', the monkey becomes man. Man has lost the tail but he has still all the waywardness and unsteadiness of that animal. The totality of such animal traces must be sacrificed on the altar of the mind, as part of the inner yajna.*
[SSS Vol. 14, P 199-200]

Q 337. What are the six mental states?

A. *After attaining the awareness of divinity, the divine consciousness that 'I am Brahman' and the oneness of all living things, there is a third stage, which has been characterised as the Aarohana-Avarohana stage – the "Ascent-and-Descent" stage. Man has six different kinds of minds. They are: 1. The Ordinary Mind; 2. The Super Mind; 3. The Higher Mind; 4. The Illumined Mind; 5. The Intuitive Mind; 6. The Over Mind.*
[SSS Vol. 21, P 44-45]

Q 338. Which are the lowest and the highest mental states among these and how to attain *Poornatva -* fullness?

A. *The starting base for the six levels of minds is the ordinary mind. At the summit level is the Over-Mind. In the mental process, what goes on is an ascent from the ordinary mind*

*to Over-Mind as well as a descent from the Over-Mind
to the lowest level. It is when the ascending process and
the descending process meet that there is fullness in the
human being.*

[SSS Vol. 21, P 45]

**Q 339. Is Consciousness experienced at different levels
and in different mental states really differential?**

A.   *There is no difference between one kind of consciousness
and another. All consciousness is alike because it is a
manifestation of Brahman (the Absolute). It is Brahman
that has manifested as the Cosmos.*

[SSS Vol. 21, P 45]

**Q 340. What does one experience while moving from
mind to Super Mind, to Higher mind and finally
to Illuminated Mind?**

A.   *When you are at the level of Super Mind, you think that
you are different from others. This is dualism. It is said:
"A man with dual mind is half blind". Gradually, go up
to the Higher Mind where you understand your true
nature. Then you reach Illuminated Mind. Once you
experience this unity in totality, you attain Over Mind.
That is your goal. That is everything for you. All spiritual
practices are meant to attain this goal.*

[SSS Vol. 33, P 316]

Q 341. How many different levels of the mind are there?

A.   *There are different levels of the mind, viz., Super
Mind, Higher Mind, Illuminated Mind and Over
Mind. Man will reach the stage of totality only when he
attains the level of Over Mind.*

[SSS Vol. 33, P 304]

**Q 342. To what level of consciousness is Super Mind
related?**

A. *Super Mind is related to body consciousness. The source of body consciousness is the principle of Atma that pervades the entire body.*

[SSS Vol. 33, P 304]

Q 343. What is the level of consciousness of the Higher Mind?

A. **Body consciousness becomes thought consciousness when one reaches the level of Higher Mind.** *Body consciousness is limited to physical level, whereas thought consciousness has no such limits and can travel to any distance. That is why thought consciousness is termed as Higher Mind. Higher consciousness transcends the five elements. To reach this transcendental state one has to begin with Super Mind.*

[SSS Vol. 33, P 304]

Q 344. What would be the experience and the state of a person settled at the level of the Illuminated Mind?

A. *There is current in the human body from top to toe. The body itself is a big generator. Illumined Mind, which is related to the current in the body, is very powerful. When one attains this level, one will have current even in one's nails and hair. A worldly person will not feel any pain when his nails are clipped, but after attaining the level of Illumination Mind, one will get a shock when one tries to clip the nails. This is the reason why the ancient sages and seers used to grow their nails. But the person at the level of Illumination Mind will feel the shock when his nails are clipped.*

[SSS Vol. 33, P 305]

Q 345. After attaining the level of Illuminated Mind, does one get totally saturated with Divinity?

A.   *The thoughts, words and deeds of one with*
        Illuminated Mind are suffused with Divinity. That
        gives rise to a very powerful 'three phase' current in the
        body. Such people will have current even in their hair.
        You can feel the shock when you touch their hair.

[SSS Vol. 33, P 305]

Q 346. What spiritual *sadhana* leads to attaining the state
        of illumination Mind?

A.   *Start practising love. That is the correct spiritual*
        practice. Share your love with more and more people.
        You will experience oneness. Once you start sharing
        your love with everybody, then the whole world will
        become one family. After expanding your love in this
        manner, control your external thoughts and turn
        inward. Then you will attain the state of Illumination
        Mind where there are absolutely no thoughts and no
        action.

[SSS Vol. 33, P 308]

Q 347. Is an Illumination mind equipped with any special
        subtle powers also?

A.   *At the level of Illumination Mind, one's mind*
        undergoes a great change and becomes the subtle
        force. This subtle force has three powers – Prana
        Sakthi, Mano Sakthi and Vijnana Sakthi. No
        scientist, doctor or engineer can understand this. You can
        give rest to any limb of the body but not the heart. The
        heart continues to function even in your sleep. Which
        doctor or scientist can understand this? The eye looks so
        small but there are 13 lakh light rays in it. Who has made
        it? All this is God's creation. God's creation is the most
        mysterious, sacred and wonderful. All that is seen outside

is nothing but the reflection, reaction and resound of the inner.

[SSS Vol. 33, P 306]

Q 348. What constitutes the Illumination Mind?

A.   *The illumination Mind comprises the causal body. It transcends worldly thoughts and feelings. There is no trace of desire, anger, greed, ego, pride and jealousy in it.*

[SSS Vol. 33, P 307]

Q 349. When is the state of Illumination Mind achieved?

A.   *The level of Illumination Mind is reached only when all the worldly thoughts are subdued.*

[SSS Vol. 33, P 307]

Q 350. What *sadhana* is to be undertaken by the seeker to attain the level of Super Mind?

A.   *The fundamental basis to attain Super Mind is to cultivate super love, i.e., love without any desire. That is why I often tell you, love is God, live in love. Start the day with love, spend the day with love, fill the day with love and end the day with love. This is the way to God.*

[SSS Vol. 33, P 304]

Q 351. How does the control on external thoughts lead to attaining the level of Illumination Mind?

A.   *After expanding your love, control your external thoughts and turn inward. Then you will attain the state of Illumination Mind where there are no thoughts and no action...**The duality of good and bad annihilated by the Illumination Mind. In spiritual parlance, this is called samadhi state. Samadhi means Sama + Dhi (equal-mindedness).** The Illumination Mind unifies good and bad and develops the spirit of oneness.*

[SS Vol. 33, P 308]

■ **Intellect**

Q 352. To what best use should we put our intelligence ?

A.   *God has gifted this intelligence to you so that you may be able to understand yourself and realise your own true nature. Make an attempt in the first instance to find out who you are. It is this enquiry that will automatically become the enquiry of the Self and lead to the questions like – who am I? Am I this body? Am I this mind? Am I this intelligence? etc. When you examine each of these questions, you will realise that you are none of these...you are in the body, you are in the mind, you are everywhere, but they are not you. They belong to you but they are not the same as you.*

[Summer Showers 1977, P 33, 34]

Q 353. Which faculty of man best reflects the attributes of Atma?

A.   *The Buddhi is very close to the Atma and therefore well located to receive 90% of the Atmic energy and illumination.* The mind derives its power from the Buddhi, the senses from the mind, and the body from the senses. In this process of the flow of power from the Atma to the body in stages, there occurs a gradual quantitative and qualitative diminution of the power.

[Summer Showers 1990, P 90-91]

■ **Ego**

Q 354. What leads man into attachment and consequent suffering and bondage and how to get over it?

A.　　*Attachment results in bondage; detachment leads to liberation. It is the ego, the 'I' consciousness which tells you that you are the body, with its pack of senses that drive you into attachment. Be vigilant that it does not lead you into desires that are harmful.*

[SSS Vol. 8, P 161]

Q 355. What is the most effective means for the elimination of ego?

A.　　*The chief among these measures is the bhajan. Have bhajans (group singing of devotional songs) on as many days as you can, in your village or area. Have them in places where all can come and join. Have them as simple as you can, without competitive pomp or show; reduce expenses to a minimum, for God cares for the inner yearning and not the outer trappings. Your egoism will be shattered when you sing in the streets in full view of your neighbours. You will forget in your enthusiasm all pride and self-esteem. Thus, Nagarasankeerthan is a great sadhana.*

[SSS Vol. 8, P 109, 112]

Q 356. What is the significance of breaking a coconut?

A.　　*When you take a coconut to be offered in the temple, you take it, after removing the fibre; then, you offer it to God., breaking it into two halves. This is the symbol for destroying the ego and surrendering to the Lord. So you have to remove the fibre of desire for sense-objects and then, go before the Lord devoid of kama and krodha; there you declare that you are ego-less by breaking the coconut into two. You will be accepted then, not before.*

[SSS Vol. 5, P 112]

Q 357. How does ego enter the mind?

A.   *It enters your mind when you give up the path of truth. You become egoistic when you do not know your true Self and develop worldly thoughts and feelings.*

[SSS Vol. 35, P 341]

Q 358. How does ego obstruct the spiritual progress?

A.   *It is impossible to acquire wisdom without getting rid of ego. To have the vision of the effulgent light of Atma, you have to remove the soot of ego covering your mind.*

[SSS Vol. 35, P 341]

Q 359. Why is the mind always interested in earthly things?

A.   *The presiding deity of the mind is the Moon. The Moon represents coolness and fluidity. Fluids like water have a tendency to flow down and find their level. The mind, because of its very nature, has the tendency to move downwards to get interested in petty things. Efforts have to be made to make the mind look upwards.*

[SSS Vol. 21, P 219]

Q 360. What are the basic constituents of the four limbs of the *Antahkarana* – the mind, buddhi, ego and *chitta*?

A.   *The mind, the intellect, the will (chitta) and the ego are made up of the five elements, which are all emanations from the Supreme – the Sath-Chith-Ananda (Being-Awareness-Bliss). This is their Primal Source from which they have emanated like innumerable sparks from a fire. Man should realise that he has also come from the same Divine Source.*

[SSS. Vol. 21, P 219]

Q 361. Which is the worst enemy of man?

A. *Man cannot claim to be a man until the ego that prompts him to ruin others and ride over others is destroyed by sadhana (spiritual discipline)...Rare indeed is the hero who has demolished his ego and escaped from its nefarious urges.*

[SSS Vol. 14, P 83]

Q 362. How is one to get over this enemy of pride?

A. *The Geetha directs man to be "nir-mamo, nir-ahamkarah" (without 'mine' and 'I'). The Divine in him can manifest only when the dark forces of 'mine' and 'I' are rendered ineffective.*

[SSS Vol. 14, P 83]

Q 363. What is the significance of animal sacrifice?

A. *The real meaning of animal sacrifice is the sacrifice of the animal nature in man. Everyone has to get rid of Ahamkara and Mamkara (Ego and the sense of 'mine'). Without sacrificing these animal tendencies, sacrificing dumb animal is unworthy of human beings.*

[SSS Vol. 25, P 167]

■ Chitta

Q 364. What is *Chitta Suddhi*?

A. *The purification of the mind of man from ego and all its brood of blemishes – This is Chitta Suddhi, the cleansing of all levels of consciousness.*

[SSS Vol. 14, P 123]

Q 365. How is *Chitta-suddhi* attained?

A. *The basic chitta (inner consciousness) has to be freed from down-dragging impulses... Ceaseless effort is*

*necessary to gain and possess chitta suddhi. One has
to be ever in sathsang (holy company) and in activities
devoted to the service of God in all human forms.*

[SSS Vol. 14, P 123-124]

Q 366. What is it that God looks for in the devotee?

A.   *God looks for your devotion. He looks into your chitta
(mind) rather than at your vittha (wealth).*

[SSS Vol.27, P 81]

■ Viveka

Q 367. How to distinguish between the real and the unreal?

A.   *So long as you are entangled in the sensual world, you
cannot distinguish the Real from the unreal. But, you have
to discover the real, through discrimination; there is no
avoiding that responsibility; you have to do it, now or later.*

[SSS Vol. 3, P 131]

Q 368. What is *Nischayatmika Buddhi*?

A.   *However efficient the body, the senses and the mind may
be, they serve no purpose in the absence of the charioteer,
namely Nischayatmika Buddhi. It means the decision-
making capacity.*

[Summer Showers 1990, P 88]

Q 369. What is to be done to attain *Buddhi yoga*?

A.   **When the desire to attain the fruit of action is
renounced with full intellectual awareness, then it
becomes what Krishna calls, "Buddhiyogam". The
intellect has to be purified and trained; otherwise it
is impossible to give up attachment to the fruits of**

action and to continue doing things as either duty or dedication. Such a purified intellect is named "Yoga-buddhi'.

[Geetha Vahini, P 41]

Q 370. How is one to lead the senses along the right path?

A. *The pleasures the senses draw from the objective world are weeds; the crop is the attachment to God. The mind is a bundle of wishes; and unless these wishes are removed by their roots, there is no hope of destroying the mind. So, the first thing to be conquered is Kama, the demon of desire…Desires are objective; they belong to the category of the "seen". The conviction that "I am the see-er only, not the seen", releases from attachment.*

[Geetha Vahini, Page P 47-48]

Q 371. How does one develop the inner vision?

A. *Fix your consciousness always on the Atmic Reality and discard the body and the senses as unreal and impermanent. Atma is the Eternal; so establish yourself only in that and not in the transient non-Atmic illusions or objects.*

[Geetha Vahini, P 253]

Q 372. What is the difference between *Buddhi-sakthi* and *Medha-sakthi*?

A. *Buddhi is the power of discrimination exercised over the sensations and perceptions, pertaining to the five sensory organs of sight, hearing, touch, taste and smell. Medha-sakthi is associated with supra-sensory perceptions, extrasensory perceptions, intuition and spirituality. It transcends the sensations and perceptions provided by the phenomenal world.*

[Summer Showers 1979, P 153]·

Q 373. What is true wisdom?

A.   *Real wisdom consists in recognising that man is pure bliss; bliss that persists from the past into the present and the future. "If you seek this steady, genuine pure state of bliss, you must be attached to Me," said Krishna.*

[Geetha Vahini P 147]

Q 374. Can discrimination or *viveka* come by reading books?

A.   *Mere reading of books will not vouchsafe viveka. That which is seen, heard or read must be put into practice in actual life. Without this, reading is mere waste of time. If anything is read to pass time, it passes with time and nothing remains...Only those who, by means of discrimination, practise what they read can realise the Truth and enjoy everlasting Bliss.*

[Prema V, P 4-5]

▣ Vairagya (Detachment), Renunciation, Tapas, Sacrifice

Q 375. What is real *Tyaga* (sacrifice)?

A.   ***The control of the senses is the Tyaga (sacrifice) that leads to Immortality.*** *Sacrifice of wealth is no sacrifice at all. It is the sacrifice of the senses (the desires caused by them) that is the highest sacrifice.*

[SSS Vol. 27, P 80]

Q 376. Does *Tejas* (effulgence) come from *Tapas* or sacrifice?

A.   *The more one sacrifices, the greater will be one's Tejas. Though I eat very little, my Tejas is ever increasing.*

Everyday after the morning Bhajan, I take a little Ragi Sankati (gruel made of coarse grain) and Chutney or curry made of leaves. This is what I used to take earlier and it is the same now also. There has been no change in it. I eat very little food, yet I have tremendous Tejas. The Tejas comes not because of food but because of the spirit of sacrifice. One gets a lot of strength when one involves oneself in social welfare activities.

[SS – Jan. 2001, P 18]

Q 377. What is it that should be renounced? Are external objects to be given up?

A. *No. These things can be renounced easily. But, this is not real sacrifice. The real renunciation, which one has to make, is the giving up of the evil qualities of Kama (desire), Krodha (anger) and Lobha (greed).* **"Kamam Karma Nasanam" (Desire is the destroyer of action). "Krodham Jnana Nasanam" (Anger is the destroyer of wisdom). "Lobham Bhakthi Nasanam" (Greed is the destroyer of devotion).**

[SSS Vol. 21, P 143]

Q 378. What is the essence of *Tapas*?

A. *Standing on your head and squinting your eyes is not penance! Trikarana Suddhi – unity and purity in thought, word and deed - is penance...When thought, word and deed are not one, only tamas (darkness) will result instead of tapas.*

[Summer Showers 1991, P 51]

Q 379. What is the relation between *Tyaga* (renunciation, sacrifice) and *Bhoga* (worldly enjoyment)?

A. *The Isavasya Upanishad proclaims that all pleasures (bhoga) should be enjoyed with a feeling* *of renunciation (tyaga). The Upanishad reveals that when you perform actions without ego and when you experience the world without attachment, there remains no distinction between bhoga and tyaga. Work without ego and attachment is selfless work – a pleasurable sacrifice. All selfless work is nothing but renunciation.*

[Summer Showers 1991, P 44]

Q 380. How will the seeds of desire burn?

A.   *The fire of detachment will fry the seed of desire, down to the last trace of life in it. Mere transitory fits of renunciation will not succeed in preventing sprouting. Detachment has to be supplemented by the knowledge of the hollowness of the objective world.*

[SSS Vol. 7, P 164]

Q 381. How is renunciation cultivated?

A.   *It is necessary to analyse and discriminate every act of man, for, the spirit of renunciation is born out of such analysis. Without it, renunciation is difficult to get.*

[Prema Vahini, P 108]

Q 382. Should one retire into a forest to do one's *sadhana* of finding God?

A.   *There is no need to retire into a forest or a cave to know your inner Truth and to conquer your lower nature. As a matter of fact, you have no chance to exercise your anger there and so the victory achieved there may not be lasting and genuine. Win the battle of life; be in the world but yet be away from its tentacles.*

[SSS Vol. 1, P 91]

Q 383. How should a seeker view the family relations on the spiritual path?

A. *Affection for family and relations is limiting. Before birth, who is the mother and who is the child? Before marriage, who is the husband and who is the wife? These relations are cultivated mid-way through our eternal journey. They are 'passing clouds'.*

One must neither desire nor fear such temporary associations. Life is a vast ocean with short-lived waves of samyoga (union) and viyoga (separation). Therefore, spirituality must come first. The Upanishads propagate methods to achieve Divinity and Immortality. "Na Karmana Na Prajaya Dhanena, Tyagenaike Amritatvamanasuh – Not by good deeds, children or wealth, but only by sacrifice is immortality attained.

[Summer Showers 1991, P 40, 42]

Q 384. **What is essentially needed to wash off the impurities that have stuck to the mind?**

A. *Vidya (Knowledge) and Tapas. Only when both are used can the levels of consciousness be thoroughly cleansed. No man can be rendered holy without Vidya and Tapas.*

[Vidya V, P 69]

Q 385. **What is the reward of *vairagya* – renunciation?**

A. *Don't you see that only those who gave up, renounced, sought the more difficult road of God-realisation, instead of easier path of World-realisation, are honoured everywhere?*

[SSS Vol.3, P 136]

Q 386. **What is the lesson of renunciation man must learn so as to become eligible for attaining Moksha?**

A. *One has to give up assumed relationships and artificial* *attachments through rigorous analysis of their nature and give them up as quickly as possible. This is what the world teaches as the lesson of renunciation.*

[Sutra Vahini, P 23]

Q 387. What was the true spiritual significance of *Ashwa Medha Yaga* (horse sacrifice) that used to be performed in ancient times?

A.   *By Ashwa (horse) is meant that which is restless. The horse cannot remain steady even for a moment. It will always be shaking one part or the other of its body. The horse is an animal, which represents the unsteady mind. The word Medha in Ashwa Medha literally means the mind. Thus to perform the horse sacrifice really means to offer the restless mind to God.*

[SSS Vol.25, P 168]

Q 388. What leads to the attainment of Immortality?

A.   **"Na Karmana Na Prajaya Dhanena Tyagenaike Amrutatvamanasuh" (immortality is not attained through action (karma), progeny or wealth. It is attained only by sacrifice).**

[SSS Vol. 34, P 97]

■ Control Of The Senses And The Mind, Purification

Q 389. How to keep the mind and the senses under control?

A.   *You must watch the working of the mind, from outside it; you should not get involved in it. The faculty of the mind is like a strong current of electricity. It has to be watched from a distance and not contacted or touched.*

Touch it, you are reduced to ashes. So too, contact and attachment give the chance for the mind to ruin you. The farther you are from it, the better. By skilful methods, you have to make the best use of it for your own welfare.

[Geetha Vahini, P 48]

Q 390. What is the method for sense control?

A. *The mind must be withdrawn from its present comrades, the senses. It must become loyal to its real master, the intellect (buddhi). That is to say, you must separate the grain from the chaff, through the exercise of discrimination (viveka) and then fix your desire on the things that last, rather than on things that are flashy and corroding.*

[SSS 5, P 18]

Q 391. How does a pure mind lead to oneness with the Divine?

A. *The original Divine Spirit, the individualised spirit, which is the image, and the objective world of which the body is a part – these are the three entities called Ishwara-Jeeva-Prakrithi. Success in sadhana is won the moment you are able to either deny the objective world as a delusion, or recognise it as nothing but the Supreme Spirit itself. Purify the mind to cognise God in everything.* **In ordinary day-to-day arithmetic, three minus one is equal to two; but in the arithmetic of the Atma the three (Ishwara-Jeeva-Prakrithi) minus one (Prakrithi) is equal to not two, but one (Ishwara) for, once the image (Prakrithi) goes, the image (Jeeva) also disappears! When the mirror is eliminated, two entities disappear, the mirror and the reflection it can cast. And you merge in the Divine.**

[SSS Vol. 10, P 63]

Q 392. What *sadhana* should be done to control the mind?

A.   *All sadhana is done by the mind, for the satisfaction of the mind. How can an effort of the mind turn around and control the mind itself? Can a thief arrest himself? Similarly, the mind cannot control and destroy itself. We must reach the state of a-manaskam – mindlessness. Absence of all thought is a-manaskam. One should restrain thoughts.*

[Summer Showers 1991, P 38]

Q 393. *But mind-control is so difficult, beyond the reach of all. It is so wayward, never halts at one place. How can one enter upon yoga with such mind?*

A.   *It is not an impossible task; the mind can be mastered, however difficult the task might be. **By systematic practice (abhyasa) and by relentless inquiry (vichara) and detachment (vairagya)- the mind can be mastered.***

[Geetha Vahini, P 116]

Q 394. What should we seek to acquire on the spiritual path?

A.   *We must acquire "diamonds". How? When we destroy the mind, which pursues worldly matters, that state of "die "mind is "diamond". Therefore, we must restrict the movement of the mind into mundane matters.*

[Summer Showers 1991, P 128]

Q 395. What is the secret of attaining immortality?

A.   *Bend the body, mend the senses, and end the mind – that is the process of attaining the status of 'the children of immortality', which the Upanishads have reserved for man.*

[SSS Vol. 9, P 62]

Q 396. What is the most effective discipline to attain purification at all levels of consciousness?

A.   *To attain this lofty goal is the control and conquest of the five senses. Avoid the errors and evils that the eye, the ear, the tongue, the mind and the hand are prone to commit. These are called the pancha-doshas (five vices).*

[SSS Vol. 13, P 209]

Q 397. How to remove the *pancha-doshas* (five vices)?

A.   *Surdas pleads with the tongue to call out the names – Govinda, Damodara, Madhava. When the eye, ear and tongue are under control and capable of being used for self-improvement, the mind and the hand can also easily be held in check.*

[SSS Vol. 13, P 209]

Q 398. How can life be sanctified?

A.   *Cultivate and develop only sacred thoughts and thus sanctify your lives. If you want to have good thoughts, you must resort to the spiritual sadhana. The starting point for spiritual path is Satsang – holy company. **The company of the wise begets detachment, detachment leads to the destruction of delusion, followed by the acquisition of steady wisdom, and culminating finally in Jivanmukti – liberation, while alive.***

[Summer Showers 1990, P 76]

Q 399. Why can't the impure Antahkarana reflect the reality?

A.   *The mind is like a clean mirror. It has no intrinsic power of its own to directly experience the sense objects except through the concerned sense organs.... Antahkarana is subject to four kinds of defects. The four defects result in malfunctioning of the Antahkarana. Thus the mirror of*

*man's mind gets covered up with dust accumulating on
the surface of the mirror. On account of this Mala, man
is unable to see clearly the reflection of his real identity in
the mirror of the impurities covering it.*

[Summer Showers 1990, P 78, 79]

**Q 400. What should be done when one gets excited or
angry?**

A.   *When such a situation comes to you, you should try and
sit alone and give some thought to it and find out what is
right and what is wrong. When some thought comes into
your mind, you should not immediately act with
excitement. This kind of action will take you to great sin.
Take time and discriminate, find out whether it is going
to lead you to a good act or bad act. This discrimination is
very necessary.*

[Summer Showers 1977, P 159]

■ Thoughts And Desires

Q 401. How does thought control lead to Self-realisation?

A.   *Every thought that emerges must be directed
towards the Atma. This is called sayujya – merger
with God. Therefore, if Self-realisation is the goal,
we must align the body, senses and mind as per the
prompting of the Atma. When one merges all
thoughts into the Atma, one becomes the Atma –
The knower of Brahman becomes Brahman Himself.*

[Summer Showers 1991, P 38]

**Q 402. There is no end to the thought waves that emerge
from mind. Is it possible for man to arrest these
vibrations in order to attain purity of mind?**

A.　*In fact it is not necessary to restrain and arrest these mental vibrations. Though this body is mortal, the thoughts are immortal. The power of thought vibrations runs round the world. As the heat waves, the electrical waves and light waves radiate, the mental waves too radiate. The thought vibrations are the cause for man's joy and sorrow, health and disease, birth and death. The entire world is suffused with mental vibrations. Hence, it is necessary to direct our thoughts on noble paths.*

[Summer Showers 1993, P 35]

Q 403. How do thoughts shape man's future?

A.　**We sow the seed of thought and reap the fruit of action, we sow the seed of action and reap the fruit of nature, we sow the seed of nature and reap the fruit of character, we sow the seed of character and reap the fruit of destiny.**

[Summer Showers 1993, P 36]

Q 404. What is the effect of harbouring evil thoughts?

A.　*By harbouring the evil thoughts of hatred, envy, anger and ego, man brings his own downfall. Man harbours evil thoughts to harm his fellow men. But, the harm that he does to his fellow men boomerangs on him with all its power and strength.* **By abusing, criticising, hurting and scandalising his fellow men, man is in fact abusing, criticising, hurting and scandalising the Lord Himself. Utterly ignorant of the presence of Divinity in others, man indulges in such heinous conduct.**

[Summer Showers 1993, P 36]

Q 405. How is one to control the *Sankalpa* (thoughts) and *Vikalpa* (confusion, doubts) of the mind?

A.　*When the stone of thought is cast on the lake of the mind, the ripples started by it fill all the senses and limbs in the body. When the thought is a pure and sacred one, the ripples emanating in the mind fill all the senses and limbs in the body, from head to toe, with pure reactions...If the thoughts are impure, they travel in the ripples to the senses and induce to indulge in unholy acts. Hence, the well known saying* **"The mind is made up of thoughts and aberrations." It follows that people should not give room for bad thoughts, bad associations or bad relationships.**

[SSS Vol. 27, P 145]

Q 406. How is one to proceed with the process of self-correction should the bad thoughts arise in mind?

A.   *Those who wish to use the body properly and ensure that they entertain good thoughts, perform good acts and reap good results should scrupulously follow two things, viz., regulation of diet and regulation of other living habits. You should not consume any and every type of food merely to appease hunger or the palate. You must eat only Satwic food. Our thoughts are determined by the kind of food we consume...As is the food, so is the head – thoughts. Our thoughts, therefore, are the result of the type of food we eat. The body is cleansed by water, while the mind is purified by Truth. It is only when we take food that is conducive to truth that we can pursue the path of truth. As the body is a sacred shrine, you should strictly avoid taking any intoxicating substances and articles of food.*

[SSS Vol. 1990, P 14-15]

Q 407. How can we translate good thoughts into good actions?

A.   *Chant the Name of God incessantly. It should be like your* *pulse beat. Body becomes lifeless, if there is no pulse beat. Likewise, you will become a living corpse if you do not chant The Divine Name. Consider whatever happens as good for you. When you foster such good thoughts, they will naturally turn into good actions, which will set an ideal to others.*

[SSS Vol. 33, P 299-300]

Q 408. How to control the worldly thoughts?

A. *In order to control the worldly thoughts, one has to reach the level of Super mind. Super Mind is nothing but superior mind, that which transcends the ordinary mind.*

[SSS Vol. 33, P 307]

Q 409. How will the bound soul get freed from the clutches of the mind and how and wherein will it finally merge?

A. *Cultivate good thoughts. Good thoughts lead to good actions. Good actions lead to Satsang (good company). Cultivate love. Everything is based on love and love alone. Man is born in love, is sustained in love and ultimately merges in love.*

[SSS Vol. 33, P 317]

Q 410. What was Lord Krishna's advice for checking *sankalpas* and escaping their consequences?

A. *Good thoughts lead to good actions and bad thoughts are responsible for bad actions. Man is the embodiment of sankalpas and vikalpas (thoughts and aberrations). All sankalpas are caused by body attachment. Krishna therefore exhorted man to give up body attachment. One of the main principles propounded in the Bhagavad Gita is given in the Sloka:*

"Sarvadharman Parityajya Maamekam Saranam Vraja, Aham Twa Sarvapapebhyo Mokshaishyami Ma Suchah" (*Surrender unto Me and perform all your actions as an offering to Me. I will destroy all your sins and confer liberation on you.*)

[SSS Vol. 35, P 238]

Q 411. Can one offer one's evil intentions and bad qualities and thoughts also to God?

A. There is a soiled and tattered currency note with you. No one is prepared to accept it from you. But when it is tendered to the Reserve Bank, which issued it, it is bound to accept it and issue a new note in return. Likewise, who is competent to accept one's bad thoughts, perverse feelings and evil intentions? Only the Almighty can accept them. He is the spiritual Reserve Bank that will accept the soiled notes of your mind and give in return good currency (in the form of good thoughts).

[SSS Vol. 25, P 167]

Q 412. For realisation of the Self, man has to conquer both the external and the internal tendencies. Out of the two, which are difficult to conquer?

A. *For him who has struggled with external tendencies and conquered them, the internal tendencies become easily controllable. The external tendencies have name and form and are attracted by becoming objects of experience. So, to overcome them is a matter of some difficulty. The internal tendencies have no form, taste or weight. They can be tamed with greater ease.*

[Prema V, P 92]

Q 413. How do desires rob man of his happiness?

A. *Kama (desire) has a 2-headed son, Krodha-Lobha by name, the twin-headed monster anger-greed. Through the malignant designs of these three, you are robbed of lasting happiness.*

[SSS Vol. 4, P 47]

Q 414. Can the desires be overcome by firm resolution?

A. *It is not the resolution that matters; it is resoluteness. Resolution is just a string of words. You may know the 700 slokas of the Bhagavad Gita by heart; but the time you spend in learning by rote, and in reciting it, is all waste, if you do not resolutely act upon even a single sloka. That learning might even be a handicap; for the skill has affected your head, and made it swell with pride.*

[SSS Vol. 4, P 49]

Q 415. How can we put an end to the cycle of birth and death?

A. *Man does not realise that the end of this cycle of birth and death is in his own hands. The tree came from the seed and the seed from the tree and so on, from the beginning of time. Yes, you may not know which came first, tree or seed; but you can easily put an end to the cycle, by frying the seed (desires). It won't sprout again.*

[SSS Vol. 3, P 170]

Q 416. How is one to go about on the journey of life for final success?

A. *Reduce the luggage you carry about on the journey of life. Remember, all that is not 'you' is luggage! You are not the body. So, the body is an item of luggage. The mind, the senses, the intelligence, the imagination, the desires, the plans, the prejudices,*

the discontent, the distress – all are items of luggage.
Jettison them soon, to make your travel lighter, safer
and more comfortable.

[SSS Vol. 9, 124]

Q 417. How and when will the true virtue manifest in man?

A.   *Desire and bondage to the objects desired and the*
plans to secure them are the attributes of the
individualised selves, not of the Self or Atma
resident in the body. The sense of me and mine, and
the emotions of lust and anger originate in the body-
mind complex. Only when this complex is conquered
and outgrown can true virtue emanate and manifest.

[Sutra Vahini, P 22]

Q 418. How is one to escape the consequences of *Kama* (desire) and *Kala* (time)?

A.   *Birth is the consequence of Kama (desire, lust):*
Death is the consequence of Kala (Time). The God of
Desire (Kama) was reduced to ashes by Shiva; the God of
*Time is Kala or Yama. He was subdued by Shiva. **So,***
one has to surrender to Shiva (God) if one has to
escape the consequence of these two frightfully fatal
forces.

[SSS Vol. 7, P 179]

Q 419. If desire is the cause of future birth, how is one to eradicate desires?

A.   *Man is burdened with desires. He plans to brighten the*
future, and wipe out the past. The tiny seed of desire grows
soon into a mighty tree; so you have to fry the seed in the
fire of Tapas, so that it may not sprout.

[SSS Vol. 7, P 164]

■ Samskaras

Q 420. What does *Samskara* mean?

A.   *Samskara means elevating culture and is the basis of rebirth. Our present actions become seeds of samskaras that decide the fruit in the next life.*

[SSS Vol. 26, P 249]

Q 421. Are Samskaras the residual effect of all good and bad activities of man ?

A.   *There are two types of activities, good and bad. The effect of both on the life of man has to be considered. The acts and activities that have transpired and that have been thrust back into forgetfulness by subsequent events have left a trace of their consequences on the mind. The residue is there. This residue is called samskaras... Only the chief events are registered clearly. The rest turn hazy and recede and disappear. These few that are registered and retained are samskaras.*

[Prema Vahini, P 43]

Q 422. Do the samskaras of the present life affect the coming life?

A.   **The samskaras of life, some stronger than the rest, stand out to the last. The net result of all the life is that which comes to memory at the last moment of life at the time of death. Therefore, direct the entire current of life towards the acquisition of that samskara which you feel best for the last moment. Fix your attention upon it, day and night. The feeling that dominates the moment of death works with great force in the coming life. This truth must guide man for the journey of this life too, for** samskaras are the wherewithal for this journey, as well as for the journey after this.

[Prema Vahini, P 46]

Q 423. How is one to earn holy *samskaras* in life?

A. *It is to earn holy Samskaras that one has to maintain the flow of high thoughts and feelings uninterrupted. The hands should be used to perform good deeds. Have the Lord's name within, and the practice of Swa-dharma without...The holy stream of good Samskaras must flow full and steady along the fields of holy thoughts and finally abide in the great ocean of Bliss at the moment of Death.*

[Prema Vahini, P 48]

Q 424. How do good *samskaras* help one reach the goal of life?

A. *The Samskaras make or mar the Jivi; they are the steps that take all Jivis to the goal. Through good Samskaras alone can man attain the Lord. So, every Jivi has to be wholly engaged in Sathkarma. Sathkarma is the authentic Puja. Be engaged in such Karmas. Revel uninterruptedly in the thought of the Lord. This royal road to the goal you have to reach.*

[Prema V, P 50]

Q 425. How is one to save oneself from the effects of bad Samskaras of the past?

A. *Man can attain everlasting bliss by getting immersed in good works and by saturating the mind with the love of God. Then the evil tendencies dare not hamper the path.*

[Prema V, P 49]

Where there is Faith, there is Love
Where there is Love, there is Peace,
Where there is Peace, there is Truth,
Where there is Truth, there is Bliss,
Where there is Bliss, there is God.

[SSS Vol. 25, P 33]

6
CONSCIOUSNESS LEVELS, BRAHMA-JNANA

Q 426. What is *Akasha*? What are the different levels of Consciousness in Akasha?

A. *Akasha is the name for sphere of Consciousness. Bhoota akasha is outer Cosmic Consciousness; Chitta akasha is the inner Consciousness of the Chitta (seat of intellect), the centre of discrimination of living beings, while Chit-akasha is the pure, unalloyed consciousness that flows from the Atma.*

The Bhoota akasha is the vast limitless space in which the Sun and planets are but tiny knots of energy. It is so extensive that the light from some of its stars, millions of light years away, has not yet reached the earth. Light travels, they say, at 1,86,000 miles per sec (in fact the speed is 1,88, 000 miles per second). So you can imagine the enormous size of the Bhoota akasha.

The Chitta akasha subsumes such an immeasurable Bhoota akasha, for the Consciousness illumines and becomes aware of all that exists. The Chitta akasha is prompted into activity by the Chit-akasha, the Chit of Sat-Chit-Ananda (different from the inner instrument of discrimination named Chitta). An infinitesimal fraction of the Atma is enough to activate the Chitta so that it can draw into Itself the cosmos, the entire objective Universe.

[SSS Vol. 14, P 228]

Q 427. **In what three different forms does God live in the human body?**

A. *'Purusha' signifies the shining and self-effulgent Brahman. This kind of self-effulgent Brahman is present in the human body in three different names, that is, Vishwa, Taijasa and Pragya (Prajna). In the world the same Brahman is present in three different aspects of Virat, Hiranyagarbha and Avyakrita.*

[Summer Showers 1974, P 206]

Q 428. **By what different names is the Divinity present in its three aspects in the Universe known?**

A. *Indra is one who has the form of Virat and gives all Aishwaryas or wealth. Surya the sun will have the form of Hiranyagarbha. Vasu stands for one who eradicates the sorrow.*

[Summer Showers 1974, P 206]

Q 429. **In which state of consciousness can we perceive these aspects of the Divine?**

A. *Indra is present in the waking state. The Sun is present in the dream state and Vasu is one who is present and takes care of the deep sleep state.*

[Summer Showers 1974, P 207]

Q 430. **Do these forms of Divinity in the Universe function independently in these states?**

A. *These three are not functioning independently in these* *states. These three are not fully independent and so do not act on their own in these states. Brahman remains fully independent and remains as the basis and makes them function according to His own wish.*

[Summer Showers 1974, P 207]

Q 431. How is the one Divine Principle Brahman present in various states of Consciousness?

A. *The Upanishads have elaborated on the principle of Brahman through three names: Virat, Hiranyagarbha and Avyakrita. These three forms of Divinity relate to sthula (gross), sukshma (subtle) and kaarana (cause) and to the three states of waking, dream and deep sleep.*

[Summer Showers 1991, P 131]

Q 432. What is *Prajnana*?

A. **Man is not just a combination of body and mind. He possesses prajnana – constant integrated awareness. Prajnana is the permanent witness or awareness pervading the Antahkarana (inner instrument).**

[Summer Showers 1991, P 46]

Q 433. What is the meaning of '*Ayam Atma Brahma*'?

A. **It means that this Atma is identical with Brahman.** *Atma is not something which is distinct from us. This Atma is present in everyone, in all beings and in all things. That Atma is identical with Brahman and has got a form that is indestructible. It is filled with shabda or (astral) sound. Om is the Ek-aksharam Brahman. The one single letter Om is Brahman. This has associated with it four aspects. The four aspects are: the waking stage, the dreaming stage, the deep sleep stage and the Turiya stage (beyond the deep sleep stage).*

[Summer Showers 1977, P 133]

Q 434. **What is the form of the waking state and how does the Atma experience the external world through it?**

A.   *In the waking state, one is fully awake. This waking stage has got a gross form and is connected intimately with our desires of the material world and is promoted by the five working organs and the five sense organs which we have together with the five pranas and four other features of the antahkarana: mind, intellect, ego and chitta. These are all present in the waking stage. This stage is also referred to as Viswa.*

[Summer Showers 1977, P 133]

Q 435. **What is the form and the functional aspect of the dreaming stage?**

A.   *The dreaming stage has got a subtle form. This stage is called Taijasa. Whatever one has experienced in the waking stage attaches itself in some form with the mind and continues to appear in the dreaming stage. In this stage all the 19 aspects, which we have mentioned earlier, will still appear as subtle forms with a subtle phase.*

[Summer Showers 1977, P 133]

Q 436. **How are the mind and intelligence involved in the waking and dreaming states?**

A.   *Mind, in the Manomaya Kosha and intelligence in the Pranamaya Kosha, play an important role. Both the waking stage and the dreaming stage are somewhat on the same footing and are equally important.*

[Summer Showers 1977, P 134]

Q 437. **What happens in the deep sleep stage? Has it got any connection with the material world?**

A.   *This (deep sleep stage) is also termed as Prajna (Pragya).*

In this stage of deep sleep, there is no connection whatever either through the gross form or through the subtle form, with the material world. Take the example of reflection of the sky in the pot. Once the pot is removed, the reflection disappears and the sky in the pot becomes identical with the original big sky. So also in this state of deep sleep, we lose all connection with the material world, the gross and the subtle forms and we are independent of them. In this state the 19 facets (Tattvas) mentioned above, are neither in the material form nor in the subtle form. The deep sleep state is quite distinct and separate from them. In this state, various organs of the body do not function at all.

[Summer Showers 1977, P 134]

Q 438. What is the aspect of the *Turiya* stage?

A.   *The aspects of Turiya are indescribable in ordinary words by any one. This state in its totality reflects the spirit of Atma. As we cannot see our own eyes, so also Atma cannot see itself. To understand this aspect, take the example of a doll made of salt and ask that doll to go and experience the taste of the ocean. The salt doll will go into the ocean and will get lost by dissolution and merger. As in this analogy, if the Jiva is looking for the Atma, he will completely merge into the Atma when he gets close to it.*

[Summer Showers 1977, P 134]

Q 439. What is the experience of this state of oneness of the *jiva* with Atma?

A.   *This aspect (of merger of the jiva into Atma or God) is described as omnipresence. This is also another feature of Atma and it is able to be present in all the living beings.*

[Summer Showers 1977, P 135]

Q 440. How is this state of omnipresence of Atma or Brahman described?

A.   *This state has been described by calling '**Prajnanam Brahma**' in the Veda. It has also been described as '**Tat Twam Asi**' or **That Thou Art**. It is also '**Ayam Atma Brahman**' or **Atma is Brahman**. This is same as saying '**Aham Brahmasmi**' or **I am Brahman**. These are the four **mahavakyas** that constitute the spirit of the Vedas.*
[Summer Showers 1977, P 135]

Q 441. How is one to achieve the third stage called *Prajna (Pragya)*?

A.   *No one can live without being dependent to some extent, on the material creation around him. At that time he is in the first stage or the waking stage, which is described as the Viswa.*

*Later when we can acquire faith in the Divinity, then we transform into the next higher stage described as Taijas. **If we do not stop at this stage, and if we develop the next higher stage and identify ourselves with Atma, that can be described as Pragya.** In this stage of Pragya there will be a commendable determination to fulfil a task. That determination is permanent and unwavering.*
[Summer Showers 1977, P 137]

Q 442. What is *Prajnana (Pragyan)*?

A.   *The aspect of unity with Atma or Paramatma can be referred to as the aspect of Prajnana. Prajnana enables you to stand out only as a witness and experience everything around you...We say this is my hand...who is this claimant? Veda has been telling us the answer by saying: That is you, thou art that, I am*

Prajnana and I am Brahman; in that way it makes you stand out as a witness and not become identical with your body or hand.

[Summer Showers 1977, P 138]

Q 443. How are all these states of consciousness contained in Brahma?

A.   *The one all-pervasive Brahman permeates the entire universe of animate and inanimate objects. This all-inclusive Brahman has assumed the audible form of the primordial word AUM. There are four inseparable elements in this Supreme Para Brahman. They are Viswa, Taijas, Prajna and Turiya...The Turiya-avastha is the highest state of consciousness in which the essential nature of the Atma is experienced.*

[Summer Showers, P 99, 100]

Q 444. Is the consciousness that we experience in different states really differentiated?

A.   *There is no difference between one kind of consciousness and another. All consciousness is alike because it is a manifestation of Brahman (the Absolute). It is Brahman that has manifested as the Cosmos.*

[Summer Showers 1977, P 45]

Q 445. If the consciousness at all levels is one, why does the external world and our inner consciousness appear to be different? How is one to correct the distorsion?

A.   *Do not look at the world with a worldly eye. Look upon it with the eye of Atma, as the projection of Paramatma. The One is experienced as many because of the forms and names man has imposed on it. That is the result of the mind playing the game. Uparathi (a state of mind beyond dualities)*

promotes inner exploration – Nivrithi, not outer
enquiry and activity, Pravrithi. Along Nivrithi lies
the path of Jnana.

[Sutra Vahini, P 14]

Q 446. What are the characteristics of *Prajna avastha* (state)?

A.   *Prajnavastha is a transcendental state of consciousness*
in which the dichotomy between grossness and subtlety
disappears in Super-consciousness. It is pure Prajna or
consciousness of Divinity. In Prajnavastha, the
differentiating and diversifying faculties of the mind
become inoperative. That is why it is said that prajnanam
is Brahman.

[Summer Showers 1979, P 99-100]

Q 447. What are the characteristics of *Turiyavastha*?

A.   *Turiyavastha is the highest state of consciousness in which*
the essential nature of the Atma is experienced. It is a
pure, tranquil and steady state of superconsciousness in
which all discriminating gunas (attributes) are
transcended and dissolved in the eternal and absolute
reality of Brahman.

[Summer Showers 1979, P 100]

Q 448. How does Prajna express itself in the human body
and where does it manifest?

A.   *It is the principle which pervades equally the body, the*
mind, the Will and the Antahkarana (inner instrument).
It has been defined as 'Constant Integrated Awareness'.
It expresses itself as 'I' and shines forth in its fullness. It
manifests itself throughout the world.

[SSS Vol. 25, P 211]

Q 449. How does one comprehend the meaning of 'I' in
the human nature?

A. *This 'I' shines as an entity that is pure, unsullied and unselfish. In modern parlance this is called "Conscience". Whatever action one does, the "Conscience" declares whether it is right or wrong...This is the voice of Prajna—principle which is related to the Universal Consciousness.*

[SSS Vol. 25, P 212, 213]

Q 450. What truth does *Prajna-sakthi* teach about the relationship between the object and the image?

A. *The Prajna-sakthi teaches that when a person sees his reflection in a trough of water, the reflection resembles him, but he is not the reflection...The image is you, but you are not the image. If someone beats you, you are hit but the image is not affected by beating. If you and the image were identical, the blow that hit you should affect the image equally. Therefore it is clear that you and the image are not the same. But this image identifies itself with you.*

[SSS Vol. 25, P 214]

Q 451. If *Prajna* (Constant Integrated Awareness) is present in all the constituents of the body and the mind, then it is a common factor. How is it identified?

A. *Prajna is present in all the constituents of the body and the mind, but under different names and forms. Just as sugar is the common factor in a variety of sweets with different labels, Prajna is a common factor. This common factor is identified with 'I' (nenu).*

[SSS Vol. 25, P 215]

Q 452. How does it happen? How to cognise this common factor 'I' in all?

A.   *This infinite "I" principle appears in a myriad objects in multifarious forms. All these objects have emanated from the infinite 'I'. They are fragments of the Infinite. Similarly, in the body, the mind, the intellect, etc. the Prajna-sakthi (the integrated awareness) of "I" is present. All these have emerged from the Infinite and are manifestations of it. We should attempt at expounding the unity that underlines the diversity.*

[SSS Vol. 25, P 216]

Q 453. How should we proceed in the *sadhana* for attaining 'Prajna-tattva'?

A.   *People indulge in what they call meditation in 'ekaantam' (solitude). It is not seclusion in a room or a cave or a forest that constitutes solitude. It is the one-pointed contemplation of God that is true meditation. It means merging the mind in thoughts of the Divine exclusively. The mind is a prey to continuous fickleness. The only way to achieve concentration is to merge the mind in the Prajna-tattva, the integral awareness of the 'I'. Prajna is also termed as Brahma-Jnana or Advaita-Jnana (knowledge of the Absolute). It is also called Atma-jnana.*

[SSS Vol. 25, P 219]

Q 454. What are the different levels of Consciousness associated with these bodies and by what name is the Atma known in these states?

A.   *The Atma when it is associated with the physical body is called **Annamaya Purusha**. This is the state of ordinary consciousness. When the spiritual consciousness is associated with the Vital Consciousness (the Pranamaya Kosha), the Atma is known as **Pranaswarupa** (Life*

Consciousness). When the Atma is associated with the mental consciousness, it is known as **Manopurusha.** *The fourth consciousness transcends the human senses. It is called* **Ateeta-Maanasatvam – Transcendental Consciousness.** *The Vedas and Upanishads have described this state as* **Brihat and Rita.** *It transcends human limitations and comes close to divinity.* **It is called Super Mind. The Atma in this state is called Vijnanapurusha. Above this state is the Anandamaya Purusha – the enjoyer of Bliss. It is a state of Super-Consciousness, which expands in due course to merge with the Universal Consciousness.**

[SSS Vol. 21, P 43-44]

Q 455. What is Universal Consciousness?

A. *The all-pervading Universal Consciousness is the highest consciousness, which encompasses all other levels of consciousness and is the basis for all of them.* **That is the Suddha-Satva (Pure Consciousness), the "all-effective Will", the "Super-Divine Life". This is the Sai-tattva (The Sai Principle).**

[SSS Vol. 21, P 44]

Q 456. How does the Divine Primal Will act through different beings?

A. *The Divine Will has three aspects of achievement through the three modes – the sathvic, the rajasic and the tamasic…when maya prompts us into the sathvic mood of that Will, we become progressive seekers of Jnana (spiritual wisdom) that reveals the Unity. Overwhelmed by the rajasic quality of that Will, we are deluded into the pursuit of worldly victories and ephemeral wealth and renown. The tamasic nature of that Will seeks the quickest and easiest* *ways of happy living. The facets of that Will are called Jnana-sakthi, Iccha-sakthi and Kriya-sakthi.*

[SSS Vol. 14, P 159]

Q 457. How do the three facets of the Divine Will affect us?

A.   *Maya inheres in every being and every activity of that being. It has three aspects of achievement through the three modes and moods of that Will – the sathvic, the rajasic and the tamasic. The three modes affect beings and things in various proportions and permutations and so we have all the variety and diversity of the objective world. Atma (whether individualised or universalised) is only One. The jeevatma and Paramatma are One and indivisible.*

[SSS Vol. 14, P 159]

Q 458. Wherefrom does the Cosmos arise? Who is Brahman?

A.   *The Macrocosm and the microcosm – the Brahmanda and the Pindanda – the Universal and the individual – all arise from the One Truth. Though they are manifestations from the Truth, It is not affected by either. It is known as Brahman.*

[SSS Vol. 14, P 157]

Q 459. What is *Chaitanya?*

A.   *The Atma is synonymous with Brahma, which is nothing but Chaitanya permeating every human being. Man has a name and form but Chaitanya has no form.*

[SS – Feb. 2003, P 48]

Q 460. What is the difference between *Chaitanya,* Conscience and Consciousness?

A.   *The Chaitanya that is present in the human body is called 'conscience'. The all-pervasive Chaitanya is called 'consciousness'. When the individual understands the principle of unity in diversity, the 'conscience' gets transformed into 'consciousness'.*

[SS – Feb. 2003, P 48]

Q 461. How does Consciousness act?

A. *Resolution, decision, design – these are acts of Consciousness. Non-conscious entities are incapable of such exercises of Will.*

[Sutra Vahini, P 55]

Q 462. What is the meaning of "Jyoti" as mentioned in the Upanishads with reference to Brahman?

A. *The Jyoti illumines Heaven and beyond, It reveals even Brahman. That which makes known, by its splendour, the era preceding the origin of living beings, and the regions beyond even the farthest and the highest, "That" is indicated by the word Jyoti. It shines in that super most among supreme Loka (region).*

The same Jyoti shines everywhere, at all times, in all beings. It comprises Sath-Chith-Ananda. For every living being, why, for the very Cosmos itself, the invisible Brahman, is the Basis. It is this Para Brahma, the Omni-Self that causes the Cosmos to shine.

[Sutra Vahini, P 92]

Q 463. By what other names is this Upanishadic "Jyoti" referred to? How does it operate in human beings?

A. *Jyoti is the word appropriate only for this Light and not the limited, inferior physical light. It is Param-Jyoti (Supreme Light), the Advaita Jyoti (the Jyoti without a second), the Akhanda Jyoti (the Eternal Light). In other words It is Para-Brahman Itself, for all this is revealed only through It (Para-Brahman). Jyoti is embodied in Brahman; it operates in and through Brahman only.*

Brahman is immanent in all and so, Jyoti reveals all and shines in all. This Jyoti brings to light the fire that pervades the regions (Lokas), that warms the body and resides in the stomach, the gleam in the eye.

[Sutra Vahini, P 92]

Q 464. What experiences does the individual soul have during the dream and deep-sleep states? Can the soul have the experiences of its past lives also?

A.   *The Jivi (embodied soul) is the deity enshrined in the body, its temple. The Jivi experiences all that is seen, heard and contacted by the mind in the outer worlds. Besides these, the Jivi might construct and experience in dreams and witness such experiences undergone during previous lives. It depends on the activities stamped on the mind of each one. The Bliss the Jivi is, the authenticity of the Param-Atma. During dreamless sleep, the Jivi enters and revels in the region of Bliss. But this experience doesn't last; it is quite temporary. The person who has gained the Awareness through the purification of the mind and the clarification of the intellect (sadhana) will have the unchanging Bliss of mergence in Param-Atma.*

[Sutra Vahini, P 79]

■ Knowledge Of The Divinity

Q 465. Of all the Vidyas which one is the true and the highest *Vidya*?

A.   *If we can understand and acquire the essence of the Atma Vidya, then every other vidya will become available. All these material vidyas that we learn for the sake of the material world are like individual rivers. But the*

Adhyatmic vidya is like the ocean…That is why it is said, "Adhyatma vidya, vidyanam." Among all vidyas, Adhyatmic vidya is the only true vidya.

[Summer Showers 1977, P 191]

Q 466. What is *Brahma Vidya* (Knowledge of Divinity)?

A. *Brahma Vidya is solely connected with the knowledge of Atma. Brahma indicates Omnipresence, Brahma also indicates totality and completeness. In its aspect of totality, Brahma Vidya deals with the spiritual world and all the ethical aspects of our life.*

[Summer Showers 1977, P 186]

Q 467. When does one become eligible for attaining *Brahma Vidya* (knowledge of God)?

A. *We become eligible for Brahma Vidya only when we understand the relation between Brahma and man in the cosmic cycle of creation and destruction. Brahma means vast, infinite principle.*

[Summer Showers 1991, P 130]

Q 468. What do we mean by knowledge about one's own self?

A. *It is the knowledge of the Atma. To know the Atma and to know one's own self is the most useful aspect of one's learning.*

[Summer Showers 1977, P 46]

Q 469. Where has Prana come from? Who makes the eyes see and the mind think?

A. *Upanishads call this power "Brahman". They declare that Brahman makes the world shine. Brahman lends His illumination to others, but* *nothing makes Brahman Himself shine. Brahman's effulgence makes the eyes see, but they cannot see Brahman! The mind can think only with Brahman's power, but it is unable to grasp Brahman Himself... Kathopanishad declares that Brahman is the life of prana, the mind of the mind, the eye of the eyes.*

[Summer Showers 1991, P 57]

Q 470. What is *Brahmananda*?

A.   *Divine Bliss, Brahmanandam, is composed of two words – Brahma + Anandam. Brahma and Anandam are separate. Man journeys from food to bliss. Man's aim is bliss alone. When this bliss joins with Brahma, it acquires the form of Brahmanandam.*

[Summer Showers 1991, P 130]

Brahmanandam, Parama Sukhadam, Kevalam jnanamurtim,

Dwandwateetam, Gagana Sadrisham, Tattwamasyadi Lakshyam,

Ekam, Nityam, Vimlam, Achlam,

Sarvadhee Sakshibhutam, Bhavateetam, Trigunarahitam.

(God is the embodiment of supreme bliss, He is wisdom Absolute, the One without the second, beyond the pair of opposites, expansive and pervasive like the sky, the goal indicated by the Mahavakya Tattwamasi, the eternal, pure, unchanging, the witness of all functions of the intellect, beyond all mental conditions and the three Gunas)

[SSS Vol. 34, P 144]

Q 471. What is *Atmananda*?

A.   *Atmananda (bliss of the spirit) is Amritananda (the* *eternal bliss). That is within you. It is Brahmananda. All qualities are within you.*

[SSS Vol. 34, P 206]

Q 472. How can this Divine Bliss be attained?

A.   *Divine Bliss can dawn with the conquest of worldly attachments, fear and anger, but only to a certain extent…Love for God must be cultivated as well.*

[Summer Showers 1991, P 131]

Q 473. How can we understand the principle of Brahman – the Divine principle?

A.   *The Upanishads have elaborated on the principle of Brahman through three names: Virat, Hiranyagarbha and Avyakrita. These three forms of Divinity relate to sthula (gross), sukshma (subtle) and Karana (cause) and to the three states of waking, dream and deep sleep.*

[Summer Showers 1991, P 131]

Q 474. What is the concept of *Poornam* (Fullness) of Para Brahma?

A.   *This material objective world is what is visible to our eyes, what pleases our senses, what fascinates our minds and what informs our brains. But in and through this very world, there is one reachable non-material subjective world. When that is known, both worlds reveal themselves as partial expression of the same invisible Consciousness (Chaitanya). The two supplement each other into the one fullness (Poornam). From the Para Brahma (the Full), the jiva (the individual soul) arises. When the jiva sheds the material corpus in which it is encased, the eternal Universal Consciousness is again the One Fullness (This is Full), the Para Brahma Principle.*

Poornam Adah, Poorrnam Idam, Poornaath Poornam Udachyathe, Poornasya Poornam Aadaaya, Poornam Eva Avasishyathe. (That is Full, This is Full, From the Full arose the Full, From the Full when the Full is taken out, Full itself remains).

[Vidya V, P 4]

Q 475. What happens when one attains Supreme Wisdom?

A.   *When one attains the Supreme Wisdom or the highest knowledge, the discrimination between the opposites – Atma and Anatma, Vidya and Avidya, Vikasa and Vinasha (growth and decay) fades away.*

[Vidya V, P 5]

Q 476. How is one to acquire Supreme Wisdom?

A.   *The sacred wisdom cannot enter hearts which are dark and dirty. When one is anxious to destroy the darkness of ignorance and the dirt of desire, awareness of the Atma (Atma-jnana) or, in other words, knowledge of Brahman (Brahma Vidya) has to be gained. Darkness can be ended only with the help of light.*

[Vidya V, P 7]

Q 477. If a person is a master of the *mantra 'Aham Brahmasmi'*, does he attain unity with Brahman?

A.   *No, ceaseless striving through countless births, loyal performance of scriptural duties, these purify the mind. In such a mind, seeds of devotion sprout and when tended with care and knowledge, flowers bloom, fruits appear and ripen and get filled with sweetness and fragrance. When the fruit is eaten, man becomes one with the Supreme, the power that permeates all things and which is eternally present and conscious and blissful. A person may enunciate the formula – Aham-Brahmasmi correctly; etymology may be perfect; but It is not mastery of the words and their meaning that count, it is awareness and experience – these are fundamentals.*

[Prema V, P 40]

Q 478. What is the *Adwaitic* experience?

A. *It is Brahman alone, upon which all is super imposed, that exists. There is nothing else, besides Atma. That is the Adwaitic experience. Mud alone is real. The pot-consciousness is born of ignorance regarding mud; mind is the basis, the substance of the pot. How can the pot exist without mud? How can effect exist apart from the cause? The world appears as multiplicity only to the ignorant. To a Jnani, Brahman alone is. This is Adwaitic experience.*

[Prema V, P 40]

Q 479. What is the difference between *Adwaita*, *Dwaita* and *Visishta-adwaita*?

A. ***That which teaches the highest knowledge of this Unity is known as Adwaita; that which teaches the principle of the Lover and the Loved, the Jiva and the Brahman is known as Dwaita; that which teaches about all three, Love, Lover and Loved, Prakriti, Jiva and Brahman, is known as Visishta-adwaita. But these three are one***...*From milk, butter and buttermilk emerge. Milk, which contains all is Adwaita. Butter, which contains the two categories is Dwaita; after that is rated the buttermilk which remains as Visishta-adwaita. Though, their tastes differ, the colour of all these is the same always. This, which is the same in all, is the Nirguna Brahman.*

[Prema V, P 63]

Q 480. Are those living in the families eligible to follow the path of Brahman?

A.   *It is not that those who are in the family, living as a part thereof, do not have the right to follow the path of Brahman. The family life is like a chariot. Husband and wife are the horses. Dharma is the charioteer. Family or the bundle of worldly desires is the path and Moksha is the goal. Thus the horses namely the husband and the wife can lead the chariot of life to Moksha if they follow the path of dharma. It is not right to think that only yogis, jnanis and rishis are entitled to moksha. The destination is available for everyone... When one aspires to reach the right destination, God is always ready to respond to everyone with the same attitude. He is even prepared to lead them to the destination.*

[Summer Showers 1974, P 64-65]

Q 481. How and when do the differences and distinctions of the physically seen world disappear and the Universal Consciousness is attained?

A.   *The expression 'God is nowhere' can remain unchanged. There is no need to contradict it. The only thing necessary is to read the 'w' in 'God is nowhere', in conjunction with the previous 'no', so that it becomes 'God is now here'. The negative suddenly becomes positive. Similarly, by merely unifying in one direction the multidirectional vision now directed on the universe, the distinctions and the differences disappear and the many become One.*

[Vidya V, P 8]

Q 482. What is meant by *Pratyaksha* and *Paroksha*?

A.   *Knowledge itself is of two kinds; patent and latent, direct and indirect, Pratyaksha and Paroksha, real and apparent. Pratyaksha or Aparoksha (the patent knowledge) is gained through the ear and other sense organs. The Paroksha (or the latent), the real knowledge knows no plurality. It analyses and understands the attractions and objects, which haunt the mind. It purifies the mind and widens the vision of the heart.*

[Vidya V, P 12]

7
ATMA

■ **Atma**

Q 483. What is that by knowing which one knows everything?

A.   *This is the Atma principle.*

[Summer Showers 1991, P 127]

Q 484. Is Atma the object of Knowledge?

A.   *Atma is not the object of Knowledge; it is the very source and spring of knowledge. Knowledge is that which shows the way to the ripening, fruition, the freedom, the immortality, the eternal happiness, the eternal peace. He who is carried away by the vagaries of the senses cannot attain the Atma. (Atma) Brahman is the one, unchanging, in this changing world.*

[Prasanthi V, P 4]

Q 485. How is Atma defined?

A.   *The Atma is, really speaking, nothing positable. It is neither this nor that. It can be said to be only It, the Atma, the Brahman. Brahman itself has become*

Sathya, Prema, Light, Santhi, Jnana and Paramananda. Through any of these paths, you can attain Brahman; have no doubt about that. It is the Truth. The Atma is not these five senses, nor buddhi, nor the pranas – the life force. It can only be described as what it is not, not by what it is. No one can say it is this etc.

If anyone says it is thus and thus or it is this or it is that, we can take it that he does not know a wee bit of it at all. About something unknown, much can be said; anything, any name can be ascribed to it. In short, the Atma cannot be communicated by words; it is impossible to describe it whoever may try.

[Prasanthi V, P 5]

Q 486. What is the one common factor in all living beings that links them together?

A. *There is only one common feature for all living things in the world and that is the eternal spirit. In all manifold forms of creation in unity and in diversity, we find only the spirit of Atma and nothing else. It is the realisation of this aspect that constitutes the essence of all learning.*

[Summer Showers 1977, P 46]

Q 487. We know that the body, mind and intellect are instruments of the *Atma* to enable it to relate with the outside world. Is the life-force in the body or the *prana* as it is called, the same, as Atma or it too is an instrument of the Atma?

A. *The life principle or the prana in us is such that when we go to sleep during the night, it loses all the ability to find out even whether the prana exists or not. The prana or*

*the life in us, does not know whether the body is breathing
in or breathing out. In that state of sleep, because all the
sensory organs have become passive, they are not working.
In those conditions, along with the organs, even this life
prana is also not working...Here also it becomes clear to
us that prana should be classified as one of the other
instruments or organs and not Atma.*

[Summer Showers 1977, P 48]

**Q 488. What is the nature of the Atma? How does it
experience the outside world?**

A.   *This Atma, which is present in everyone, experiences
the world with the help of the organs. Even in the
dreaming state, in a very subtle manner, the Atma
experiences the intelligence and the mind. The
experience, which the Atma has in the waking state
and in the dreaming state, is also possible in the
deep sleep state. We thus conclude that the quality
of Atma is such that in all the three states i.e, the
waking state, the dreaming state and the deep sleep
state, it does not change.*

[Summer Showers 1977, P 48]

Q 489. What is the true nature of the Atma?

A.   *The Atma should be regarded only as a witnessing
consciousness when alone it will be true Atma. You
are only a witness.* You, through the help of your organs
and your body are witnessing all the things around you.
Atma is present everywhere. There is no place in the world
where there is no Atma. That kind of omnipresent Atma
enters a container, a form, and through that container,
the human body, it makes use of you.

[Summer Showers 1977, P 50]

Q 490. **What is that state of Atma that is called 'Prajnanam Brahma' in the Vedas?**

A. *This is another feature of Atma and it is able to be present in all beings. This state has been described by calling 'Prajnanam Brahma'. It has also been described as 'Tat Twam Asi' or That Thou Art. It is also 'Ayam Atma Brahma' or Atma is Brahman. This is same as saying 'Aham Brahmasmi' or I am Brahman. These are the four mahavakyas that constitute the spirit of the Vedas.*

[Summer Showers 1977, P 135]

Q 491. **If Atma has the form of sound or *Sabda* as revealed above, then are Atma and *Sabda* the same?**

A. *Atma, which is the form of sound or sabda and the sound, the Omkar, are both one and the same. Those who propound Vedanta have been explaining the truth by saying that the combination of A-kara, U-kara and M-kara is A U M, and is nothing but Brahman. Either in the gross form or in the subtle form, or in the supreme form of the Turiya, what is contained is the same and it is Omkar. This Atma which is identical with divinity is present everywhere. It takes the form of Pragya in the created form in order to establish the identity between the jeevatma and Paramatma.*

[Summer Showers 1977, P 136]

Q 492. **How will the Atma in man shine?**

A. *All beings in the world have different names and forms as embodied beings. When the embodiment is taken away only the one Atma in all of them remains. The sense of separateness is a creation of* *the mind. When this feeling born of ignorance goes, the Godliness in man will shine.*

[SSS Vol. 25, P 11]

Q 493. What are Atma and Anatma?

A.   In reality, there is no such thing as Anatma. Anatma is merely the inability to perceive the Atma.

[SSS Vol. 25, P 202]

Q 494. What makes man turn away from Atma?

A.   *It is the mind that turns men away from Atma. It is because one has lost the vision of the Atma that he is caught up in the Anatma Bhaava (vagaries of the mind). Forgetting the effulgence of the Sun (the Atma), man relies on the mind, which is like the moon that sheds the reflected light from the sun.*

[SSS Vol. 25, P 202]

Q 495. Should one engage himself in spiritual exercises to get rid of *Anatma* or control the mind?

A.   *All special practices in which people are engaged today are related to the mind only. Spiritual exercises should not be performed mentally. The mind is like a thief who cannot be expected to catch a thief. The mind, instead of seeking the Atma, interests itself in other things. It turns man away from the Atma and involves him in illusory pleasures of the world. Hence, spiritual exercises based on the mind cannot lead man out of the darkness of ignorance. When the Atma is experienced, the mind will cease to exist.*

[SSS Vol. 25, P 202-203]

Q 496. Is there still the need for mind control after one has experienced Atma?

A. *When the mind is absent, there is no need for control of mind. Once the Atma is experienced, the mind control becomes superfluous. It is like the light of the moon fading in the presence of the sunlight.*

[SSS Vol. 25, P 203]

Q 497. What is the best way to experience Atma?

A. *If man enquires earnestly into the nature of 'I', his enquiry will lead him to the experience of the Atma.*

[SSS Vol. 25, P 203]

Q 498. Why does man not recognise the effulgence of the Atma in spite of its presence within him?

A. *The Sun shines in all its glory, but its light is not felt inside a house because of the walls around and ceiling above. The body is a divine temple and the indwelling Spirit is the eternal Jiva. But man has created the walls of Moha and Mamakara (attachment and possessiveness) around it and covered it with the ceiling of Ahamkara (egoism). It is only when these walls and roof are removed that the divine 'I' principle will be revealed in its full form as the effulgent 'Prajna'.*

[SSS Vol. 25, P 211]

Q 499. Is it the body or the Atma that derives joy from looking at objects? What is it that relishes and enjoys the taste of the food eaten? Is it the body or the Atma?

A. *The eye is an instrument. How can we identify this instrument with Atma? What applies to the eye, applies to the ear, which hears, the tongue, which tastes, the hand, which does work, the nose that smells. All these organs have to be regarded as instruments. Then, how can the human body, which is composed of these organs, be anything other than an instrument? The mind is only a device by which we can distinguish or think and it cannot be identified with the Atma. Intelligence is also an instrument, which can be used at the command of the Atma.* **The Atma, which is present in everyone, experiences the world with the assistance of these instruments.**

[Summer Showers 1977, P 47-48]

Q 500. Who was the first Sage to discover the power of the Atom?

A.   *Kanada was the one who experienced and propagated the truth that God is all-pervasive. Anoraneeyan Mahato maheeyan (Brahman is subtler than the subtlest atom and vaster than the vastest object).Kanada recognised the existence of God in every atom. He even described God as Anuswarupa (the very form of atom). The world cannot exist without the atom. Earlier nothing existed in the universe.*

[SSS Vol. 35, P 189-190]

Q 501. What was Sage Kanada's finding on the divine principle of the atom (Anu)?

A.   *Saints and sages of yore undertook spiritual practices. Kanada also performed penance. Ultimately, he realised that he had originated from the atom and would merge into it. He gave up body attachment. So long as there is selfishness in man, he will not be able to understand the divine principle of the atom. One may do japa, dhyana and penance, but one's mind should always be steadily fixed on the principle of the atom. Everything is contained in this. Our body, mind, intellect, etc., are nothing but the manifestations of the atom, which is verily divine.*

[SSS Vol. 35, P 196]

Q 502. Wherefrom does the life force come in the atom?

A.   *People think that the atom has no life in it. It is a wrong notion. The life force that holds the entire universe together is present in the atom also. Hence it is said, God is present in microcosm as well as in macrocosm.*

[SSS Vol. 35, P 194]

Q 503. Do the sense of 'doer' and 'enjoyer' affect the Atma?

A.   *The sense of doer and enjoyer of 'agentship' might appear to affect the Atma but they are not part of the genuine nature of the Atma.*

[Sutra Vahini, P 22]

Q 504. Do the wrong actions of a deluded person affect the state of his Atma?

A.   *Things get mirrored and produce images but the mirror is not tarnished or even affected thereby. It remains as clear as it was. So, too, the man of virtue might be subjected to some contaminating activities due to back-log of acts (karmas) in previous lives, but they cannot mar or obstruct his present nature or activities. The jivi or individual has as his genuine basic attributes: purity, serenity and joy.*

[Sutra Vahini, P 22]

■ Jivatma

Q 505. Is 'becoming' of Paramatma into Jivatma real? Does it mean fragmentation of the One Paramatma? Why are we not able to cognise the Oneness?

A.   *In spite of 'becoming', which is only illusion imposing multiplicity on the One Being, It remains One. So long as inquiry is postponed, only the multiplicity is cognised. The multiplicity is neither real nor unreal. It is relatively real, pragmatically real, Mithya, not Sathya, but an*

*amalgam of sathya (truth) and asathya (untruth) –
apparently real but fundamentally unreal, real for most
practical purposes (Vyavahar) but unreal when the basic
nature is unraveled. Mithya is the mixture of Sathya and
Asathya, the knowledge of the snake, which is negated
when the knowledge of the rope is won.*

[SSS Vol. 14, P 157-158]

**Q 506. What is the relationship between God, Jeevatma
and the objective world? What is the Reality
behind the three?**

A.   *Maya is the Will that causes all three. It is a clear
flawless mirror. When the satvic nature is reflected
in that mirror, God results. When the rajasic nature
is reflected, the Jeeva or individualised self-
results...All three are Paramatma from whom the
three derive their Reality as Its reflections. While
undergoing reflection, they attain different forms
and combinations of characteristics. The One
becomes many. Every one of the many is Real only
because of the One in it.*

[SSS Vol. 14, P 159-160]

■ Reality, Tattva

Q 507. What is that 'I' we so often talk of? What is our Reality?

A.   *When we talk of the 'I', we note that there are two
kinds of 'I'. 'I' in one sense is the recognition of your
external human form and the body. This is the eye
with which you experience the external aspect. There
is a second 'I' referring to the inner aspect. These
two relate to two aspects, the body and the Brahman*

inside the body. *Between these two extremes there is also an intermediate state and that is the identification of the 'I' with the jiva in you. To say that you are identical with the jiva in the intermediate state between the body and the Brahman is like the dreaming state. To say 'I am the body' corresponds to the waking state. To say 'I am Brahman' corresponds to the deep sleep state.* **These states are however, simply reflections of the Atma and they cannot be identified with the Atma. There is a state, which is higher than all these three states and is referred to as the Turiya state.**

[Summer Showers 1977, P 49]

Q 508. What is real 'I' in man and how to comprehend this real 'I' principle?

A. *It is true that it is the "I" that sees, hears and experiences. But when a man uses the 'I', he identifies it with the body sense and not with an awareness of its Prajna nature. Hence, there are two kinds of 'I'. One may be equated with the term 'eye' and the other with the single letter 'I'. The 'I' that corresponds to the 'eye' is related to the body. The single letter 'I' proclaims the power of the Prajna (Constant Integrated Awareness).*

[SSS Vol 25, P 211-212]

Q 509. What does *Tattvam* mean?

A. *Tat is 'That', 'tvam' is 'this'. What is 'That'? What is distant is referred to as 'that' and what is near is called 'this'. Our senses determine what is near and what is far. The physical body in close proximity to the senses was called 'this' by the rishis. The principle beyond the reach of the senses is 'That', the Atma…Thus, we have the Vedic injunction –* **Tat Tvam Asi – That Thou Art.**

[Summer Showers 1991, P 32]

Q 510. **How do we cognize *Prajna* (Constant Integrared Awareness) present in all the constituents of the body and the mind?**

A.   *One declares "This is my body". "My" is an expression of "I". Again one declares: "This is my mind". Here again "I" is affirmed. "This is my chitta" (will), "These are my sensory organs". In all these statements, the 'I' is repeatedly affirmed in the possessive case. The declaration "this is my body" also carries by implication the meaning "I am not the body". Similarly when one says 'this is my mind', he affirms that he is not the mind. The use of 'my' describing one's body and mind etc. means that he is different from the body and the mind...In the body, the mind, the intellect, etc., the Prana-sakthi (the integrated awareness) "I" is present. All these objects have emanated from the infinite "I".*

[SSS Vol. 25, P 215-216]

Q 511. What is *Ritham*?

A.   *Ritham is that which is changeless in three periods of time – past, present and future. That is true wisdom.That which undergoes change is marakam and that which is changeless is tarakam.*

[SSS Vol. 35, P 348-349]

■ Atmic Experience

Q 512. Can we see the Lord?

A.   *The Lord is all Love; so He can be seen only through Love. The moon has to be seen only through its own light, no other light can illumine the moon...The Lord can be seen only by the light that He is, namely, the light of pure prema (love).*

[SSS Vol. 1, P 87]

Q 513. How is one to attain the vision of God?

A.   *Krishna said: "The vision is achieved only by the Bhakta who is devoted to Me, with Ananya-Bhakti; devotion which does not admit of the least distraction." Such Bhaktas see only the Lord; whatever they do, they do as worship to the Lord. They have no other form before their eyes; no other thought in their minds; no other act for their hands. At all times and places, they see only My Form, they utter only My Name; they think only about Me...It is such Oh! Arjuna, that attain this vision."*

[Geetha Vahini, P 221]

Q 514. God is said to be beyond the sensory perception of man. If that is so, how can we experience God?

A.   *To be able to experience the aspect of God, which is above sensory capacities, we should also rise above the senses...The world is filled with Brahman. Without Brahman there is no world. The whole universe is only an illusory manifestation of Brahman. One does not have to search for Brahman in some distant chosen place. If with some reason and depth we make an enquiry there is a chance of finding Brahman in our own heart and within ourselves. Provided we get into a state of meditation, we can enjoy the bliss of recognizing Brahman everywhere. If the mind is made steady and unwavering we can enjoy the permanent bliss and see the aspect of Brahman.*

[Summer Showers 1974, P 54-55]

Q 515. While remaining a part and parcel of the creation, how can one experience the divinity in the heart?

A.   *While the fruits on a tree are important, in order to get such fruits we have to protect the tree, the leaves and the* branches. *In a similar manner, the Atma is most important for us but we have to protect the body and the sensory organs, which help us to recognise the Atma. These roots of the tree, which are invisible, can be compared with our faith and belief in the Atma. It is only when we undertake to water the roots and protect the tree, will we be able to get the fruit of Moksha.*

[Summer Showers 1977, P 58]

Q 516. What promotes communion with God? What is it that God looks for in the devotee?

A. *Sacrifice promotes Yoga (communion with God). God looks for your devotion. He looks into your chitta (mind) rather than your vittha (wealth).*

[SSS Vol. 27, P 81]

Q 517. Scriptures say that man should seek *darsan* (vision), *sparsan* (touching the Feet) and *sambhashan* (hearing speech) of the Lord. What benefits will accrue from these?

A.   ***Darsanam paapa naasanam*** *(vision of the Lord destroys all sin)*
Sparsanam karma vimochanam *(touching the Feet frees one from bondage)*
Sambhashanam sankata naasanam *(conversing with the Lord dispels all distress).*

[SSS Vol. 27, P 114]

Q 518. Why is it not possible to describe the glory of God?

A.   *The glory of God cannot be described in words. Man describes Him on the basis of his own imagination. Truly speaking, God is beyond all definition. Man, however, tries to know God by various types of Pramanas in this world.*

[SS – Feb. 2003, P 50]

Q 519. What are the various types of *Pramanas* ? Can God be known through *Pramanas*?

A. *Truly speaking, God is beyond all definition. Man, however, tries to know God by various types of Pramana (proofs) in this world. They are Pratyaksha Pramana, Anumana Pramana, Dwaita Pramana and Adwaita Pramana, etc. (proofs based on direct perception, inference, duality and non-duality). God is beyond all these Pramanas.*

[SS – Feb. 2003, P 50]

Q 520. What is *Aprameya*?

A. *As God is beyond all Pramanas, He is known as Aprameya (cannot be described by analogy to any concernable object). God is beyond all limitations. He is extolled as Aprameyaya Namah (salutations to the One who is incomparable.*

[SS – Feb. 2003, P 50]

Q 521. What are *Pratyaksha* and *Anumana Pramanas*?

A. *Man tries to know God by various means and Pramanas. When you see the fire directly, it is called Pratyaksha Pramana (direct proof). If you see only the smoke from a distance and not the fire, you presume that there is fire behind the smoke. It is only a possibility. It is Anumana Pramana. It is possible that fog may appear as smoke; actually, there may not be fire at all! Therefore, Anumana Pramana too gives rise to doubt. Love in man is the Pratyaksha Pramana of divinity in a human being. God is present in the heart of every man with all His divine powers.*

[SS – Feb. 2003, P 50]

Q 522. What is the call of the enlightened sages?

A. *"Uttishtatha Jaagratha Praapya Varan nibodhatha"*

– "Arise, awake and achieve your goal, O men in
the sleep of ignorance."

[Summer Showers 1991, P 19]

Q 523. What did the ancient sages say about God-
experience?

A.   *"Uttishtatha, Jaagratha, Praapya Vara annibodhatha
– Arise, awake and achieve your goal, O men in the
sleep of ignorance", the sages declared. "Witness the
Divine effulgence for yourselves. We have seen Him.
Where? Antar Bahischa Thath Sarvam Vyaapya
Narayana Sthitaha – God is present inside, outside,
everywhere".*

[Summer Showers 1991, P 19]

Q 524. How does God look like? How have the sages who
have seen God described Him?

A.   *"Vedaaha metham Purusham Mahantham, Aditya
Varnam Tamasah Parastaat" – we have witnessed
that Great Person, who is brilliant like the Sun and
who is beyond darkness.*

[Summer Showers 1991, P 19]

Q 525. Where does God abide?

A.   *"Beyond darkness (tamas)." Unless we transcend the
darkness of ignorance, we cannot experience Him.*

[Summer Showers 1991, P 19]

Q 526. How is one to unlock the closed inner door?

A.   *Your heart (spiritual) wherein God resides may be
compared to a lock. It is not possible to open it with
any key. Mind alone is the key. When you insert the
key of the mind into the lock of your heart and turn
'right', it opens. When you turn 'left', it locks. When
we turn our vision to the world, we develop*

attachment. *When we turn to Divinity, detachment results. Therefore, for attachment and liberation, our direction alone matters, while the lock and the key are the same. Cultivate inner view.*

[Summer Showers 1991, P 11]

Q 527. When does one get the vision that can see the Lord within?

A. *You go to a temple in order to have the vision of God. But when you stand in front of the idol, you close your eyes and pray. The inner meaning of this is that one has to see God not with the physical eyes, but with the eyes of wisdom. You will get the eyes of wisdom only when you turn your vision inward. That is the reason people meditate with their eyes closed and visualise God within.*

[SSS Vol. 33, P 306]

Q 528. How is one to understand and experience the Atmic principle? On what lines should the *sadhana* to this end be undertaken?

A. *The principle of Atma is one and the same in all, be it a Yogi (renunciant), a Bhogi (pleasure seeker), a Jogi (itinerant) or a Vairagi (dispassionate one). It is present in theists and also in atheists. Forgetting this all-pervasive Divinity, you undertake various spiritual practices, limiting Divinity to a particular name of your individual* preference. Spiritual practices should confer the awareness that Divinity is all-pervasive.

[SSS Vol 32 Part 2, P 189]

Q 529. What brings on divine effulgence?

A. *Consider service to humanity as your very life breath. Then, you too will have divine effulgence.*

[SSS Vol. 33, P 297]

Q 530. Is divine current present even in an ordinary individual? If so, wherefrom does it rise and how does it spread in the body?

A.   *Even in an ordinary individual, there is electric current in the body. The electricity present within spreads in the entire body because of the pumping of the heart. The doctors say that the lungs purify the blood with oxygen and send it to the heart. But actually, the life force present in the lungs becomes current through vibration. This current can travel a long distance. Each time the heart pumps, the blood travels a distance of 12,000 miles in the body. How can we say this? When we join all the blood vessels in the body, both small and big (arteries, veins, capillaries, etc.), they cover a length of 12,000 miles. Just as a generator can illumine a bulb connected to it even at a distance of 100 miles, likewise the current originating from the sacred feelings in the heart can travel up to any distance. This is the power of Illumination Mind.*

[SSS Vol. 33, P 305-306]

Q 531. How is one to get more and more bliss from God?

A.   *God is the ocean of bliss. As is the size of your container, so is the amount of water that you can collect from the ocean. If you want to collect more bliss from the ocean of bliss, i.e., God, you have to increase the size of the container, which means you have to cultivate expansion of love. Expansion of love is life; contraction of love is death. Develop love in you and share it with others.*

[SSS Vol. 34, P 281]

***

8
EDUCATION, KNOWLEDGE, SCRIPTURES

■ Education

Q 532. Where should education and knowledge lead a man?

A. *The end of education is character and the end of knowledge is love. Education does not mean mere knowledge of books and acquaintance with them.*

[SSS Vol. 13, P 50]

Q 533. What is true education?

A. *True education is that which inculcates in the students the noble qualities like truth, devotion, discipline, compassion and sense of duty. What is the use of possessing high intelligence if one lacks virtues? Mere intelligence is not enough. Is not a fox also intelligent? Intelligence should be coupled with virtues.*

[SS – June 2000, P 176 (Summer Course Discourse on 15-5-2000)]

Q 534. What is lacking in modern education?

A. *Modern education bestows only information; it does not* *lead to transformation. Culture alone can bring about transformation. Education without culture can be compared to a field without water supply, an electric wire without power supply, a house without light, a school without a teacher and a temple without deity.*

[SS – June 2000, P 169 (Discourse on 15-5-2000)]

Q 535. What is the difference between education and educare?

A.   *The word 'education' is derived from the root word 'educare'. Education refers to acquiring information from outside while 'educare' means to bring out or to elicit that which is inside. Man should bring out the sacred qualities that are latent in his heart and put them into practice. The worldly education is related to the head and subject to change. But the human values like compassion, forbearance, truth, which originate from the heart, are changeless. That which is filled with Daya (compassion) is Hridaya (heart). It is the source of bliss.*

[SS – June 2000, P 170 (Summer course inaugural address on 15-5-2000 at Brindavan)]

Q 536. What are the aims of the secular and the spiritual education and how are we to achieve those aims?

A.   *It is said, **secular education is for happiness in the mundane world and spiritual education helps man to achieve the goal of life.** In order to acquire spiritual education, one must spend some time in inquiry. Spiritual education cannot be acquired from secular education. It is said, "**Adhyaatma Vidya Vidyanam** "(spiritual education is true education) and "**Saa Vidya Yaa Vimuktaye**" (true education is that which liberates).*

[SS – Dec. 2002, P 365 (22-11-2002)]

Q 537. What are the hallmarks of a truly educated person?

A.   *"Sarve Loka Hite rataha" (work for the welfare of the entire world), "Sarve Jnanopasampanna" (acquire all forms of knowledge), "Sarve Samudhita Gunaihi" (be a paragon of all virtues). These are the hallmarks of a truly educated person.*

[SS – June 2000 P 11 (Summer Course Discourse on 15-5-2000)]

■ Knowledge, Wisdom

Q 538. What is the difference between wisdom and science?

A.   *There is a gulf of difference between wisdom and science. Science is related to the power of the mind and machine, whereas wisdom originates from the power of the Atma.*

SSS Vol. 33, P 312

Q 539. Is secular knowledge not essential?

A.   *No doubt, secular knowledge is essential, but it should be based on the fundamental principle present within…Heart is the source of fundamental knowledge, which is also known as Atma Vidya (knowledge of the Self). This knowledge is the power of wisdom. One should not be content with the acquisition of physical knowledge alone.*

[SS – June 2000, P 170-171 (on 15-5-2000)]

Q 540. What is the difference between *Adwaita, Dwaita* and *Visishta-adwaita*?

A.   *That which teaches the highest knowledge of this Unity is known as Adwaita; that which teaches the principle of the Lover and the Loved, the Jiva and the Brahman is known as Dwaita; that which teaches about all three, Love,*

Lover and Loved; Prakriti, Jiva and Brahman, is known as Visishta-adwaita. But these three are in fact, one...That which is the same in all is the Nirguna Brahman.

[Prema V, P 63]

Q 541. What do the words 'Swabhava' and 'Swa-ichha' mean?

A. _The word 'Swa' relates to Atma. In common parlance we interpret the word 'swabhava' as the natural condition of man. This is not correct. All ideas emanating from the mind cannot be described as swabhava. 'Swa' has to be taken to imply something, which relates to the Atma or Brahman. The word swa-ichha also has 'swa' in it and swa-ichha does not mean that we can move about in an uncontrolled manner. Swechha can be described as the desire, which comes from the depths of one's heart or the seat of Atma. And 'swabhava' would mean the state or condition emerging from the seat of the Atma or existing at the level of the depth of one's heart._

[Summer Showers 1974, P 61]

Q 542. How is one to distinguish between the aspects of _Karma, Dharma_ and _Brahman_?

A. _One who is in the path of Karma will be thinking 'I am in the light'. One who is following the path of dharma will be thinking ' the light is in me'. One who has moved on to the aspect of Brahman and learnt to experience Brahman in everything will say 'I am the light'. Thus 'I am the light' is the aspect of Brahman while 'I am in the light' is the aspect of Karma and the 'light is in me' is the aspect of Dharma. To say that you are in the light is to imply that you are dependent on the light. The dual aspect is introduced by implication. In the aspect of Brahman, there_ *is no duality. One's own self is the aspect of Brahman and to recognise this aspect of Brahman in everyone is the state of bliss, which we should seek.*

[Summer Showers 1974, P 64]

Q 543. What do the terms *Dharma-jignasa*, *Brahma-jignasa* and *Karma-jignasa* mean?

A. *Dharma-jignasa means desire to know Dharma. Brahma-jignasa is the desire to know Brahman or knowledge of Brahman. Karma-jignasa is knowledge relating to karma.*

[Summer Showers 1974, P 60]

Q 544. How are *Dharma-jignasa*, *Karma-jignasa* and *Brahma-jignasa* related to each other?

A. *From the Karma follows the doing of Dharma and from doing Dharma follows the realisation or the feeling of lack of real happiness or Ananda (in the world) and therefrom follows Brahma-jignasa – the desire to know God – the knowledge of Brahma.*

[Summer Showers 1974, P 62]

Q 545. What does *Adhi-bhutam* mean?

A. *Everything that declines and dies, everything that has name and form, is included in Adhi-bhutam. Adhi-bhutam is Apara-prakriti, all the embodied things. As Paramatma is the Primal cause and so He is all the effects too. He is also Adhi-bhutam.*

[Geetha Vahini, P 158]

Q 546. What is *Adhi-daivas*?

A. *The deities that serve the Divine Purpose are Adhi-daivas.*

[Geetha Vahini, P 160]

Q 547. What is meant by *Adhi-yajnam*?

A. *This is the entity that consumes joy and grief, the result of the multifarious karmas. God is the recipient of the sabda, sparsa, rasa, and gandha; through the five senses in all beings, He is the Adhi-yajna Principle.*

[Geetha Vahini, P 161]

Q 548. What is *Sraddha*?

A.   *Strong and unwavering faith is Sraddha. Sraddhavan Labhate Jnanam (one with steadfast faith attains wisdom). The Upanishads have expounded the principle of Sraddha in varied ways. Wisdom attained through Sraddha is **Tharakam** (liberating). Knowledge acquired without Sraddha is **Marakam** (binding).*

[SSS Vol. 35, P 339]

Q 549. How is *Sraddha* liberating?

A.   *In spirituality, Sraddha is the Taaraka mantra, which is eternal, immortal and changeless in all the three periods of time. Man can attain Jnana (wisdom) only by understanding and practising **Sraddha, Ritam (oneness of thought, word and deed), Satyam, Yoga and Mahatattwam (Self).***

[SSS Vol. 35, P 339]

Q 550. Why are we not able to see *divya jnana jyoti* (the divine flame of wisdom)?

A.   *Take for instance a glass chimney placed over a lamp. After sometime, a thin layer of soot gets accumulated over the glass. Consequently, light becomes dim. It is only when you clean the glass, can you see the light clearly. The soot can be compared to ego that envelops your mind. **It is because of ego that you are not able to visualise the 'divya jnana jyoti'. Ego enters your mind when you give up the path of truth.***

[SSS Vol. 35, P 341]

Q 551. **What is the difference between individual discrimination and fundamental discrimination?**

A. *There are four kinds of knowledge. The first is bookish knowledge, i.e., superficial knowledge. The second is general knowledge, the third discriminatory knowledge, the fourth practical knowledge. People fall into error even in discriminatory knowledge. There is individual discrimination and fundamental discrimination. Individual discrimination is based on selfish gains. It is not right.* **Fundamental discrimination is based on the well-being of all people. Your conscience should assert repeatedly and firmly what you are doing is right.**

[SSS Vol. 33, P 258]

Q 552. Who is truly a man of wisdom?

A. *Everything is governed by the Divine Will. Whatever happens in this world is only the Divine Drama. He who understands this is truly a man of wisdom.*

[SSS Vol. 33, P 328]

Q 553. **What is the significance of the** *Saptaha Veda Purusha Jnana Yajna* **performed at Prasanthi Nilayam?**

A. *Saptaha Yajna is the offering of the Seven Sounds within us to the Divine. The completion of the Yajna is described as Sampati. Sampati means Brahma-Prapti (attainment of Brahmic Consciousness). The seven-day yajna is performed for this purpose. The seven days are spent on thoughts of the Timeless Divine and in the activities dedicated to the Lord who is beyond Time.*

[SSS. Vol. 21, P 238]

Q 554. What is the fundamental principle of Wisdom?

A.   *'Aham Etat Na' (I am not this) is the fundamental
           principle of wisdom. It means that I am not the body which
           is transient and ephemeral; I am the eternal Atmic principle.*
                          [Sanathana Sarathi – May 2003, P 130]

**Q 555. What is the meaning of the declaration: 'Sahasra
Seersha Purusha' (God has thousands of heads)?**

A.   *'God has thousands of heads' - this declaration was made
           prior to this when the population of the world was in
           thousands. Today the world population is nearly 600
           crores. Every one of them is a manifestation of divinity.
           Every human being is a divine incarnation. You should
           not think that is separate from you. Ekam Sath Viprah
           Bahudha Vadanti (God is one but the wise refer to Him
           by various names).So every individual is the embodiment
           of God.*
                          [Sanathana Sarathi – May 2003, P 130]

**Q 556. When asked, "Where is God?" is it proper to reply,
"He is present in my heart"?**

A.   *It is not a proper answer. This is not the truth. The truth
           is, you are in God. Everything is in God.*
                          [Sanathana Sarathi – May 2003, P 130]

**Q 557. What is the difference between Atma and
Paramatma?**

A.   *Truly speaking, the indweller who is in the form of the
           Atma, is verily God Himself.*
                          [Sanathana Sarathi – May 2003, P 137]

**Q 558. What is the meaning of the declaration 'Na sreyo
Niyamam Vina'?**

A.   *'Without discipline, there can be no well-being'. Desires
           should be under limit.*
                          [Sanathana Sarathi – May 2003, P 133]

Q 559. What does man bring with him at the time of birth?

A.   *When man emerges from the womb of his mother, one does not find any garland around his neck. There are no jewels made of pearls nor are there glittering golden ornaments. There are no chains studded with precious stones like emeralds and diamonds. There is no garland of flowers either. But there is one garland around his neck. Brahma strings together the consequences of his past deeds into a garland and puts it around his neck at the time of his birth.*

[Sanathana Sarathi – May 2003, P 133]

Q 560. Why does man fail to manifest his innate divinity?

A.   *As man does not have fear of sin, he is unable to manifest his innate divinity.*

[Sanathana Sarathi – May 2003, P 132]

Q 561. Of the six inner foes, Kama, Krodha, Lobha, Moha, Mada and Matsarya, being the obstacles in the path of the seeker, what exactly is Kama?

A.   *Desires for riches, property, honour, status, fame, children; why list the lot? Attachment to all things of this sensory world, this false, temporary world.*

[Prasnottara Vahini, P 32]

Q 562. What exactly is Krodha?

A.   *Yearning to harm others and cause ruin to them.*

[Prasnottara Vahini, P 32]

Q 563. What is Lobha?

A.   *Determination that no one else should partake of even a small fraction of what one has earned or what one has; also, that even in times of distress, one's possessions should not be diminished by use.*

[Prasnottara Vahini, P 32]

Q 564. What is the meaning of Moha?

A.   *The delusion that some people are nearer to one than others and the desire to please them more than others, leading to earning and accumulating for their sake.*

[Prasnottara Vahini, P 32]

Q 565. *What is Mada?*

A.   *Mada means the swagger that develops when one feels that he has either scholarship or strength or riches or fame, more than others. Mada is extreme egoism.*

[Prasnottara Vahini, P 32]

Q 566. What does *Matsarya* mean?

A.   *When others are as happy as yourself, it makes one miserable; one cannot tolerate it.*

[Prasnottara Vahini, P 32]

■ Scriptures

Q 567. What is the essence of the study of Sastras, Puranas and Vedas?

A.   *It is to develop Love for God. If that love is not there, all these studies are worth nothing. Spiritual exercises lacking in love of God are like fruit without juice.*

[SSS Vol. 20, P 184]

Q 568. Is reading of good books also an indispensable item of spiritual *sadhana*?

A.   *Much reading confuses the mind; it fosters argumentation and intellectual pride. What I insist upon is putting the things read into practice – at least, a thing or two. Moreover, you must always remember that the book is only a pointer, a guide, a signpost. Reading is not*

*completion of the journey. It is only the first step. Read
for the sake of practising, not for reading's sake.*

[SSS Vol.8, P 111]

Q 569. Which Vidya awards permanent happiness?

A. *Permanent happiness can be secured only through one
Vidya, the Upanishadic Vidya. That is the science of God-
realisation. That alone can save man and grant him peace.
There is nothing higher than that.*

[Prema V, P 37]

Q 570. What is the essence of the Bhagavata?

A. **Krishna is the embodiment of the 5 elements – ether,
air, fire, water and earth. He is also the embodiment
of the five life breaths – Prana, Apana, Samana,
Udana and Vyana. "Kleem Krishnaya Govindaya
Gopi-jana-vallabhaya Swaah" – this mantra
contains the essence of the Bhagavata.** *The five names
represent the 5 Pranas (vital airs). Kleem refers to earth.
Govindaya refers to Agni (the Fire God). Gopi-jana-
vallabhaya refers to Vayu (Air). Swaah refers to ether.*

[SSS Vol. 22, P 252]

Q 571. Why is the Veda called Sruthi?

A. *Sound is the very core of Veda. Sound is associated with
harmony and melody and hence has to be heard and ecstasy
derived therefrom. It is not to be analysed, commented
upon and judged. This is the reason why the Veda is called
Sruthi (that which is heard).*

[Vidya V, P 1]

Q 572. What does Vedanta mean?

A. *The term Vedanta is generally used by many to indicate
a school of philosophical thought. But Vedanta is only a*

special section of Vedic literature. All the Upanishadic texts form part of Vedanta. Vedanta is the consummation of Vedic thought. The Vedas themselves are invaluable guide towards the Highest.

[Vidya V, P 2]

Q 573. What do the four Vedas contain?

A.   *The rks or hymns of Rig Veda are ecstatic effusions from the spirit of man extolling the delight derived while contemplating the orderliness and beauty of Nature outside them.*

The Sama Veda is the precious verbal treasure, which enables man to praise in song the Creator and His Creation. The mystery of this world and of the worlds beyond is elaborated in the texts which are comprehensively called Atharva Veda. The formulae (mantras) for rites and ceremonials either beneficial or merit-yielding or sacrificial have been called as the Yajur Veda.

[Vidya V, P 2]

Q 574. Which other branches are there in Vedic literature?

A.   **The Vedic literature grouped into these four (Rig, Sama, Atharva and Yajur) collections – each under a different name – has four more branches – the Mantras, the Brahmanas, the Aranyakas and the Upanishads.**

The Mantra texts are also called Samhitas (Collections); all sacred formulae (mantras) are grouped together. The texts, which describe the means and methods of utilizing them and benefiting by their proper recital, are known as Brahmanas. The word Brahma has many meanings. In the expression Brahmanas, it means Mantra. The

Brahmanas deal mostly with ceremonial and kindred external activities. The Aranyakas, however, deal with the inner significance and internal disciplines like withdrawal of senses and elimination of attachments.

The Upanishads attempt, by philosophical analysis, to harmonize the two paths. They form the final phase of Vedic studies, and are called Vedanta. They can be considered as even the essence of Vedic teachings.

[Vidya V, P 2-3]

Q 575. What constitutes the *Prastana Traya*, the Authentic Triad in Indian philosophical thoughts?

A. *The Upanishads, the Brahma Sutras and the Bhagavad Gita – these are the basic roots of Indian philosophical thought. They are together known as Prastana Traya, the Authentic Triad.*

[Vidya V, P 3.]

Q 576. What is the most important exhortation of the Upanishads?

A. *The most important exhortation is – "One must realize in this body itself, before death takes its toll, the Eternal Truth and the relationship between Man and that Truth. The Kathopanishad exhorts: "Uttishtatha Jagratha Praapyavaraan Nibodhatha" – (arise, awake, get initiated from the great).*

[Prema V, P 101]

Q 577. Which is the most important lesson taught by the *sastras* to the seekers?

A. *The taste of food or of anything eaten cannot be grasped if the person is ill or even if the mind is immersed in something else. So also, even if one is engaged in*

Namasmarana, Bhajan, Japa or Dhyana, if the heart is
full of Tamas, or if it is wayward, no joy can be
experienced...Therefore, those who aspire to attain the
Holy Presence of the Lord must acquire certain habits,
disciplines and qualities. The usual, accustomed ways of
life will not lead to God. They have to be modified by means
of sadhana. All the sastras teach but this one lesson: keep
God constantly in view and subdue the mind which makes
you wander from the path.

[Prema V, P 98]

Q 578. What do the words *Adhyayana* and *Swadhyaya* mean?

A. *These words apply to Vedas, which are referred to by many*
names. Adhyayana also means practice (of Brahma-yajna).
Adhyayana begins with Brahma-yajna. In the context of
our attempting to know the inner meaning of the word
Adhyayana, we come to the conclusion that Veda and
Brahman are one...As regards swadhyaya, scholars like
Jaimini and Badarayana have interpreted this word by
calling it Dharma-jignasa and Brahma-jignasa; that is
the desire to learn the meaning of Dharma and Brahma.

[Summer Showers 1974, P 60]

Q 579. Is it necessary for a devotee to read and hear scriptures?

A. *God's name is to be recited and listened to. For some*
ailments, medicines are prescribed for external
applications while for others, they are given for internal
use. But, for this universal ailment of Bhava-roga, the
cycle of birth and death, Sravan and Kirtan and other
medicines are prescribed for external and internal use.
One has to utter as well as hear the Lord's Name.

[Prema V, P 33]

Q 580. Which are the two most important spiritual commandments?

A.   *You must fasten yourself firmly to the scriptural commandment: Sathyam Vada. When you give a word to do a thing, you MUST do it. Failure on your part to do is tantamount to falsehood. Such an act is not only untruthful but betrayal and deceit too. The second scriptural commandment is: Dharmam Chara (practise Dharma). Swayed by self-interest and selfishness, man performs activities he likes. Unless we practise what we learn, we cannot gain much in this world.*

[Summer Showers 1996, P 80]

Q 581. What are the three cardinal principles of welfare, wisdom and virtue enshrined in the scriptures?

A.   *"Sarvaloka Hite Ratah" (one should be engaged in the welfare of all). "Sarvajnanopasampannah" (one should master all forms of knowledge), "Sarvasamudhita Gunaihi" (one should be the embodiment of all virtues). The key to these three cardinal principles, namely well-being, wisdom and virtue, is contained in three P's – purity, patience and perseverance.*

[SS – Nov. 2000, P 356
(Summer Course discourse on 18-5-2000)]

Q 582. What are the symbolic meanings of the characters of Ramayana?

A.   *Soon after his entry into Ayodhya in the company of Sita as Maya, Rama had to enter the jungle of life. These ordeals are the concomitants of those who are associated with Maya. As a result, he had to embark on a search for Sita. On the way, he met Sugriva. Sugriva and Vali – the brothers – represent the qualities of*

viveka (discrimination) and dheeratva (valour).
Rama made common cause with Sugriva to overcome Vali.
*He got the friendship of **Anjaneya (Hanuman) who***
symbolises dhairyam (dauntless courage). With the
help of Sugriva and Hanuman, Rama crossed the
***ocean of moha (delusion)** to enter Lanka. Once again*
he encountered the three gunas – satva, rajas and
tamas (qualities of serenity, passion and passivity)
– in Lanka in the form of Vibhishana, Ravana and
Kumbakarna. He vanquished Ravana and Kumbakarna
(rajo and tamo gunas) and crowned Vibhishana (satva
guna) as King. He recovered Sita who now assumed the
form of Anubhavajnana (wisdom born of experience) and
re-entered Ayodhya with her.

The Ramayana epic carries these significant
messages when the symbolic meaning of the
characters and events are properly understood. *The*
ruler of Lanka was the ten-headed Ravana. Although he
was endowed with all powers, he was perpetually
immersed in Moha (infatuation for women). He had the
appellation "Dasagriva" – the one with ten heads. In
Ayodhya, Dasaratha was the ruler and in Lanka it was
*Dasagriva. **Dasaratha had ten Indriyas (sense***
organs) as his chariot. Ravana was the one who was
enjoying the ten senses as a sensualist. Whatever
one's scholarship or wealth or strength, if he has no
control over his senses, he descends to the depths of
degradation. Without control over the senses, a
person who may have conquered the three worlds,
***will be a slave of his impulses.** The bad traits of Ravana*
were shared by all the people of Lanka. As is the ruler, so
are the subjects, says the adage. When the ruler indulges

in sensual pleasures, the subjects also do likewise. Lanka was thus immersed in carnal pleasures. The people were not aware of human virtues, much less of divine qualities... Lanka contained within it the forces of evil and wickedness. The conversion of such an abode of evil into a kingdom of righteousness by the installation of Vibhishana is the climax of the Ramayana story.

[SSS. Vol. 20, P 50-51]

9
RELIGION AND SPIRITUALITY

■ Religion

Q 583. What are the essential aspects of religion?

A.   *Religion is three-fourths character. No person can claim to be religious if he merely observes the sacraments and rules and fails to be upright and compassionate.*

[SS Vol. 9, P 159]

Q 584. If the purpose of religion is to bind man to God, what is the essence of the true religion?

A.   *There is only one caste,*
The Caste of Humanity.
There is only one religion,
The Religion of Love.
There is only one language,
The Language of the Heart.

If these basic ideals are followed, there will be no room for petty differences and mutual recrimination.

[SSS Vol. 19, P 20]

■ Spirituality

Q 585. Should a spiritual aspirant discuss his belief and his conviction with others?

A. *No one, not even an Avatar can ever escape criticism and blame. But he does not bend. The real nature of the Avatar is realized by those who indulge in criticism or blame only after wading through unbearable trouble and then, they too start to praise. The aspirant should keep away from all such wavering and ignorant persons and desist from discussing with them his belief and conviction. Let him immerse himself in holy books and in the company of the devotees of the Lord. Later, rich with the experience of realisation and courageous on account of that contact with reality, they can mix in any company without danger and endeavour to direct other minds on to the truth which he himself has seen.*

[Prema V, P 24]

Q 586. How is Paramatma attained?

A. *Paramatma cannot be known without faith and steadfastness. Only through Prema, comes Sraddha; only through Sraddha comes Jnana; only through Jnana comes Parabhakti; only through Parabhakti is Paramatma obtained.*

[Prema V, P 29]

Q 587. What is the true meaning of spirituality?

A. *People imagine that spirituality means meditation on God, bathing in sacred waters and visiting holy shrines. This is not the correct meaning of spirituality. Spirituality means destroying the animal nature in man and making him realise his divine consciousness.*

[SSS. Vol. 25, P 163]

Q 588. Does spirituality mean journey from the gross material world to the Divine?

A.   *Spirituality does not mean proceeding from the human to the Divine. It seeks to unfold the divinity in man. Spirituality does not mean passing from the mundane to the Divine. Spirituality means making man manifest the divinity in him. Spirituality is the realisation of the role of the Atma in daily life. It is a way of life.*

[SSS. Vol. 25, P 164]

Q 589. Does spirituality mean leading a lonely and secluded life?

A.   *True spirituality calls for the recognition of the oneness of all mankind and to demonstrate the spiritual truth underlying this Divine unity.*

[SSS. Vol. 25, P 164]

Q 590. Does spirituality mean performing good deeds?

A.   *The good deeds by the external instruments (hand, feet, eyes, tongue etc. of the body) cannot be deemed spiritual. The very first thing one has to do is to destroy the animal nature in man. Without eliminating the animal nature, all rituals and acts of charity are of no avail.*

[SSS. Vol. 25]

Q 591. Is participation in Bhajans a spiritual act?

A.   *This is doubtless a good act, but it is only an auxiliary element in spiritual discipline. Without getting rid of animal qualities, without transforming one's attitude and without getting rid of bad feelings, the continuous participation in Bhajans is of no value. Without removing the*

*animal nature, a singer of Bhajans continues to be
a sinner...Without the conquest of animal nature
all forms of external worship are of no use.*

[SSS. Vol. 25, P 165]

Q 592. What is real spirituality?

A. *It is not the reading of scriptures or the performances of
rituals. It is to live up to the truths one has learnt.*

[SSS Vol. 27, P 80]

Q 593. What is the sign of the beginning of a spiritual journey of man?

A. **So long as one is dominated by sense pleasure, it
cannot be said that his spiritual life has begun.** *Now,
many clamour for the experience of spiritual bliss, but few
earn it, because they find themselves too weak to reject the
clamour of the senses...You have to feel that each moment
is a step towards Him. Do everything as dedicated to Him,
as directed by Him, as work for His adoration or for serving
His children.* **Test all your actions, words, and
thoughts on this touchstone: "Will this be approved
by God? Will this rebound to His renown?"**

[SSS Vol. 8, P 242]

Q 594. What timetable should a *sadhaka* follow for his spiritual sustenance?

A. *A breakfast of pious repitition of Lord's name (japa)
and meditation (dhyana), a lunch hour of ritual
worship of the Lord (puja), 'tea and snacks' of reading
scriptures or sacred books (pravachana) in the afternoon
and a light dinner of devotional music (bhajan) in
the early hours of the night. If you follow this regimen,
you can sleep soundly and wake up refreshed.*

[SSS Vol. 5, P 84-85]

Q 595. How has a *sadhaka* to resolve the three *gunas* on his spiritual journey?

A.   *The three gunas (qualities of the mind) have to be transcended one after the other, thamas (lethargy) being transmuted into rajas (passionate activity) and rajas into sathwa and sathwa (serenity and poise) too, at last into characteristiclessness. The gunas bind man and leave 'impressions'. Thamas is like the worms that creep and crawl in offal; rajas is like the fly that sits on foul things as well as fair; sathwa is like the bee that visits only fragrant flowers. But all three are drawn towards objects, whereas one should be free from all traces of attachment. When hearts are infested with flies and worms, the spray of Namasmarana has to be used for disinfecting the place.*
[SSS Vol. 4, P 133]

Q 596. What is the basic lesson for a spiritual seeker?

A.   *Take the base (Adhara) as more real than the structure (Aadheya); the Lord as more real than the world. This is the basic lesson of Indian thought. Among all the lessons of Vedanta, this is a pearl.*

[SSS Vol. 4, P 63]

Q 597. What is the first sign of spiritual life?

A.   *The first sign of spiritual life is vairagyam (detachment). If you have no vairagyam, you are illiterate so far as spiritual scholarship is concerned. Vairagyam is the ABC of sadhana. Vairagyam must become strong enough to make you discard the bondage of the senses.*

[SSS Vol. 3, P 135]

Q 598. Has age any relevance in the spiritual realm?

A.   *It is not age that matters. A person may be old, but his* *heart may be fresh and tender, full of enthusiasm for service and willingness to sacrifice. That will ensure your getting the passport to the spiritual realm. Divinity is only the terminus of the journey of human life, like the ripe fruit being the terminus of the journey from bud through blossom, from blossom to the fruiting, the sour bitter fruit to the sweet juicy ripeness. Grace is the sunlight, which will ripen the fruit. Sadhana is the sap, which rises from the earth. Both are needed by the tree, in order that it may yield fruit.*

[SSS Vol. 9, P 122-123]

Q 599. Why is spiritual progress a slow process?

A. *Influences of the past can and do hamper spiritual progress. Hence, transformation does not come easily; it has to happen slowly but steadily. That is why I repeatedly say: "Start early, drive slowly, reach safely."*

[SS – Nov. 2000 (Summer Course discourse IV of 18-5-2000)]

Q 600. How can one find God in the world of activity?

A. *You cannot easily detach yourself from activity. The mind clings to some thing or other. Make it cling to God. Let it do all things for God and leave the success or failure of things done to God, the loss and the profit, the elation or dejection. To get the attitude of surrender, of dedication, you must have faith in God. This world is a play; it is not an empty dream. It has a purpose and use. It is the means by which one can discover God. See Him in the beauty, the grandeur, the order, the majesty of Nature. These are but shadows of His Glory and His Splendour. That is why the Vedas have three sections or Kaandas: Karma,*

Upasana and Jnana. Karma leads to consciousness of the ever-present, immanent, all-powerful God. Upasana or adoration of that God leads to the knowledge that He is in all; when you experience that there is no Second, that is Jnana!

[SSS Vol. 5, P 105]

■ Spiritual Sadhana

Q 601. What does the word 'sadhana', which is considered essential for realisation of divinity, mean?

A.   *The literal meaning of Sadhana is the effort you make to achieve the object you desire or to reach the goal you have in view. Sadhana is thus the primary means to realise your aim or objective. A second meaning of the term is Sa-dhana, that is wealth that is associated with Divinity. Dhana is described in three ways as Aishwarya, Sampada and Dhana (material wealth). All of them refer to the same thing.*

[SSS Vol. 21, P 114]

Q 602. What is the best period in man's life to start *sadhana*?

A.   *Start today the sadhana that has to be done tomorrow. Start now the sadhana that has to be done today. One does not know what is in store next moment; therefore there should be no delay in engaging oneself in the sadhana that has to be done. Physical stamina is also necessary for this sadhana, and so, the body has to be tended, though over tending causes damage.*

[Prema V, P 69]

Q 603. What *sadhana* is expected of man to know Atma?

A. *We only need to reject whatever does not pertain to Atma.*
Then we come face to face with that Reality.

[Summer Showers 1991, P 38]

Q 604. On what factors does the success of *sadhana* depend, to adhere to the path of Truth?

A. *In spiritual matters, faith is the very essence. Doubt shakes*
the foundations of sadhana and is therefore, to be avoided.
Have faith in the wisdom of the ancients; do not pitch
your tiny little brain against the intuitions of the saints
and their discoveries.

[SSS Vol. 5, P 183]

Q 605. What is the purpose of spiritual *sadhana*?

A. *The fruit comes from the tree. But can the tree know the*
nature of the fruit? When two sticks are rubbed against
each other, fire emerges. But do the sticks know that the
fire is latent in them? Likewise, the Divine is latent in man.
It is through the process of enquiry and sadhana that man
can discover the Divine in him. It is like churning
buttermilk to get the butter in it. Through sadhana and
pure love (Bhakti) man can manifest his divinity.

[SSS Vol. 19, P 126]

Q 606. The mind of man revels in external objects and in purposeless pursuits. How is one to attain perfection?

A. *There have always been, there are and there will always*
be teachers who reveal to man and who instruct him to
attain, the heights which he can reach by the fullest
manifestation of his physical, mental and intellectual
powers, through one-pointed steadfastness...The first
sadhana is to search for the faults and weaknesses within
oneself and strive to correct them and become perfect.

[Prema V, P 7]

Q 607. How is one to grasp the oneness of Atma and Paramatma?

A.   *The relationship of the jiva and the Lord, the kinship between the two can be grasped by everyone who acquires three chief instruments: (1) A mind unsullied by attachment and hatred (2) a speech unsullied by falsehood and (3) a body unsullied by Violence.*

[Prema V, P 29-30]

Q 608. What is the most effective *sadhana* for experiencing Divinity?

A.   *"Mamaivaamso Jeevaloke Jeevabhutah Sanatanah" (The eternal resides in every being in the world as a fragment of Mine), says the Lord in the Gita. We have to develop the faith that it is the same Lord who dwells in all beings as a spark of the Divine.* You are not the body. You are a fragment of the Divine. This is the great truth that everyone has to realise fully. Without achieving this conviction, there is no use in performing any sadhana or worship for years. Once this conviction is obtained, the vision of the Divine is experienced automatically.

[SSS Vol. 20, P 119]

Q 609. When does God reward a dedicated *sadhaka*?

A.   *Strive – that is your duty. Yearn – that is your task. Struggle – that is your assignment. If only you do these, sincerely and steadily, God cannot keep back long the reward of Realisation.*

[SSS Vol. 13, P 201]

Q 610. What is the essence of real *sadhana?*

A.   *You must see no evil but see only good.*
        You must hear no evil but hear only good.
        You must speak no evil but speak only good.

You must do no evil but do only good.

This is real sadhana. You need not do japa, dhyana and thapas.

[SSS Vol. 27, P 104]

Q 611. What *sadhana* is prescribed for seeking God within?

A. *For sadhana, the nine-fold path of devotion (Nava-vidha Bhakti) has been prescribed for humanity.*

[SSS Vol. 27, P 104]

Q 612. What should be the primary object of *sadhana*?

A. *The attachment, the love that is inherent in man, should not flow wildly in diverse channels; it should flow uninterruptedly in the direction of God.*

[Geetha Vahini, P 230]

Q 613. Why is *sadhana* so essential in life?

A. *Sadhana is essential because the effects of karma have to be removed by karma alone, as a thorn is removable by another thorn.*

[SSS Vol. 4, P 191]

Q 614. What tends to spoil one's *sadhana*?

A. *The most tasty dish will become uneatable if a drop of kerosene falls on it. One bad Karma will spoil the spiritual discipline.*

[SSS Vol. 5, P 21]

Q 615. Can one achieve the spiritual goal by practising puja rituals, religious ceremonies and performing pilgrimages?

A. *No. These are only beneficial acts. Aadhyathmik, in its real sense, relates to two progressive achievements or at least sincere attempts towards these two achievements: (1) elimination of the*

*animal traits still clinging to man and (2)
unification with the Divine.*

[SSS Vol. 14, P 162-163]

Q 616. **Generally how long has one to remain engaged in
the** *sadhana?* **Is** *sadhana* **required even after
realisation?**

A.   *A ladder has to be at least as tall as the height you want to
reach; your sadhana has to be as long as the time taken to
reach the goal. When the walls are completed, the
scaffolding is removed; when the Vision of Reality is
attained, japa, vrata, puja, archana, sravana, keertana –
forms of spiritual disciplines can be dispensed with.*

[SSS Vol.5, P 27]

Q 617. **How does God assess our progress in** *sadhana?*

A.   *You get the marks that your answers at the
examination deserve, not more, not less. Sometimes,
if you secure only 5 or 6 out of total of 100, even the 5
or 6 may be cancelled and you will be assigned just a
zero. For, there is not much to choose between zero
and the 5 or 6 you were able to collect. But, if you get
a number very near the minimum needed for a pass,
the 2 or 3 that you fall short of will be added on as
grace marks and you are very likely to be promoted.
This is true of sadhana also. Poor progress in it is as
bad as failure, whereas good progress will be
appreciated and Grace will pull you through.*

[SSS Vol. 9, P 75]

Q 618. **Where and how to find the surety and the security
for success in the** *sadhana* **on Godward path?**

A.   *This bank helps you to keep your money safe when you
deposit it with them. They will allow you to make use of it*

when you are in difficulty. There is another Bank which receives deposits and maintains accounts strictly and confidentially. Every little sum is entered and accounted for: deeds, thoughts, words, good, bad and indifferent. Open a deposit account there, in that Bank, for your prosperity here and hereafter. That deposit, growing by your spiritual efforts, will give you joy and peace. This bank will give loans if you mortgage your house or lands, property that has come down to you from your ancestors. That Bank also will allow you to draw upon the accounts of previous births, and deposits made then.

Sometimes this bank will grant you overdrafts, so that you tide over temporary crisis; the extent of the overdraft is settled by the Manager with reference to your reliability and capabilities. It is like the Anugraha (Grace), that God will confer on you when you have earned it by Sath karma, Sath chinthana, Sath bhaava, Satsanga and Namasmarana (good deeds, good thoughts, good feelings, good company and constant contemplation on the name of God and the glory it seeks to express).

[SSS Vol. 6, P 99-101]

Q 619. Is practice of economy and avoiding wastage also conducive to spiritual progress?

A. *If we want to eliminate bad qualities like hatred, envy, pride and ostentation, we have to employ Sathya, Dharma, Shanti, Prema and Ahimsa as the cleansing agents. You have to cultivate the human values and undertake spiritual sadhana. In cultivating human values, emphasis should also be placed on avoiding wastage of money, food and time. In matters concerning expenditure, my attitude is strict. For anything that is legitimate and*

*essential I am prepared to offer even lakhs of rupees.
But I will grudge giving even a paisa for something
unnecessary and useless. This is because money
breeds all evils in the world. You should avoid
extravagant and wasteful use of money.*

[SSS Vol. 19, P 50, 52]

■ Sadhana And Food

**Q 620. Besides regular *sadhana* what else is conducive to
the attainment of spiritual growth?**

A.   *'Sathwic' food is conducive to the progressive attainment
of the four states of spirituality viz.,* **salokya, samipya,
sarupya and sayujya.** *Salokya is entrance to the field of
Theo-centric reality. Samipya is proximity to the
fundamental spiritual substance of the universe. Sarupya
is the assimilation of the form of the deity. Sayujya is the
liberation and ultimate union with the Godhead.*

[Summer Showers 1979, P 93]

Q 621. What aids in achieving *dharana* in concentration?

A.   *Correct posture, right type of food and right place, sathwic
food, satsang, etc., assist the sadhaka to some extent. They
develop the habit of concentration.*

[Summer Showers 1979, P 92]

**Q 622. How should a seeker conduct himself in daily life
and what food habits should he observe?**

A.   *A spiritual aspirant need not live in monastic isolation.
He should practise universal compassion. Food plays an
important part in the cultivation of universal compassion.
Sathwic food enables the sadhaka to apprehend the
omnipresent reality of Divinity. He progresses through*

the four stages of the life-divine. These four phases of spiritual advancement are 'salokya', 'samipya', 'sarupya' and 'sayujya'.

[Summer Showers 1979, P 92]

Q 623. Is it right to keep talking and thinking of other activities while taking our food?

A. *When we take our bath, when we sit for dhyana or when we take our food, we should not think of other activities and other ideas. Too much talk, while we eat our food, will also cause harm to us.*

[Summer Showers 1977, P 172]

Q 624. What is the meaning and significance of this verse "Brahmarpanam"?

A. *The meaning of this verse is that God Himself, who is in the human form in you is taking the food. Therefore, this changes our food to food for God.*

[Summer Showers 1977, P 172]

Q 625. Is the aspect of cleanliness of food equally important?

A. *In the matter of food there are three aspects regarding the cleanliness of which we should take great care. One is cleanliness of the material, which we use for cooking the food. The second is the cleanliness of the vessel in which we want to cook the food. We can certainly clean the materials, which constitute the food and also clean the vessel in which it is cooked. The third aspect relates to the cleanliness of the process of cooking. This is not easily possible. Until the material gets cooked to its final stage, our ideas should be good for this to be achieved.*

Even if there are lapses in these aspects of cleanliness, namely the vessel, the materials used for cooking and the process of cooking, if we offer the food to Paramatma before we eat, then the food will become clean.

[Summer Showers 1977, P 173]

Q 626. At one moment man is full of love but in the very next moment he bursts into a fit of anger. What is the reason for this unpredictable habit?

A. *Such a tendency is the result of improper food and habits. You should maintain balance in life.*

[SS – May 2003, P 133]

Q 627. How does the quality of food one takes affect *sadhana*?

A. *The spiritual technique of dhyana mentioned in the Gita cannot be beneficial in the absence of comprehensive sathwic food which should feed the entire body with sathwic sights, sounds, smells and tactile sensations. Limited food and sathwic food are essential for spiritual progress. Such food should give satisfaction to all the sensory organs.*

Rajasic food generates virulent thoughts. By consuming non-vegetarian food, we develop brutal mentalities. Those who are practising meditation must abstain from meat. We should also remember constantly that ahimsa or non-violence is the supreme dharma. It is sin to kill innocent animals for the sake of filling our stomachs. We must remember that God dwells in all creatures. 'Isa vasyam idam sarvam' (all this is pervaded by God), says the Isa Upanishad.

[Summer Showers 1979, P 95, 96]

Q 628. What constitutes *Sathwic* food?

A. *Each organ of perception must be provided with its proper* *spiritual sustenance. Thus, sathwic food does not mean the moderate consumption of milk, curds, ghee and fruits alone but the enjoyment provided by noble thoughts, sacred sounds, holy sights, and spiritual discussion as well.* **Sathwic nature is developed by feeding the eyes with sathwic sights. The tongue is meant to sing the glory of God. The ears are meant for feasting on the glorious manifestations of the divine.**

[Summer Showers 1979, P 94]

Q 629. How is one to be free from physical and mental health?

A. *Regulate food habits; restrain the greed of the tongue. Eat only sathwic (conducive to equanimity) or pure food; engage yourself only in sathwic recreation. Then you can be free from physical and mental ill health.*

[SSS Vol. 8, P 187]

Q 630. In what way do our food habits determine our thoughts and ideas?

A. *While taking our food, if we use inciting words, such ideas that are related to these words will sprout in us also.*

The nature of the fire will determine the type of smoke that comes out. The kind of smoke that comes out will determine the type of cloud that it forms. The type of cloud that is formed will determine the type of rain, which the cloud yields. The type of rain determines the harvest. The kind of harvest determines the food that we get out of it. The kind of food we eat will determine our ideas. For all our ideas, it is our food that is responsible.

[Summer Showers 1977, P 172]

Q 631. What should we think and pray while taking food?

A.   *We should not give room to any type of talk when we take our food. With a happy heart and with a sacred word, we must undertake to utter 'Brahmarpanam' mantra and then take our food. In this way, whatever has been offered to Brahman will become the 'prasad', which comes to us as a gift of Brahman.*

[Summer Showers 1977, P 172]

Q 632. How to stop unsacredness entering the heart?

A.   *Before partaking of food, chant the sacred mantra. Then, no unsacredness would enter your heart. "Annam Brahma; Raso Vishnu; Bhokta Devo Maheswara" (food is Brahma; essence is Vishnu; one who partakes of it is Maheswara). These three correspond to the body, mind and action respectively. Purity of thought, word and deed is true wisdom. You don't need to undertake any other spiritual practice.*

[SSS Vol. 35, P 348]

Q 633. How does wine harm a person?

A.   *First the man drinks the wine,*
        Second the wine drinks the wine,
        Third the wine drinks the man.

[Summer Showers 1990, P 112]

■ Sathsang

Q 634. What is the main benefit of *sathsang*?

A.   *Through sathsang you develop freedom from delusion, through freedom from delusion you develop faith in Truth and through faith in Truth, you attain Liberation itself.*

[SSS Vol. 13, P 258-259]

Q 635. How far does keeping the company of the holy help in spiritual endeavour?

A. *The easiest and most fruitful method of keeping yourself free from dust and rust is sathsang (good company). The company of the good and the godly will slowly and surely chasten and cleanse the persons prone to straying away from the straight path towards self-realization.*

[SSS Vol. 13, P 86]

Q 636. How is Sathsang considered as a first step for one's liberation?

A. *From keeping good company, detachment follows as a consequence. From acquiring detachment, removal of all illusory relationships follows as a consequence. From the removal of all relationships, steadiness of mind follows as a consequence. From the steadiness of mind, liberation of the jiva follows as a consequence.*

[Summer Showers 1973, P 45]

Q 637. What is the quality of the good company?

A. **When a sharp axe is used to cut a sandalwood tree, the sandalwood tree does not feel hurt by the axe, nor does it get angry with it. On the contrary, the sandalwood tree hands its fragrance to the axe ... this is the quality of good people.**

[Summer Showers 1973, P 53]

Q 638. How does sathsang lead one to the spiritual path?

A. *The Sathsang, the gathering of Godward-bound seekers, is a must for the sprouting of spiritual desire and its fulfilment. Even the tardy will soon develop a keen enthusiasm for the spirit through the influence of sathsang.*

[SSS Vol 13, P 258]

Q 639. Is it necessary even for a highly evolved seeker to engage in good company to negate negative influence of the surroundings?

A. *For the one who has reached success also, holy company is valuable, for it is like keeping a pot of water inside a tank of water; there will not be any loss by evaporation. If the spiritually advanced person (yogi) lives among worldly men, the chances of his yoga (union with God) evaporating into bhoga (enjoyments) are very great.*

[SSS Vol. 5, P 12]

■ Worship, Prayer, Puja, Pilgrimage

Q 640. We worship God in the form of idols, but cannot see their physical forms. Do these forms really exist? If so, why cannot we see these forms?

A. *Since ancient times man has been accustomed to worshipping God in the form of idols. You worship Rama and Krishna in the form of idols. But can you see their physical forms now? No. You worship Easwara. But are you able to see Him? The forms of Rama, Krishna, Easwara are ever existing. But man is not able to visualise them because of his narrow-mindedness. One should always be broad minded. You find divinity installed in the heart of one with expansive feelings.*

[SSS Vol. 35, P 195-196]

Q 641. What should be one's visualisation while doing idol worship?

A. *See God in stone; do not change God into stone. That is the vision, which is highly desirable. The stone must be visualised as Divine, suffused with God, which it really* *is. This vision is the precious gift that God has given to the people of this land.*

[Geetha Vahini, P 207]

Q 642. Is the sadhana of *Puja, Japa* and *Dhyana* enough to experience the Divine?

A. *Do not waste all your life immersed in dualism. What is it you have gained from all the pujas you have done and all the discourses you have listened to? If you have not progressed in the slightest extent from the state of duality, you have gained nothing from your experience. At least from now on, try to go forwards towards a higher consciousness. Proceed from Dwaita (Dualism) to Visishtadwaita (partial non-dualism) and reach the stage of Adwaitic (non-dual) Consciousness. Do not stay put in the stage where you are like a milestone. Having performed sadhana, studied the scriptures, met the saintly men and listened to the discourses, you should realise the fruits of spiritual experience.*

[SSS Vol. 20, P 125]

Q 643. When God being omni-present and all-knowing, knows what a *Bhakta* wants, should the prayers still be said?

A. *It is your duty to ask God. Words must correspond to thought. The thought must be put into true word. It is true that the Divinity knows all, but He requires that the true word is said. The mother may know that to maintain life child requires food, but the milk is given when the child asks for it.*

[Conversations P 47]

Q 644. Does God listen to the prayers of devotees?

A. *When God is invoked by prayer that emanates from the* *heart, let it be but once, He responds immediately. From the lips the call must roll back to the tongue; from the tongue, it must go deep into the throat; from the throat, it must reach down into the heart.*

[SSS Vol. 13, P 158]

Q 645. Will the Lord gratify all that we ask for, in our prayers?

A.   *If the Bhakta dedicated his all, body, mind and existence, to the Lord, He will Himself look after everything for He will always be with Him. Under such conditions, there is no need for prayer. But, have you so dedicated yourself and surrendered everything to the Lord? When losses occur, or calamities come, or plans go awry, the Bhakta blames the Lord. Some, on the other hand, pray to Him to save them. Avoiding both these as well as the reliance on others, if complete faith is placed on the Lord at all times, why should He deny you His Grace? Men do not rely fully unswervingly on the Lord; therefore, though you have to be the agent and the instrument doing everything, keep on praying with devotion and faith.*

[Prasanthi V, P 16]

Q 646. What is the best means of praying to the Lord?

A.   *The Lord can be prayed to by means of Kirtana, Japa, Dhyana or Bhajan. In every one of these, the chief item is the Divine Name. That is why Krishna spoke in Gita of japa-yajna. When japa is done, it is better to recite aloud, and make it bhajan. This will inspire the gathering. If Bhajan is sung in a sweet voice, people will be drawn towards the Lord. Gradually it will develop into the Love for God, and His Grace will follow in due course. One should patiently wait for the grace.*

The best form of prayer is Santhi-mantra: **"Asatho maa sadgamaya; thamaso maa jyothirgamaya; mrityor maa amrithamgamaya."** *The meaning of this mantra is:*

"Oh Lord, when I am deriving happiness through the objects of this world, make me forget the unreal objects and show me the way to permanent happiness;

Oh Lord, when the objects of the world attract me, remove the darkness which hides the all-pervading Atma, which every such object really is; and

Oh Lord, bless me through Your Grace with immortality or Paramananda, resulting from the awareness of the effulgence of the Atma, immanent in every object."

[Prasanthi V, P 18]

Q 647. Why do not all get immediate response to their prayers from Swami?

A.   *The man who dies, prays to Me to receive him; the persons who weep at his departure, pray to Me to keep him alive. I know both sides of the picture, the past and the present, the crime and the punishment, the achievement and the reward, and so I carry out what is just, though modified by Grace. I am not affected one way or the other, by the arrival into the world of some or the departure from it of some others. My nature is Nitya-anandam. You can share in that Anandam by following My instructions and practising what I say.*

[SSS Vol. 3, P 160]

Q 648. Should one pray to God for Moksha?

A.   *When God's grace is won, one need not pray*

separately for Moksha or liberation. He knows best what you should get and when. He will give what you deserve and benefit from. Yearn for Him, suffer anguish for Him; there is no need to yearn for Moksha then. If that is done with no second thought, He will destroy all your sins. Hold fast to Him; He can make you immortal. Those who want to escape from this cycle of birth and death, must obey the command of the Lord as laid down in the Gita and surrender to Him.

[SS – May 2001, back title page]

Q 649. How should the day be started and ended?

A.   *Rise everyday as if you are rising from death. Say, "Thus am I born. Make me speak soft sweet words, make me behave coolly and comfortingly towards all, let me do deeds that shower happiness on all and form ideas in my mind which are beneficial to all. May this day be worthwhile by Thy Service" — pray like this, sitting on your bed, before you start the day's schedule. Remember that pledge throughout the day. When you retire at night,* sit up and examine quickly all the experiences of the day, see whether you have caused pain or displeasure to any one by any word or deed. **Then pray, "I am now dying and falling into your lap. Pardon me for any lapse; take me under your loving shelter." After all sleep is a short death and death a long sleep.**

[SSS Vol. 7, P 23-24]

Q 650. How should the prayers be said?

A.   *A person driving a car concentrates on the road, for he is anxious to save himself and others from accident. Fear is what induces single-mindedness in this case. Love is greater force for giving concentration. If you have steady* *and resolute love, the concentration becomes intense and unshakeable. Prayer begins to yield fruit, under such conditions. Pray, using the Name as a symbol of the Lord; pray keeping all the waves of the mind stilled.*

[SSS Vol. 2, P 134]

The tongue is enough to win Him, the tongue that speaks the language of the pure mind.

[SSS Vol. 3, P 79]

Q 651. Does God grant everything we pray for?

A. *God is always ready to give you all that you want, but you do not seem to know what is good for you and what you really want.* **Since you do not know what you should want and under what circumstances, it is better and easier to surrender yourself completely to God and simply ask for His Grace.**

[Summer Showers 1973, P 13]

Q 652. What is the right thing to be asked in prayer from God?

A. *Our devotion and prayer to God should not be for the sole purpose of obtaining something or fulfilling some desire of ours. This should be for the sake of Atma or for the sake of becoming one with the Lord.*

[Summer Showers 1974, P 176]

Q 653. Who should man address in prayers and worship for one's worldly problems?

A. *The cosmos is governed by the three principal deities. I am letting you into a secret. So far as Creation is concerned, propitiate Brahma and establish links with the deity. As regards protection, establish links with Vishnu (by propitiating Him). With regard to destruction, establish association with Easwara -*

*Siva, (by propitiating Him). However, if your heart
is totally pure, you can establish direct connection
with God. You need not approach the lesser deities.
For this, there is a way. That is the way of total
surrender. Through surrender, you can establish a
direct link with God, heart to heart.*

[SSS Vol. 28, P 50]

■ Japa, Bhajan

Japa

**Q 654. How does *Japa* cleanse the mind and help in
realisation?**

A.   *You know there is butter in the milk. But you have
to subject it to the process of turning into curd and
then churning it to get butter. Similarly, in the pot
of the body there is the milk of Divinity. You have
to churn it using Buddhi as churning rod and Bhakti
as the rope. Out of churning comes butter, which is
Self-realisation. You get it from what is already
there inside you.*

[SSS Vol. 26, P 135]

**Q 655. Should one be very particular about purity and
impurity while engaged in the *sadhana* of *Japa* and
Dhyana?**

A.   *Do not care for the vagaries of the mind. Carry on Smarana
and Dhyana of the Nama and Rupa you like best, in the
manner you are accustomed to. In this way, you will acquire
Ekaagrata (concentration); you will realise your heart's
desire. Do not entertain in your mind the idea of purity*

and impurity while doing this sadhana of Dhyana. There is nothing impure in the world. When the Lord is immanent everywhere in everything, how can anything be impure? Even if something appears to the ulterior eye as impure, the moment it contacts the Name of the Lord, it becomes purified.

[SS – June 2002, P 185]

Q 656. **The *Japa-malas* have 108 beads. What is the significance of 108?**

A.   *The japa-mala teaches you the Unity, though it has* **108 beads!** *If it is a sphatika maala (garland of crystal beads) you can see the string running in and through each bead, the inner reality on which all this is strung! If the beads are not transparent, you still know that the string passes through, holds together and is the basis for the maala to exist!* **Why 108 beads? 108 is the product when 12 is multiplied 9 times, 12 is the number of Adityas (luminaries), that reveal the objective world, and so, symbols of the Saakara aspect (the world of name and form, of manifoldness, the seeming variety, the fleeting pictures).** *9 is the screen on which the pictures appear, the basis, the rope which deludes you as the snake in the dusk, Brahman, the Nameless, Formless, Eternal Absolute.* **9 is the Brahman Number, for it is always 9, however many times you multiply it! It is immutable, for 9 multiplied by any number finally adds up to 9 only.** *So, when you turn the beads, impress upon yourself the fact that there is both truth and travesty in the world, that the travesty attracts, distracts and delights in deceiving you, diverts you into devious paths, the truth makes you free.*

[SSS Vol. 9, P 28-29]

Q 657. **What is the symbolism of thumb and the fingers of the hand?**

A. *The thumb represents Brahman, the eternal Absolute, the Immanent Principle. The forefinger, the index one, which indicates this and that, you and other, is the jeevi, the Individual, feeling separate and distinct. When these two are joined at the tip, held in that position, it is the Jnana-mudra, the becoming One with the Brahman. The other three fingers represent Prakriti, the Objective World, which is negated when the mergence is affected.* They are the three gunas, the sathwic, the rajasic and the tamasic (qualities of purity, passion and inertia), that by their interplay create the phenomenal world.

[SSS Vol. 9, P 29]

Q 658. *How is the rosary to be held in the fingers for rolling the beads during japa?*

A. *Hold the rosary over the middle finger, keeping the three Guna-fingers together.* This means that you are now transcending the world of attributes and qualities, of name and form, of multiplicity that is the consequence of all this transformation, and proceeding towards the knowledge of the UNITY. *The Jeevi finger now slowly passes each bead towards the thumb (Brahman), touching the tip of the Brahman finger when the bead passes over, so that the mergence is emphasised with every bead and every breath,* for, while the fingers learn and teach the lesson, the tongue too repeats the mantra (holy formula) or the Name, with the Pranava (the primal sound of OM).

[SSS Vol. 9, P 29]

Q 659. **How long should the devotee continue the use of Japa-maala?**

A.   *The japa-maala (rosary) is very useful for beginners in sadhana, but, as you progress, japa must become the very breath of your life and so the rotation of beads becomes a superfluous and cumbersome exercise in which you have no more interest.* "Sarvada sarva kaaleshu sarvatra Hari chintanam" – always, at all times, in all places, Hari (the Lord) is meditated upon. That is the stage to which the japa-maala should lead you. **You should not be bound to it forever; it is only a contrivance to help concentration and systematic contemplation.** *The belt has to be discarded when you have learnt to swim, the crutches when you are able to walk.*

[SSS Vol. 9, P 30]

Q 660. What is *Likhit Japa*? What is the fruit of this sadhana?

A.   *"Likhit Japam" has been recommended for purifying one's mind. It is a form of spiritual exercise in which one is engaged in writing the name of the Lord. This should be performed in a spirit of devotion...**It is not quantity that counts. Even the writing of a few names with sincere devotion is better than filling pages mechanically.***

[SSS Vol. 27, P 285]

■ Bhajan

Q 661. How does one dwell on the meanings of the Bhajans while singing or participating in them?

A.   *When you sing Bhajans, dwell on the meanings of the songs and the message of each Name and Form of God. Rama – the name should evoke in you the Dharma He* *embodied and demonstrated. Radha – the name should evoke in you supramental, super-worldly Love she had as the greatest of the Gopis. Shiva – the name should evoke the supreme sacrifice of the drinking of the Halahala poison for the good of the world; the cool grace heightened by the cascade of the Ganga and the moonlight from the Crescent. Do not waste time purposelessly; let every moment be Bhajan. Know the purpose of Bhajan or Namasmarana and devote yourself wholeheartedly to it; derive the maximum benefit from the years allotted to you.*

[SSS. Vol. 7, P 67-68]

Q 662. Does singing of Bhajans lead to winning the grace of God?

A.   *If Bhajan is sung in a sweet voice, people will be drawn towards the Lord. Gradually, it will develop into the Love for God, and His Grace will follow in due course. One should patiently wait for the Grace.*

[Prasanthi V, P 18]

Q 663. How is one to revel in the glory of God through Bhajans?

A.   *Bhajan must be a felt experience. Do not sing with one eye on the song that makes the effect on the listeners, and the other, on the effect it makes on God. Let your heart pant for God; then, the raaga (musical tune) and taala (musical beat) will automatically be pleasant and correct.*

[SSS Vol. 11, P 214]

Q 664. Should any edible *prasadam* be offered after *Bhajans?*

A.   *About prasadam (the edible that is usually offered to the Lord after bhajan and distributed as consecrated food to the participants), well, the edible offering is to be avoided. The Name itself is the best consecrated offering to be* shared. *You can give Vibhuti (holy ash) as prasad, that is enough. This is the most precious and effective prasad.*

[SSS Vol. 8, P 112]

■ Worship Of The Lord's Feet

Q 665. What is the importance of Lord's Feet?

A. *Just as the feet of the individual bear the burden of the human body, the subtle body of the Divine bears on its Feet the entire Universe.*

[SSS Vol. 26, P 339]

Q 666. Why is so much significance conferred on the Lord's Feet?

A. *'Feet' do not mean sandals made in silver or gold. Feet refer to the Divine that sustains everything. Viewing from the point of view of science, it will be noted that blood flows from the feet upwards to all parts of the body. It is this blood which sustains the entire body. The feet that bear the burden of the entire body are essential for life itself.*

[SSS Vol. 26, P 339]

Q 667. Can we secure a vision of the Divine form if we seek refuge in the Lord's Feet?

A. *Yes. Here is a small example from the early life of Lord Krishna in Gokulam to show what the Lord's Feet mean.*

Krishna was known as one who used to steal butter from all houses and feed his friends and playmates too. As there were a lot of complaints about this naughty child, Krishna's mother Yashoda caught hold of him one day as he was running away and asked him: "Why are you *stealing butter from other houses while I offer you so much at home? Give up this habit. Otherwise I'll tie you to a post to restrict your movements." He smiled and ran away. Yashoda went from house to house in search of Krishna. He played a small trick. Yashoda could not move fast as she had a heavy body. Krishna dipped his feet in milk in a house and ran from there, leaving behind the trail of his footprints caused by milk. **It was only with the help of Krishna's own footprints that she was able to catch him. In fact, because she was so eager to get at him, Krishna himself helped her to trace him...Yashoda was able to catch the Lord only through footprints of His Feet.***

[SSS Vol. 26, P 340]

Q 668. In what other way are the Lord's Feet glorious?

A.   *The lord's Feet are glorious in many ways. But, they will confer blessings only if they are sought with real faith.* **The Lord's Feet contain the Divine insignia of Shankha (conch) and Chakra (discus). The conch symbolises Shabda Brahman (the Cosmic Divine Sound). The discus represents the Wheel of Time. The Sound and Time together represent the different cosmic aspects of the Lord. The entire universe originated from Sound vibrations.** *These vibrations are related to Time. Sound and Time are inter-dependent.*

[SSS Vol. 26, P 340-341]

▣ Namasmarana

Q 669. Does *Namasmarana* result in the attainment of Mukti ?

A.   *Even if the attainment of Mukti is not directly* *realised as a consequence of taking up the Lord's Name, four fruits are clearly evident to those who have the experience. They are (1) The company of the Great (2) Truth (3) Contentment and (4) The control of the senses. Through whichever of these gates one may enter, whether he be a house holder or recluse, or a member of any other class, he can reach the Lord without fail. This is certain.*

[Prema Vahini, P 107]

Q 670. Which spiritual exercise will yield the maximum benefit?

A. *Believe that all hearts are motivated by the One and Only God; that all faiths glorify the One and Only God; that all names in all languages and all forms man can conceive denote the One and Only God; His adoration is best done by means of love...foster love, live in love, spread love—that is the spiritual exercise which will yield the maximum benefit. When you recite the Name of God, remembering His majesty, His compassion, His glory, His splendour, His presence – love will grow within you, its roots will grow deeper and deeper, and its branches will spread wider and wider giving cool shelter.*

[SSS Vol. 8, P 118-119]

Q 671. Can the correct recital of the *mantras* and the Name of God produce illumination?

A. *The correct recital of the Gaayathri Mantra with the orthodox Udhaatta, Anudhaatta and Swarita (modulation of the voice and the higher, lower and even accents) can produce experienceable and authentic illumination, whereas incorrect* *pronunciation and wrong accent result in thickening of the darkness!* Therefore, instead of scoffing at the disciplines of recitals, meditations, prayers, formulary worship and mantra-utterances, their values have to be accepted and their results tested and confirmed by practice and exercise.

[SSS Vol. 8, P 83]

Q 672. **Which is the greatest formula that can liberate? What is meant by Atma-Rama?**

A.   *The greatest formula that can liberate, cleanse and elevate the mind is Ramanaama (the Name of Rama).* Rama is not identified with the hero of the Ramayana, the Divine offspring of Emperor Dasaratha. Vasishtha, the preceptor, said that he had chosen that Name since it meant, "He who pleases". While every one else pleases the self, nothing pleases the caged individualised self (soul) more than the free universal Self (God). **The Self is, therefore, referred to as Atma-Rama, the Self that confers unending joy**...The Vedic declaration, Tat-Twam-Asi (That-thou-art) is enshrined in the word Rama, which consists of three sounds: 'Ra', 'aa', and 'ma'. Of these, Ra is the symbol of Tat (That; Brahman, God), Ma is the symbol of Twam (Thou, jivi, individual) and aa that connects the two is the symbol of the identity of the two.

[SSS Vol. 8, P 84, 85]

Q 673. **Are different Names of God different in status too?**

A.   *Let Me tell you that no particular Names can be raised to a status higher than the rest, for all Names are His and He answers to all.*

[SSS Vol. 8, P 85]

Q 674. Which Name of God should we recite for His constant remembrance?

A. *God has a million Names. Sages and saints have seen Him in a million Forms; they have seen Him with eyes closed and eyes open. They have extolled Him in all the languages and dialects of man.*

Select any Name of His, any Name that appeals to you, select any Form of His; every day when you awaken to the call of the brightening east, recite the Name, meditate on the Form; have the Name and Form as your companion, guide and guardian throughout the toils of the waking hours; when you retire for the night, offer grateful homage to God in that Form with that name, for being with you, by you, beside you, before you, behind you, all day long. If you stick to this discipline, you cannot falter or fail.

[SSS Vol. 8, P 119]

Q 675. What is the value of the Divine Name?

A. *You are playing marbles with the Name of God, unaware of its value. Once you realise the worth of the Name of God, you will keep it in your heart of hearts as the most precious treasure. Know that the Divine Name is the key to illumination and liberation...*

The Name undoubtedly brings the Grace of God. Meerabai, the Queen of Rajasthan, gave up status and riches, fortune and family and dedicated herself to the adoration of the Lord, Giridhara Gopala. Her husband brought a chalice of poison and she was ordered to drink it. She uttered the Name of Krishna while she drank it; it

*was transformed into nectar, by the Grace the Divine
Name evoked!*

[SSS Vol. 8, P 89, 90]

Q 676. Can *Namasmarana* alleviate the burdens of life?

A.   *The Name of God is the most effective tonic. It will
keep off all illness...This one ever-present job will
alleviate the burden of all the hundred jobs, make them
all lighter and more worthwhile. Rise every day with
the thought of God; spend every day with the Name
of God; go back to bed with the thought of His Glory
as enshrined in His Name.*

[SSS Vol. 8, P 188, 189]

**Q 677. How should one pursue *Namasmarana* as a
spiritual discipline?**

A.   *Do not indulge in Namasmarana as a pastime or a fashion
or a passing phase, or as the unpleasant part of an imposed
timetable, or as a bitter quota to be fulfilled each day.
Think of it as a sadhana, to be seriously taken up
for the purpose of reducing your attachments to
fleeting objects, purifying and strengthening you,
and liberating you from the cycle of birth and death.
Hold fast to it as the means of rescuing yourself in
every way...It has to become as much a must as
breathing; as welcome to the tongue as sugar; as essential
for happy living as sleep or food or water.*

[SSS Vol. 8, P 188, 189]

**Q 678. Is it true that Name is like an armour and a shield
for the devotee?**

A.   *Namasmarana saved Prahlada from the agony of
torture...The Name was his armour, his shield, his breath,
his life. Anjaneya (Hanuman) too demonstrates the might*

of the Name. With the Name imprinted on his heart and rolling on his tongue, he leapt across the sea to distant Lanka where Sita was. He had no space in mind for anything other than the Name of his master.

[SSS Vol. 5, P 247]

Q 679. Is *Namasmarana* a sure instrument to realise the Lord?

A. *Namasmarana is an instrument to realise the Lord. Thyagaraja started the Nama-japa of Sri Rama in his 20th year; he recited it 96 crores (960 million) times, and took 21 years and 15 days for the vow to be finished. As a result, he had the darshan (vision) of Sri Rama, "the letters of the Name taken shape", he says. The Name signifies the quality of the Lord, his guna, and so constant contemplation arouses the same guna in the reciter.*

[SSS Vol. 5, P 249]

Q 680. Does *Namasmarana* result in vision of the Lord?

A. **Man's duty is to sanctify his days and nights with the unbroken smarana (recollection) of the Name. Recollect with joy, with yearning. If you do so, God is bound to appear before you in the Form and with the Name you have allotted Him, as most beautiful and most appropriate! God is all Names and all Forms.**

[SSS Vol. 8, P 94]

Q 681. During the time of Rama, did Hanuman and others perform the great feats by the power of His Name alone?

A. *Once Anjana Devi, mother of Anjaneya (Hanuman) came to the residence of Kausalya. Kausalya enquired who she was. Anjana Devi introduced herself, saying, "I am the mother of Anjaneya, who could cross over the mighty ocean in a leap." After some time, the mother of sage Agastya also came there. On being asked, she introduced herself saying, "I am the mother of the one who swallowed the entire ocean in one gulp." Then Kausalya said to them, "Your sons could accomplish such stupendous tasks because of the mighty power of the Name of my son, Rama." As they were conversing, Rama appeared there and asked, "Mother what is that you are discussing?" Kausalya replied, "Son, we are discussing the glory of Your Name." Then Rama said, "Mother, it is not merely because of My Name that they were able to perform such mighty tasks. Their purity of heart was also responsible for this. There are many who chant My Name, but are all of them able to reap its benefits? Purity of heart is very essential."*

[SSS Vol. 34, P 84]

■ Mounam (Observing Silence), Yajna, Sacrifices

Q 682. Why is *Mounam* (silence) prescribed as a *sadhana*?

A. *The ancient sages laid down the sadhana of Mounam (silence) to maintain the purity of speech. They realised that excessive talk could lead to sins and abuses like hurting others, speaking falsehood or creating emotional excitement. That is why they recommended penance for the tongue for spiritual aspirants.*

[SS – Aug. 2000, P 251 (Discourse on 16-5-2000)]

Q 683. What does true *Mounam* signify?

A. *Mounam does not signify merely the absence of*

speech. It also signifies the absence of sankalpa (thoughts). In fact, the mind is a bundle of thoughts. If you remove the thoughts, the mind is dissolved. For this, you must control your speech. Only then can you experience Brahman.

[SSS – Aug. 2000, P 251 (Summer Course discourse 16-5-2000)]

Q 684. What is *Mounam*?

A.   *It is not the keeping of the mouth shut. It means, the getting beyond the influence of all the senses and getting established always in the consciousness of one's own Reality.*

[Prasanthi V, P 67]

Q 685. When does one get established in genuine *Mounam*?

A.   **When the mind withdraws from the external world, the tongue too becomes silent; all senses follow suit, that is the genuine Mounam.**

[Prasanthi V, P 67]

Q 686. Does *Mounam* lead to experience of Divinity?

A.   *Why did the sages go into the jungle? To sink their minds in the silent calm of the forest; to dwell ever in the thought of God whose voice is heard when all other voices cease.*

[SSS Vol. 5, P 29]

It is only in the depth of silence that the voice of God can be heard.

[SSS Vol. 8, P 185]

Q 687. What are the other incidental advantages of observing *Mounam* or the vow of silence?

A.   *Such persons will escape the viles of the intellect, which breed doubts, delusions and dualistic diversions, away from the Atmic reality.*

[Prasanthi V, P 67]

Q 688. What is *Nirvikalpa Mounam*?

A.   *When the buddhi is tranquil, Santhi envelops man; he is immersed in Tejas, splendour; he is in the Akhanda paripurna Ananda. This stage is also called Nirvikalpa, the Nirvikalpa-mounam.*

[Prasanthi V, P 67-68]

Q 689. How can one achieve the state of perfect *Mounam*?

A.   *May all sadhakas, by their disciplined lives and ceaseless effort establish themselves in the knowledge of their Swarupa, their own Reality. May they keep their minds away from the Drisya world, contemplate on the Paramatma always, acquire peace of mind, withdraw from all contact with the sensory world, saturate themselves in Ananda and know themselves as the One, without a second.*

[Prasanthi V, P 68]

■ Self-Enquiry

Q 690. What should be the mode of self-enquiry?

A.   *First, you must know your full address. Who are you? The Atman. Whence did you come? From the Atma. Where are you going? To the Atma, itself. How long can you be here? Until you merge with the Atma. Where are you now? In the unreal, the ever-changing. In what form? As An-atma. What are you engaged in? In evanescent tasks. Therefore, what should you do, hereafter? Give up these three and try the other three – to enter the eternal, to engage in never-changing tasks, and to enjoy Bliss of the Atma. This must be the chief effort of the Jivi, its perpetual aim, the greatest adventure in the world.*

All other tasks are humdrum, they glitter a moment and vanish. You will realise this Truth if only you turn your back on them and watch, wisely.

[Prasanthi V, P 46-47]

Q 691. How to start *Atmavichara*?

A. *The first step in Atmavichara (enquiry into the nature of the Atma) is the practice of the truth that whatever gives you pain gives pain to others and whatever gives you joy gives joy to others. So, do unto others, as you would like them to do unto you.*

[Sanathana Sarathi – Oct. 2002, P 297]

■ Grace Of God

Q 692. What is Grace?

A. *Prasadam means Grace that flows from God when He is propitiated. My Grace is ever with you; it is not something that is given or taken. It is given always and and accepted by the Consciousness that is aware of its significance. Win the grace of your own sub-conscious; so that it may accept the Grace of God which is ever available. God does not deny any one; it is only you who deny God. When a gift is proffered, you have to do only one little act, so that you may earn it – you have to extend your hand to receive it. That is the Grace...The Grace itself will confer on you the faith and the strength, the wisdom and the joy.*

[SSS Vol. 11, P 92, 93]

Q 693. What is the main benefit of God's Grace?

A. *Grace will set everything right. Its main consequence* *is **Atmasakshathkara** (Self-realisation); but there are other incidental benefits too, like a happy contented life here below and a cool courageous temper, established in unruffled santhi (peace). The main benefit from a jewel is personal joy; but when one has come to the last coin in the purse, one can sell it and start life again…this is the nature of Grace. It fulfils a variety of wants.*

[SSS Vol. 8, P 70-71]

Q 694. What is the secret of getting the Grace of the Lord?

A.   *Try to win the Grace by reforming your habits, reducing your desires, and refining your higher nature. One step makes the next one easier, that is the unique quality of the spiritual journey. At each step, your strength and confidence increase and you get bigger and bigger instalments of Grace.*

[SSS Vol. 5, P 197]

Q 695. How are God's Grace and individual effort related?

A.   *Individual effort and Divine Grace are both interdependent. Without effort, there will be no conferment of Grace; without Grace, there can be no taste in the effort. To win that Grace, you need have only faith and virtue.*

[SSS Vol. 6, P 61]

Q 696. Which is more powerful, Grace or *Karma*?

A.   *If you win the Grace of God, even the decrees of the adverse effect of karmas can be overcome.*

[SSS Vol. 2, P 65]

Q 697. Does Grace of God confer all one needs?

A.   *The most desirable **Aishwaryam** (prosperity) is **Easwara anugraha** (the Lord's Grace); that is to say, the most desirable form of wealth is the Grace of*

God. He will guard you, even as the eyelids guard the eye. Do not doubt this.

[SSS Vol. 4, P 264]

Q 698. Are inner consciousness and God's Grace the same?

A. *An aspirant might win God's Grace, and the Guru's Grace and the Grace of the devotees of the Lord. But all this grace would be of no avail if he does not secure also another grace, the grace of his own inner consciousness, his Antahkarana. Without this grace, he falls in the perdition, for all the rest are of no account whatsoever.*

[Prema V, P 33]

Q 699. What qualities in a devotee ensure the advent of God's Grace?

A. *Earn the qualifications – holiness, purity, faith, universal love; then, He will approach you on foot to console, comfort and save! Purity of heart and control over your desires and senses, if you have these two credentials, Grace is your right.*

[SSS Vol. 14, P 100]

Q 700. Should one pray to God for grace or will it come as a consequence of performing good deeds?

A. *Grace is showered on those who seek. Knock, and the door will be opened; ask, and food will be served; search, and the treasure will be yours.*

[SSS. Vol. 9, P 123]

Q 701. Which of the two paths- *Jnana* and *Bhakti*, brings Grace of the Lord more easily?

A. *Through devotion to God (Bhakti) alone can that*

knowledge (Jnana) be attained. **Bhakti purifies the heart and universalises the vision. It also brings down the Grace of God;** *for, the clouds have to come over the fields and pour rain; the plants cannot rise up to drink the life-giving fluid. The mother has to bend to the cradle to fondle the child.* **Bhakti has that power, to bring the Lord down.**

[SSS Vol. 4, P 69]

Q 702. How is one to win the grace of God?

A.   **The Grace of God cannot be won through the gymnastics of reason, the contortions of Yoga or the denials of asceticism. Love alone can win it, Love that needs no requital, Love that knows no bargaining, Love that is paid gladly, as tribute to the All-loving, Love that is unwavering.** *Love alone can overcome obstacles, however many and mighty. There is no strength more effective than purity, no bliss more satisfying than love, no joy more restoring than bhakti (devotion), no triumph more praiseworthy than surrender.*

[SSS Vol. 11, P 75]

Q 703. What is *Shaktipata*?

A.   **Shaktipata means that the guru hands over in one shower all the capacities to the disciple with his grace.** *This Shaktipata is given only when there is deservedness. In all individuals this Shakti is present in a hidden manner and is in a latent form. What the guru does is simply to remove the veil of ignorance, which is hiding this power.*

[Summer Showers 1974, P 44]

Q 704. Can spiritual *sadhana* succeed without grace of God?

A.   *Holding the fan by the hand will not help; you must move* *it to and fro vigorously, in order to feel the cool breeze that blows on your face. There is no breeze in the fan; it is all around you, everywhere, as air. Direct it towards yourself by sadhana. So too, direct the Grace of God that is everywhere, towards you and make yourself happy by sadhana.*

[SSS Vol. 8, P 66-67]

Q 705. What kind of sadhana is needed to acquire God's Grace?

A. *God's Grace is as the shower of rain, as the sunlight. You have to do some sadhana (spiritual practice) to acquire it, the sadhana of keeping a pot upright to receive the rain, the sadhana of opening the door of your heart, so that the Sun may illumine it. Like the music that is broadcast over the radio, it is all around you; but you must switch on your receiver and tune the identical wavelength so that you can hear it and enjoy it. Pray for Grace; but do at least this little sadhana.*

[SSS Vol. 8, P 70]

Q 706. Why does not everyone get God's Grace?

A. *When you have no faith in God, you cannot gauge the efficacy of Grace. If you discard Rama and Krishna, they cannot stand by you in your hour of need. You do not attach yourself to Sai Baba and so you do not receive His Grace. If you start with cynicism and doubt and try to criticise and discover faults, the result is deeper ignorance and confusion. Unholy thoughts fog the mind with foul fumes. How can clarity come to the vision then?*

[SSS Vol. 8, P 71]

Q 707. How is one to quicken one's redemption?

A. *Remember, you have to come to Me, if not in this*

birth, at least within ten more births! Strive to acquire Grace; Grace is the reward for spiritual practice; the highest spiritual discipline is to follow the instructions of the Master.

Years of rigorous training make the soldier, who can then stand all the rigours of warfare. The heroic fighter is not made in a day. So too, the practising spiritual aspirant (sadhaka) who can win victories, is not made in a day. Restrictions and regulations, drill and techniques have been laid down for him also. Follow them sincerely and steadily and victory is yours.

[SSS Vol. 4, P 29]

Q 708. Why can't we understand the mystery about the actions of God and His grace?

A.   *There is no constraint of time, place, distance or complexity to the actions of God. There is no creature that can impose limitations or constraints on God. God is utterly selfless. All His actions are sacred whether they seem pleasant or unpleasant to you. You are sometimes confused. You feel if Swami is God, will He do this or that? How can you decide what God should do? No one has the authority to question the powers of God. He alone decides whether to reward, punish, protect or destroy anything.*

[SSS Vol. 32 Part 2, P 193]

Q 709. What makes an individual eligible to receive God's grace without asking?

A.   *Give up all desires and cleanse your heart. Then I will grant you all that you require without your asking for it.*

[SSS Vol. 32 Part 2, P 146]

Q 710. Wherefrom can one draw strength on the Godward path while living in the midst of the Prakriti?

A. *The tiny sparrow sits on the storm-tossed bough, because it knows that its wings are strong. It does not depend upon the tossing bough to sustain it. So too, **rely on the Grace of God, earn it and keep it. Then, whatever the strength of the storm, you can survive it without harm.***

[SSS Vol 5, P 151-152]

■ Deities And Festivals

Ganesa

Q 711. What does Ganapati mean?

A. *Ganapati means the 'Master (Lord) of the Ganas (Ganaadhipathi).*

[SSS Vol. 30, P 178]

Q 712. What is the meaning of the word 'Gana'?

A. *In the word 'Gana', Ga stands for Buddhi (intellect). 'Na' means Vijnana (the higher knowledge or wisdom). Ganapati is the Lord of the intellect and the higher knowledge.*

[SSS Vol. 30, P 179]

Q 713. Ganesa is also called *Vighnesvara*? What is its meaning?

A. *Vinaayaka is also called Vighnesvara as He removes all obstacles coming in the way of devotees who pray to Him sincerely.*

[SSS Vol. 27, P 218]

Q 714. Why is Ganesa known as *Siddhi-Vinayaka*?

A. *He responds to the prayers of the devotees and hence he is* known as Siddhi-Vinayaka *(the Vinayaka who grants what is sought for.)*

[SSS Vol. 22, P 193]

Q 715. Are the intellect and the higher knowledge present in the external world or are they to be found within man? Where is Ganapati to be located?

A.   *He is present within each human being. There is no need to seek Him in the external world. Ganapati dwells in every human being in the form of intellect and wisdom.*

[SSS Vol. 30, P 179]

Q 716. Where are the *Ganas*? What is their form?

A.   *Jnanendriyas and Karmendriyas (five organs of perception and five organs of action) are the Ganas. The mind is the master over these ten organs. Buddhi (intellect) is the discriminating faculty above the mind. The ten senses, the mind and the intellect together constitute the Ganas.*

[SSS Vol. 30, P 179]

Q 717. When Ganapati is described as 'Parvati-tanaya', who is Parvati?

A.   *Parvati signifies Prithvi (Mother Earth). The meaning of 'Parvati-tanaya' (son of Parvati) is that Ganapati, who is the Lord of the Ganas, is the son of Parvati, who symbolises Sakthi (the Divine Energy). There is underlying unity between the two. The truth is both of them are all-pervading and convey the message of Eka-atma-bhavam.*

[SSS Vol. 30, P 179]

Q 718. What does the appellation 'Vinayaka' mean?

A.   *Ganapati has the appellation 'Vinayaka', because*

there is no master above him. He is all-powerful and
independent. Without recognising the esoteric
significance of the Vinayaka Principle, people look only
at the external form and offer worship in mundane terms.

[SSS Vol. 30, P 180]

Q 719. In what form does Vinayaka, the one who has no master, resides within human being?

A. *It is in the form of Atma. The Atma has no master. The mind is the master of the Indriyas (senses). Indra is the master of the Indriyas. People conceive of Indra as presiding over his own celestial realm. But, as the Lord of the Manas (mind), he resides in everyone. The Buddhi (intellect), which is the master of the mind, is the very embodiment of Jnana (wisdom or awareness). This kind of awareness of this Jnana is supreme. It is Constant Integrated Awareness. It remains unchanged, neither growing nor diminishing. It is called Vijnana.*

[SSS Vol. 30, P 180]

Q 720. What kind of *Jnana* or knowledge is this Constant Integrated Awareness or *Vijnana* and who is the preceptor for this knowledge?

A. *It is not the knowledge of the phenomenal world. It is Atma-jnana (spiritual knowledge). The Gita declares: "Adhyaathma Vidya Vidyanaam" – "Among all forms of knowledge, I am the knowledge of the Self". The true aim of life is to acquire this knowledge. Vinayaka is the preceptor for this knowledge. The preceptor is within you. The Vinayaka Principle is in everyone.*

[SSS Vol. 30, P 181]

Q 721. What is the inner significance of worshipping the elephant-faced deity?

A. *The elephant is a symbol of might and magnitude. The elephant's foot is larger than that of any other animal. The elephant can make its way through the densest jungle. In this way, it signifies the quality of a leader who shows the way for others. The elephant is highly intelligent. The elephant is also known for its fidelity and gratitude. In any circumstance, it will not forget its master. It will sacrifice its life for its master.*

[SSS Vol. 30, P 184]

Q 722. What is the significance of steam-cooked offerings to Ganesa?

A. *There are some inner secrets that should be noted in the worship of Ganesha. The food offerings to Ganesha are prepared entirely by using steam instead of heat from a burning stove. Combining rice flour with jaggery (molasses) and til (sesame) seeds, balls are prepared which are cooked in steam. In Ayurveda this edible is accorded a high place for its curative properties. The jaggery in the edible is a remedy for various ailments. The til seeds serve to purify the arteries. It also helps to improve the vision. The inner meaning of all this is that the food offerings to Ganesha have health giving properties.*

[SSS Vol. 30, P 184]

Q 723. What does Vinayaka's vehicle, the *Mushika* (mouse) signify?

A. *It represents darkness, which is the symbol of ignorance. The mouse moves about in the dark. Ganapati is regarded as controlling the darkness of ignorance.*

The mouse is also known for its strong sense of vasana (smell). The inner significance of vasana in relation to humanity is the heritage of vasanas (inherited tendencies), which they bring from previous lives. These account for the actions in present lives. They also signify desires... Vinayaka signifies the triumph of wisdom over ignorance and agelessness over desires.

[SSS Vol. 30, P 185]

Q 724. What is the spiritual significance of the Ganesa worshipl?

A. *Knowledge of the seer and the seen is the great message of Ganapathi. 'Ga' means Buddhi (intelligence), 'Na' means Vijnaana (wisdom). 'Pathi' means master. So, Ganapathi is the master of all knowledge, intelligence and wisdom. There is also another significant meaning for the word, that He is the leader of all the Ganaas who are celestial. He is also called Vinayaka, which term means that he is one who has no master above Him. He is the Supreme master. He is beyond the mindless state. One who has stilled the mind cannot have any master...He is also called Lambodara, which means Guardian of Wealth – Lakshmi Swarupa. Here* Lakshmi represents all wealth and prosperity and not only Dhanam (money) for which there is a separate deity called Dhanalakshmi, one of the eight Lakshmis. Here, wealth means Sukha and Ananda (pleasure and bliss).*

Ganapathi is the one who gives us spiritual potency and endows us with supreme intelligence. These two are termed as Siddhi and Buddhi respectively. *Siddhi and Buddhi are described as his two consorts. As He is the Adhipathi (master of Siddhi and Buddhi), he is regarded as their husband in mundane terms.*

Adoration of Vinayaka as Prathama Vandana (First deity to be saluted) has been mentioned in the Vedas. Ganapathi

Tathwa finds a place in the Vedas and Upanishads. Reference to Him is made in the Gayatri also. He is the one who instills purity in body and fearlessness in mind. It is said: "Tanno Dantih Prachodayath", giving importance to his tusk.

[SSS Vol. 27, P 216-217]

■ Siva And Sivaratri

Q 725. **What is the difference between *ratri* (night) and *Siva-ratri*?**

A. *For the man who has recognised his divinity, every night is Siva-ratri. For the man immersed in worldly concerns, all nights are the same. Those nights are marked by darkness. Siva-ratri is marked by Light.*

[SSS Vol. 26, P 67]

Q 726. **There are many different stories given in the *sastras* to explain the origin of Sivaratri dedicated to Siva's worship. What is the true significance of this night?**

A. *In sastras, there is a story that Siva-ratri is the day on which Siva danced the tandava in His Ecstasy, with all the Gods and sages taking part in the Cosmic Event. When He consumed the halahala poison that emanated from the ocean of milk in response to the prayers of the worlds, which it threatened to destroy, the heat of the fumes was well nigh unbearable, even for Him. So, it is said, Ganga was poured uninterruptedly on His matted locks (this is the explanation for the abhisheka which is offered in all Siva temples for hours on end and in some places uninterruptedly) but Siva was only partly relieved. So,* the cool Moon was placed on the head, that gave him some relief. After this Siva danced with all gods, the tandava dance.

That is the story but all this did not happen on a particular day and so Sivaratri cannot be said to commemorate that day. Some say that Siva was born on this day, as if Siva has birth and death like any mortal! The story that a hunter sat on bilva tree on the look out for animals to kill and without intending any worship, unknowingly, dropped the leaves of that tree, which happened to be a bilva, upon a Lingam beneath and so attained salvation, explains only the importance of this day; it does not explain the origin. Besides, we have not only Maha-sivaratri,. We have every month a Sivaratri, dedicated to Siva worship.

True Significance of Sivaratri

The night is dominated by the Moon. The moon has 16 Kalas or fractions; and each day when it wanes, a fraction is reduced until it is annihilated on New Moon night. After that, each day a fraction is added until it completes itself on Full Moon night. The moon is the presiding deity of the mind; "Chandramaa manaso jaatah", out of Manas of the Purusha, the moon was born. There is a close affinity between the Manas and the moon; both are subject to decline and progress. The waning of the moon is the symbol for the waning of the mind; for the mind has to be controlled, reduced and finally destroyed. All sadhana is directed towards this end. Mano-hara , the mind has to be killed, so that maya may be rent asunder and the reality revealed. Every day during the dark half of the month, the moon and symbolically its counterpart in man, the manas, wane and a fraction is diminished; its power declines and finally on the fourteenth night, Chaturdasi, *there is just wee bit left, that is all. If a little extra effort is made that day by the sadhaka even that bit can be wiped off and Mano-nigraha completed.*

The Chaturdasi of the dark half is therefore called Sivaratri, for that night should be spent in japa and dhyana of Siva, without any other thought either of food or sleep. Then, success is assured. And once a year, on Maha-sivaratri night, a special spurt of spiritual activity is recommended, so that what is savam can become Sivam by the removal of this dross called Manas.

This is the purpose of Sivaratri and so it is foolish and even harmful deceit to imagine that "keeping awake" is the essential thing in its observance.

[SSS Vol. 1, P 110-112]

Q 727. What does '*Lingam*' signify? What is '*Prapancha*' and what does '*Hrudayam*' mean?

A.   *Lingam means that in which this Jagath attains laya— leeyathe; that into which this Jagath goes—gamyathe. Examine the Lingam; the three gunas (primordial qualities) are represented by the three-tiered Peetha (platform); the Lingam above symbolises the goal of life. Lingam means 'a symbol', the symbol of creation, the result of activity of the three gunas and of the Brahman (Supreme Reality) which permeates and gives it meaning and value. When you worship the Lingam, you should do so with faith in this symbolic significance.*

The word 'Prapancha' which you use so freely to indicate the created world means, "that which is composed of the 'pancha-bhutas'—the five elements of earth, fire, water, wind and ether." Take the word 'Hrudhayam' used for "the heart". It means Hrudi (in the heart) ayam (He).

That is to say, it means not the organ that pumps blood to all parts of the body, but the seat of God, the altar where Siva is installed, the niche where the lamp of Jnana is lit.

Again, Siva does not ride on an animal called in human language, a "bull"! The bull is only a symbol of Dharma standing on the four legs of Satya, Dharma, Santhi and Prema. The three eyes of Siva are the eyes which reveal the Past, Present and the Future. Siva alone has all three…Meditate thus on Siva this day, so that one may get rid of the last lingering vestiges of delusion.

Just as OM is the verbal symbol of God, the Lingam is the symbolic form of the Godhead. It is just a form. Everything is Maya (delusion) and to grasp it, you must deal with Maya. Otherwise, you cannot realise Maya Sakthi (Deluding Power). God is in every part of the world…It is Maya, which binds and limits man; all sadhana is to conquer Maya.

[SSS Vol. 1, P 112-114]

Q 728. What is the significance of Navaratri?

A. *Navaratri is celebrated in honour of the victory that the Para-sakthi (the goddess of energy, immanent in the macrocosm and the microcosm) achieved over the A-sura of evil forces, as described in the Devi Mahatmyam and Devi Bhagavatam. That Para-sakthi is in everyone as the Kundalini Sakthi, which is liable to destroy, when awakened, the evil tendencies inside the mind. So, the Navaratri is to be dedicated by all for the propitiation of the outer as well as inner Divinity, in order that the outer and the inner worlds may have peace and joy. By means of systematic sadhana it is possible to tap the inner resources that God has endowed man with and elevate yourselves to the purer and happier realm of the Reality.*

[SSS Vol. 7, P 159]

Q 729. **What is the message of the nine-day's Festival - Navaratri?**

A.   *Look at the trainers of wild beasts. They bring the tiger, the most ferocious of animals, into the circus ring, and make it jump through the hoop of fire or lap milk from a plate, face to face with a goat, sitting on a chair. They are able to subdue the ferocity and tame it to the position of an unassuming toy. They did sadhana, they made the tiger also go through a regimen of sadhana and they succeeded! If they could succeed with the tiger, can you not succeed with the ferocious denizens of your mind? You can. That is the message of the nine-day's festival celebrating the victory of the Primal Energy.*

[SSS Vol. 7, P 159-160]

Q 730. **How does this Primal Energy manifest Itself in its various aspects in the inner and outer world?**

A.   *That energy when it is manifested in its quiet aspect (sathwic), is delineated as the Great Teacher and inspirer Maha Saraswati; when it is active and potent (rajasic), the great Provider and sustainer, Maha Lakshmi; when it is dull and inactive, but latent and apparently quiet (tamasic), as the great Dark Destroyer and Deluder, Maha Kali. Since Shakti is all-pervasive, omnipotent, infinitesimal as well as all-comprehensive, it can be contacted everywhere, in outer Nature or inner consciousness.*

[SSS Vol. 7, P 160]

Q 731. **What is the meaning of Guru Purnima?**

A.   *Guru is one who illumines your path to divinity. Purnima signifies the sacred light of full moon. Full moon stands for a mind with total illumination. It is spotless and*

blemishless. Even if there is a little trace of blemish in the mind, it will lead to darkness. It cannot give you total bliss.
[SSS Vol. 35, P 197]

Q 732. How was King Bali related to Prahlada?

A. *Virochana was the son of the great devotee Prahlada. He was, however, different from his father. He was a staunch materialist. He followed the hedonistic philosophy of Charvaka. Emperor Bali, who was the soul of goodness and purity, was Virochana's son.*

[SSS Vol.19, P 152]

Q 733. What is the significance of Onam festival?

A. *Emperor Bali wanted to ensure peace and prosperity for the entire world under his beneficent reign and commenced the Viswajit Yaga for this purpose. The Devas became jealous when Bali was performing this Yaga. They approached Lord Narayana and prayed to Him: "Bali, who is Rakshasa by birth, is attempting to bring the whole universe under his sway by performing the Viswajit Yaga. You must save the world from coming under the rule of Rakshasas."*

The Lord, who knew the greatness of Bali, his noble qualities and his devotion to God, formally acceded to the Devas' prayers but decided to confer the highest blessings on Bali. For this purpose He incarnated in Siddhasrama as Vamana and went to Bali's Yagasala to ask for a gift.

Pure-hearted as he was, Bali could instantly recognise the radiance on the face of the young Vamana. He asked Vamana: "Swami, what is it you seek at this Yaga? I have decided to renounce everything I possess to redeem my life."

Vamanamurthi was short in stature, but the whole universe was immanent in Him. He asked for an apparently small gift from Bali – nothing more than three lengths of ground measured by his feet. Bali felt that for a ruler of the vast earth, this was too small a gift and he agreed.

That very moment, Vamana assumed the immeasurable form of Trivikrama, the Supreme Lord of the three worlds. With one step, He covered the entire earth. With the second step, He covered the whole space and asked Bali where He should place his foot for the third step. Bali knelt before the Lord and said: "Oh Lord! What can I offer you except the body and heart, which you have given to me? I pray to you to place your foot on my head." Bali was thus the supreme embodiment of self-sacrifice, who did not hesitate to offer everything he had to the Lord.

Seeing the anguish of his people at this turn of events at the Yajna, Bali made one request to the Lord before he was sent to his heavenly abode by the Lord's third step. He said: " Oh Lord! I am indeed happy that I have been sanctified by Your Divine Feet and achieved the bliss of liberation. I do not, however, wish to leave my loving people in agony. Please allow me once a year, in the month of Sravan, during the constellation of Sravana, to visit my people." He asked for this boon out of his boundless love for his people. The Lord granted this boon.The Onam festival signifies the enormous love Bali had for the people of his realm. On Onam day, all the people of Kerala celebrate the Onam festival with great rejoicing.

[SSS Vol. 19, P 153-155]

■ Spiritual Significance

Q 734. What is the real significance of the Puranic story

of *Amrita-mathana,* that is, churning of the ocean
and winning of *Amrita?*

A.   *Amrita-mathana* – Churning of the Ocean for
getting Amrita

*The story tells that when the Devas (demi-Gods)
were overcome by conceit, delusion and tamas
(ignorance), the sages cursed them with age, greyness
and senility. They became easy victims for the
Rakshasas. To restore to them the lost splendour,
the Lord suggested the churning of the ocean and
winning of Amrita (nectar of immortality).*

Significance

*You have to take this story in its symbolic sense. The
Puranas (mythological stories)always deal in parables.
Each tale has a deeper meaning. This meaning is to be
practised in daily life.*

*Indra insulted Durvasa because he was blinded by the
power of office. The curse of the sage forced him to rethink
about his Reality, to rediscover his innate status. Then he
found that he was Amritam, of the same nature as
Parabrahmam (Supreme Reality) Itself. In fact, he came
to know that he was Para Brahman, moving about in the
delusion that he was Indra! The churning is the symbol
of the sadhana needed to remove the veil of delusion, more
specifically, the Rajayoga Sadhana (royal path of integral
spirituality)....*

*When the Devas fell a prey to pride and attachment,
to unreality, they had to churn their thoughts and
impulses, their feelings and emotions, their instincts
and inspirations and bring out the cream of Truth.*

*The two groups who pulled the churning rope are
the "forward leading influences and the backward
pulling influences", the Daivi and the Asuri (divine
and demonic) urges.*

[SSS Vol. 1, P 220-221]

**Q 735. What is the symbolic reference to the names Rama,
Sita, Ayodhya, Dasaratha and his three queens in
the Ramayana?**

A.   *Sita was no ordinary woman. She was the
embodiment of Maha Maya (supreme divine
illusion). Rama acquired Maha Maya as his mate.
Sita, for her part, sought oneness with Atma
principle represented by Rama. The marriage of
Rama and Sita represents the association of the
Atma and the Maya. It is in this combined form of Atma
and Maya that Rama entered Ayodhya.*

*"Ayodhya" means "invincible". Its ruler was Dasaratha.
Dasaratha means one who has made his ten Indriyas
(sense organs) – the five organs of action and the
five organs of perception – his chariot. Allegorically,
this means that Dasaratha represents the body, with
the ten organs. These sense organs are related to the three
gunas (qualities) – Satwa, Rajas, Tamas. Dasaratha's
three wives – Kausalya, Sumitra and Kaikeyi –
symbolise these three gunas.*

[SSS Vol. 20, P 48-49]

**Q 736. Krishna is called 'Navanitachora' (Butter-thief).
What does it mean?**

A.   *The name 'Navanitachora' (Butter-thief) is used for
Krishna. It does not mean a person who runs away with
the butter that people have stored. It is not the stuff called*

butter that is got by churning curdled milk that He stole. It is the butter of Faith, won by churning process called 'yearning', from the curdled milk called, 'worldly experiences'. He covets only this 'butter'. When Yashoda chided the child Krishna for this 'theft', He replied, "But Mother, they like me for stealing it; they are sorry if I do not; they churn it in the hope that I will steal it; when I steal, their hearts are illumined and they awake."

[SSS Vol. 8, P 139]

Q 737. What is the true significance of the *Uttarayana* and the *Dakshinayana*?

A. *They have both an outer and an inner significance, the inner having greater value for aspirants for spiritual progress. I do not attach much value to the outer meaning: the Sun taking a northward direction from today (Uttarayana Day); the six months from now on being holier than the six that ended today and therefore, the Uttarayana being better suited for sadhana.*

Man's life must be a perpetual sadhana. Any day is a good day for starting sadhana whether it falls in Dakshinayana or Uttarayana (southward or northward movements of Sun). *Uttarayana is a quality of the Nayana (the eye); it is a matter of drishti—attitude, point of view. It is not Ayana (half year term).* **When your drishti is on Brahman, it is Uttarayana; when it is on Prakrithi, it is Dakshinayana. Uttarayana is a matter of attitude, point of view.**

Know that there are only two entities; the substance and the shadow, (or rather, only One, and its appearance produced by ignorance), the Atma and the An-atma—the seer and the seen, the rope and the snake. When knowledge becomes part of the mental make-up, it liberates you from Maya and you see Kailasa at the end of the Uttarayana yatra. Like Kailasa, that stage is all Light, all White. The path is straight and hard, but the Goal is glorious. It is nothing less than Illumination.

[SSS Vol. 2, P 152-153]

Q 738. **What is *Ksheera Sagara* and what is the true significance of its churning?**

A. *The Bhagavata describes the churning of the Ksheera Sagara (the ocean of milk) by the Devas (gods) and Asuras (demons). They used the Mandara mountain as the churning rod. The churning gave out both poison and nectar. Initially, deadly poison emerged. The demons were frustrated and disheartened to see poison emanating from the ocean instead of **Amruta** (ambrosia). They wanted to give up the churning process. But the gods did not want to give up. They relentlessly continued the churning with courage and determination. Their sustained efforts yielded rich rewards in the form of **Lakshmi** (goddess of wealth), **Airavata** (divine white elephant), **Kamadhenu** (wish-fulfilling cow), **Kalpataru** (wish-fulfilling tree) and ultimately the divine **ambrosia** itself. In the same manner, people should churn their mind and try to know their true identity. They should not be deterred or depressed by the initial impediments and obstacles that beset their path. Those who proceed on their chosen path with determination attain the bliss of ambrosia like the gods.*

[Sanathana Sarathi – Feb. 2003]

Q 739. **What is the inner meaning of *Namaskar*?**

A. *When you do Namaskar, you join your palms and bring* them close to your heart. The five fingers of each hand symbolise the five Karmendriyas (senses of action) and five Jnanendriyas (senses of perception). These ten senses should follow the dictates of your heart (conscience). That is true Namaskar. Some people do Namaskar in a mechanical way. They do not bring their two palms together. They say Namaskar and lift their hands, as if they are going to hit you. When you do Namaskar, bring the ten fingers together and keep the two thumbs close to your heart.

[SS – June 2002, P 175 (Inaugural Address at Summer Course on 16-5-2002)]

Q 740. What does *Hridaya* stand for?

A.   *The divinity which fills the entire Cosmos, exists in man as 'Hridya'. The Vedas name this 'Hridaya' (spiritual heart) as 'Atma'. Atma has another name 'Easwara'.*

[SS – Aug. 2000, P 249 (Summer Course Discourse on 16-5-2000)]

Q 741. What is the inner significance of *Vibhuti* or holy ASH?

A.   *When any object that has a name and form is completely burnt, it is reduced to ashes. The name and form are gone. All things are one and the same in the final state as ashes.* **When Vibhuti is given, Swami wants the recipient to understand this basic oneness (Adwaitham). The devotee should get rid of his Ahamkara (egoism arising from the feeling of separateness) and sense of 'Mine' and 'Thine' (mamakara).** *These two are based on name and form and when they are destroyed, the underlying unity of the Divine can be realised.*

[SSS Vol. 20, P 121]

Q 742. What is *Prasadam* and how should it be received?

A.   *"Prasadam (eatables offered to God) also means*
        Grace, which flows from God when it is propitiated.
        My Grace is ever with you; it is not something that
        is given or taken. It is given always and accepted
        by the Consciousness that is aware of its
        significance. Win the grace of your own sub-
        conscious; so that it may accept the Grace of God
        which is ever available. God does not deny any one;
        it is only you who deny God. When a gift is proffered,
        you have to do only one little act, so that you may
        earn it – you have to extend your hand to receive it.
        That is the Grace.

                                                [SSS Vol. 11, P 92]

Q 743. In the Siva temples we find *Nandi* (image of bull) in front of the deity. What is its inner significance?

A.   *The usual reply you get is that Nandi is the vahana*
        (vehicle) of Siva, as if He could not afford to have a better
        vehicle than a bull. This is a wrong idea. The truth is that
        just as Lingam is the symbol of the Lord (Siva), Nandi
        (bull) is the symbol of Jiva (individual soul). Therefore,
        like Nandi, man should turn away from Prakriti (world)
        and direct all his attention towards God only.

                                                [SSS Vol. 25, P 169]

Q 744. What is the symbolic significance of Lord Vishnu carrying Sankh (conch), Chakra (wheel), Gada (mace) and a Lotus flower in His hands?

A.   *God is called in His Cosmic form as Vishnu, who*
        permeates everything in the cosmos. God is the cause and
        the cosmos is the effect. Vishnu is depicted as having a
        Conch in one hand and a wheel in another. In the third
        hand, He carries a mace and in the fourth, a lotus flower.

The esoteric significance of these symbols is: the Conch is the symbol of Sound. Hence, God is described as the embodiment of Sound. The Chakra (wheel) symbolises Kaal-chakra (the Wheel of Time). The Lord is the master of Time and Sound. The Mace signifies strength of power. This means that the Lord holds in His hand the strength of all beings. The Lotus in the Lord's hand is the symbol of the heart. This means that the Lord holds in His hands the hearts of all beings.

[SSS Vol. 26, P 288]

Q 745. What is the inner significance of the third step of the Lord kept on Bali's head?

A. *The Lord's first foot covered this world and the second foot covered the other world. How huge the Lord's feet should have been to cover the whole world? How can such a huge foot be kept on Bali's head for the third step of land? The inner significance of this action is that Lord entered Bali's body, mind and soul. Once the ego or body consciousness is surrendered, there is no bar to one's realisation. It is the body consciousness that stands in the way and makes you forget God. The Lord opened Bali's eyes to help him realise the Divine.*

[SSS Vol. 27, P 229-230]

✳✳✳

10
BHAKTI YOGA

Q 746. What is Bhakti?

A. *Bhakti is a word that is used only with reference to love as directed to the Lord. When this love is broken up into many streams flowing in many different directions and towards many points, it only causes grief, for it gets fixed on mortal things of the moment.*
[Geetha Vahini, P 231]

Q 747. What characteristics should an aspirant seeking the Eternal - through the path of Bhakti – strive to acquire?

A. *The aspirant must keep away from the turmoils, the cruelties and the falsehood of this world and practise truth, righteousness, love and peace. Those who seek union with God should discard as worthless both praise and blame, appreciation and derision, prosperity and adversity. They should courageously keep steady faith in their own innate reality and dedicate themselves to spiritual uplift.*
[Prema V, P 27]

Q 748. How is Paramatma attained?

A.   *Paramatma cannot be known without faith and steadfastness. Only through Prema, comes sraddha; only through sraddha comes jnana; only through jnana comes para-bhakti; only through para-bhakti is Paramatma obtained.*

[Prema V, P 5,6]

Q 749. How is one to reduce the distance between God and the devotee?

A.   *You are as distant from the Lord as you think you are, as near Him as you feel you are. Well, let me tell you this. The distance from Me to you is the same as the distance from you to Me, is it not? But, you complain that I am far from you, though you are approaching nearer and nearer. How can that be? I am as near you as you are near Me.*

[SSS Vol. 4, P 57]

750.   Can the *sadhana* of dedication of thoughts, feelings and acts lead to attainment of the Lord?

A.   *For he who aims at Liberation must first give up attachment to the body. Without that, the Atmic stage cannot be attained. The identification with the body is the expression of ignorance. The Atma must be recognised as distinct from the Prakriti.*

[Geetha Vahini, P 223]

Q 751. What assurance has the Lord held out to *Bhaktas*?

A.   *The Lord rushes towards the Bhakta faster than the Bhakta rushes towards Him. If you take one step towards Him, He takes a hundred steps towards you. He will be more than a mother or father. He will foster you from within you, as He has saved and fostered so many saints who have placed faith in Him.*

[SSS Vol. 3, P 137]

Q 752. Is the attitude of a Bhakta placing offerings on the idol with motive or desire for a specific reward acceptable?

A. *People pray to God to relieve them from pain, grief and loss, to confer on them health, strength and wealth but if you develop an intimate attachment to Him and make Him yours, then He will manage to give you all that you need. Do not demean the relationship into bargaining.*

[SSS Vol. 6, P 175]

Q 753. Is there any harm in changing the Name and Form of one's deity?

A. *Do not get shaken in mind; do not allow faith to decline. That will only add to the grief you already suffer from. Hold fast – that must be your vow. Whoever is your Ishtadevta, Vishnu or Rama or Siva or Venkateswara, hold fast to Him… Have faith in any One Name and the Form indicated by that Name. If you revere Siva and hate Vishnu, the plus and the minus cancel out and the result is zero.*

[SSS Vol. 4, P 183, 184]

Q 754. What should be the mental attitude of a seeker?

A. *The attitude of the worshipper and the worshipped is the seed of Bhakti. First, the worshipper's mind is attracted by the special qualities of the object of worship. He tries to acquire for himself these special qualities. This is the sadhana. In the early stages of sadhana, the distinction between worshipper and the worshipped is full but as the sadhana progresses, this feeling will diminish and when attainment is reached, there will be no distinction whatsoever.*

[Prema V, P 65]

Q 755. What is the chief characteristic of a Bhakta?

A.   *There is only one wish fit to be entertained by the Sadhaka; and that is the realisation of the Lord, Easwara-Sakshatkara. There is no room in the mind for any other wish...The Bhakta who desires the Supreme and seeks to attain it should have this mental attitude...Such a Bhakta will have no desires, for desires are the product of 'I and Mine' feelings. Only after the desires are uprooted, a person becomes a Bhakta.*

[Prema V, P 65-66]

Q 756. What is the greatest gift of Bhakti?

A.   *Bhakti will force the Lord to give you Himself as a gift.*

[SSS Vol. 3, P 79]

Q 757. What is the easiest way to develop devotion?

A.   *The human birth is very difficult to attain. It cannot be got for a song. The body is a caravansarai, the mind is the watchman; the Jivi is the pilgrim. And so, none of these has any kinship with the others. The pilgrim is bound for Salvation City, Mokshapuri. For a trouble free journey, there is nothing so reliable as Namasmarana, the remembrance of the Name of the Lord. Once the sweetness of that Name has been experienced, the person will not have exhaustion, unrest or sloth. He will fulfil his pilgrimage of sadhana joyfully, enthusiastically and with deep conviction. Still, for achieving this sadhana, righteousness is very important. Without fear of sin, righteousness cannot originate; love of God, too, cannot develop. This fear produces Bhakti (devotion), which results in the Worship of the Lord.*

[Prema V, P 71]

Q 758. What is the harvest of a *sadhaka*?

A.   *Bhakta should consider the body as the field, good deeds as seed, and cultivate the name of the Lord, with the help of the heart, in order to get the harvest, the Lord Himself.*
[Prema V, P 107]

Q 759. Is devotion to the Lord the real ideal of Bhakti?

A.   *Devotion to the Lord is only a form of discipline to reach the goal. The seeker should not stop with the acquisition of devotion. He should pay attention not so much to the devotion or love that he has towards the Lord, as the Love and Grace that the Lord bestows on him. He must be always eager to find out which behaviour of his, what acts of his, will be most pleasing to the Lord. Inquire about that, yearn for that, and carry out the things that will secure that objective. That is real Bhakti.*
[Geetha Vahini, P 225]

Q 760. Is God pleased with *Saakara Upasana* or *Niraakara Upasana*, that is, worship of God-with Form (*Saguna*) or God-without-Form (*Nirguna*)?

A.   *Krishna said, "Arjuna! I do not make any distinction between the two. I am pleased in whatever way I am worshipped, provided the mind is saturated with Me and there is steady Faith in every act, word and thought."*
[Geetha Vahini, P 221]

Q 761. Is *Nirguna-Niraakara Bhakti* possible for everybody to perform?

A.   *The contemplation of the Formless, Characteristicless Nirguna-niraakara is very difficult for those with Deha-bhraanti or identification of the Self with the body.*
[Geetha Vahini, P 222]

Q 762. Is Bhakti of God with Form enough?

A. *People think that the worship of God with Form and attributes is quite enough. But this discipline will only be of some help. It will guide the person along the road only for a little while. The Lord will not grant Liberation for just this.*

[Geetha Vahini, P 223]

Sadhana of the Formless Godhead alone gives illumination. ...So, Saguna Bhakti has to be adopted as sadhana and Nirguna Bhakti as the goal to be reached.

[Geetha Vahini, P 229]

Q 763. What is the best form of Bhakti?

A. *Of various types of Bhakti, Namasmarana Bhakti is the best. In the Kaliyuga, the name is the path for saving oneself. Jayadeva, Gouranga, Thyagaraja, Thukaram, Kabir, Ramdas, all these great Bhaktas attained the Lord through just this one Nama...If every sadhaka will consider the name of the Lord as the very breath of his life and, having complete faith in good deeds and good thoughts, if he will develop the spirit of service and equal love for all, there can be no better path for Mukti.*

[Prema V, P 109]

Q 764. What are the nine modes of devotion?

A. *Nine modes of devotion mentioned in the Scriptures are: 1. Sravanam – listening to the Lord's stories, leela and Mahima, 2. Kirtanam – singing His glories, 3. Smaranam – remembrance, 4. Pada Sevanam – service to the Lotus Feet, 5. Archanam – worship, 6. Vandanam – salutation, 7. Dasyam – master-servant relationship, 8. Sakhyam – companionship,*

9. Atma-Nivedanam – *offering oneself to the Lord i.e. Self-surrender.*

[Summer Showers 1990, P 80]

Q 765. Are the nine forms of devotion (Nava-vidha Bhakti) meant for realising the Atma?

A.   *These forms of worship are intended to shed the Anatma (that which is not the Atma).* **When the Anatma is cast off, the Atma shines of its own accord.**

[SSS Vol. 25, P 201]

Q 766. What is the difference between *Anurag* and Bhakti?

A.   *Love of God is Bhakti. All other love may be termed as Anurag, which results in bondage, while love of God leads to liberation.*

[SSS Vol. 27, P 221]

Q 767. Is the path of devotion external or internal approach to Divinity?

A.   *There is no path superior to that of Bhakti. Bhakti does not mean doing Puja, Bhajans, going on pilgrimage to holy shrines etc. Bhakti means diverting the pure and unsullied mind towards God.*

[SSS Vol. 27, P 221]

Q 768. Is it possible for everyone to realise the goal through Bhakti – the love of God?

A.   *You may not achieve it instantaneously, but can do so progressing step by step. By Bhajans and other forms of worship one may advance towards the goal of final emancipation.*

[SSS Vol. 27, P 221]

Q 769. Does external worship help in realisation of the goal?

A.   *You may install idols and worship them. But do not forget the inner significance of all worship. All external activities are necessary only to help you get into the spirit of non-duality and experience unity in diversity.*

[SSS Vol. 27, P 222]

Q 770. Which is the best way to serve God?

A.   *One should regard love for God (Bhakti) as the greatest treasure one can have. When you love God, you will have love towards all because the Divine is in everyone. Love all, Serve all. The best way to serve God is to love all and serve all.*

[SSS Vol. 27, P 191]

Q 771. Through what stages do the devotees progress on the Nine-Fold path of devotion?

A.   *Different people experience the bliss derived from devotion in different ways. One devotee begins with repeatedly reciting the word, daasoham, daasoham (I am His servant), expresses his devotion as a servant of the Lord. In course of time, by frequent repitition of this word and reminding himself of the Lord, he reaches the stage where the 'daa' drops away and only 'soham' remains. He begins to realise that he and the Lord are one. Starting as the servant of the Lord, he realises his identity with the Lord.*

[SSS Vol. 27, P 186]

Q 772. How many types of Bhakti find mention in the Vedas?

A.   *The Vedas say that there are three types of Bhakti: Bhouthika, Ekantha and Ananya Bhakti.*

[SSS Vol. 15, P 222]

Q 773. What constitutes *Bhoutika Bhakti*?

A.   *Shravana (listening), Manana (contemplating and*

*digesting what has been learnt) and Nidhi-dhyasana
(practising what was learnt), the rituals connected with
Yajna, visiting various places of pilgrimage and various
types of service (seva) such as charity (daan and dharma)
are all classified as Bhoutika Bhakti (devotion related to
created or living beings). Japa, tapa and sandhya rites are
all connected with the first type of Bhakti. Constructing
temples and rituals connected with these are also Bhoutika
Bhakti. These are all connected with the physical. This
type of Bhakti constitutes the first step.*

[SSS Vol. 27, P 222]

Q 774. What is meant by *Ekanta Bhakti*?

A.   *Many people think that dedication to one idol or Form
and experiencing mental vision of that one Form sitting
in exclusive privacy is Ekanta Bhakti. It is incorrect.*

**Ekantha Bhakti is a subtle state achieved by
effective control of the mind and experiencing one's
inner Self (Antharatn.a).**

[SSS Vol. 15, P 222]

Q 775. What are the disqualifications of a *sadhaka*? What qualities should he imbibe?

A.   *Anger is the enemy No.1 of the sadhaka. It is like spittle
and has to be treated as such. And untruth? It is even more
disgusting. Theft ruins life...The sadhaka should avoid all
thoughts of the nature of the sad and depressing thoughts.
Depression, doubt, conceit, these are Rahu and Ketu to the
spiritual aspirant...it is best that the sadhaka should be
under all circumstances, joyful, smiling and enthusiastic.*

[Prema V, P 108]

Q 776. What are the signs of a genuine *Bhakta*?

A.   *During Treta Yuga when Narada asked Sri Rama about*

the nature and characteristics of His true Bhaktas, the
Lord answered: *"Whoever with Viveka and Vairagya,
and Vinaya and Vijnana, with discrimination and
renunciation, with humility and wisdom, are aware of
the knowledge of the Reality, whoever are always
immersed in the contemplation of my Leela (sport),
whoever dwells on My name at all times and under all
conditions, and who sheds tears of Love whenever the Lord's
name is heard from any lip, they are my genuine Bhaktas."*

[Prema V, P 82]

Q 777. **Which traits of a Bhakta qualify him for receiving
Lord's protection at all times?**

A. *The Lord will protect in all ways and at all times
those who worship Him in complete and
uncontaminated Bhakti, just as a mother protects
her infants, and the eyelids guard the eye, effortlessly
and automatically.*

[Prema V, P 82]

Q 778. **Which path of Bhakti should be followed by the
sadhakas who yearn to find God?**

A. *Sabari asked Sri Rama while He was gladly partaking of
the feast of roots and fruits, selected and reserved by Sabari
for him after tasting every individual item: "Lord! I am
but a woman. In addition I am of feeble intellect. Above
all, I am lowborn. How can I praise you? I do not know
what to do or how!"* **Then, Sri Rama smiled and said:**
*"Sabari! My mission is only the kinship of Bhakti. Of
what use is it to have status, wealth and character, without
Bhakti?* **Bhaktas reach me through nine paths; any
one of them takes them to Me."Sravanam; Kirtanam;
Vishnu-smaranam; Padasevanam; Archanam;**

Vandanam; Dasyam; Sakhyam; Atma-nivedanam.

If the devotee sincerely practises any one of these paths He can attain Me." I am bound by these nine forms of Bhakti.

[Prema V, P 83]

Q 779. Does worship of an idol with devotion and love in a closed room constitute *Ekaanta Bhakti*?

A.   *No. This cannot be called Ekaanta Bhakti. After all the idol is only a created object. You should experience your Atma-swarupa and not created object. You should have a vision of the Primordial Divinity, whose reflection is your Atma. Worshipping of idol is necessary as a first step. But do not devote your lifetime on the first step.*

[SSS Vol. 15, P 224]

Q 780. How does *Ekantha Bhakti* lead to Self-realisation?

A.   *By continuous training and practise of Ekantha Bhakti, you will be able to know the Atma within yourself. The Atma is in you. You cannot see it because of impurities and waves of likes and dislikes hovering around. When you remove these impurities, the mind rests in a pure state. At that stage, if you turn your eye inward you will have the vision of Divinity – the Saakshaathkaara. Ekaantha Bhakti is realised only when you turn the vision inward, away from sensory objects and experience the pure Atma. Ekanta Bhakti is Antar-drishti (inner vision), while Bhouthika Bhakti is Bahir-drishti or outer vision. After earning Bhouthika Bhakti and Ekantha Bhakti, Ananya Bhakti will be easy to attain.*

[SSS Vol. 15, P 225]

Q 781. What is *Ananya Bhakti*?

A.   *Ananya Bhakti can be described as 'unquestioning*

faith'. *Sage Shuka described the devotion of the Gopis as the highest state of Bhakti. It was Ananya Bhakti in the highest sense.*

[SSS Vol. 15, P 226]

Bhakti without any other thought or feeling is Ananya Bhakti. It is unbroken contemplation of God without any other interposing thought or feeling.

[Geetha Vahini P 251-252]

Q 782. Which is the royal road to reach God?

A. *There are many ways of realising God. All other paths merge in the path of Love. Pure Love is therefore the royal road.*

[SSS Vol. 25, P 233]

Q 783. What is the most important aspect in *Japa* and *Bhakti* sadhana?

A. *All hearts are motivated by the One and only God. His adoration is best done by means of love.Cultivate that Eka-bhava, attitude of Oneness. When you recite the Name of God, remembering His majesty, His compassion, His Glory, His splendour, His presence – Love will grow within you.*

[SSS Vol. 8, P 118]

Q 784. Is it true that women have more devotion than men?

A. *I wish to emphasise in this context that during the lifetime of any Avatar, it is only the women who recognise His divinity first. They are the ones who lead their husbands to the path of divinity.* It is only because of the devotion of women that men cultivate devotion to some extent at least. But for women, men will not have devotion at all.

[SSS Vol. 35, P 232]

Q 785. Are women drawn to Bhakti more than *Jnana*?

A.   *Women are identified with Bhakti (devotion) and men are identified with Jnana (wisdom) since times immemorial. Women can enter even the inner precincts of a palace, where men are permitted to go only up to the Durbar hall (court room). It means that Jnana will lead you up to God. Bhakti, on the other hand, will take you to His heart. That is why such a great value has been attached to Bhakti. In fact, it was the Gopikas who were responsible for the spread of Bhakti Tatthwa (path of devotion) in the world.*

[SSS Vol. 35, P 233]

11
KARMA YOGA

Q 786. Can *Karmas* be overcome?

A. *Brahman alone is true. When such Jnana (knowledge) dawns, the dark shadows of three types of Karma – the Agaami, the Sanchitha and the Prarabdha Karma can be overcome. For, the Will of God is Omnipotent and Omnipotence, there can be no limit or exception. When through sadhana, you win the Sankalpa of the Lord, you can with that Sankalpa achieve victory over Prarabdha also. Do not be discouraged on any score.*
[Prema V, P 41]

Q 787. What type of good deeds help purifying the mind?

A. *Every man must undertake good deeds to purify the mind. Without an eye on results, without selfish intent, all actions performed are Nishkama karma (desireless actions). Nishkama karma is nothing but Bhoga (pleasure) and Tyaga (renunciation).*
[Summer Showers 1991, P 47]

Q 788. Which are the three strong convictions of the ancient Indian culture?

A.   *Indian culture stands on certain strong convictions:*

1. *Karma Theory* – *results of karmas are inescapable.*
2. *Avatar-hood* – *God incarnates in human form as an Avatar.*
3. *Permanence of God* – *Everything in the world is a form of God, and is naturally sacred.*

[Summer Showers 1991, P 49]

Q 789. What is the real karma of a devotee?

A.   *Karma which pleases the Lord is superior to the karma which fulfils the yearning of the devotee.*

[Geetha Vahini, P 225]

Q 790. How does *Karma* crop up? How does one get bound in *Karma*?

A.   *Attachment is caused by ignorance. Attachment results in identification of 'I' with the body, senses, mind etc. Attachment leads to desire; desire results in anger; anger blinds reason and promotes ignorance; ignorance breeds dualities of 'mine' and 'thine', good and bad etc; these produce consequences of merit and demerit (punya and paapa). They have to be consumed in this life or future lives. So, one has to go through suffering. Karma is due to belief in dwaita (duality). Dwaita is the result of ajnana (ignorance).*

[SSS Vol. 15, P 252]

Q 791. Is it necessary to perform *Karma*?

A.   *Every one has to bow to the demands of karma. It is inevitable. Krishna said: "Do the kartavya-karmas, karmas that is your bounden duty. Being engaged in karma is to be preferred to not being engaged. If you desist from karma, the task of living becomes difficult, nay impossible.*

[Geetha Vahini, P 55]

Q 792. Which *Karmas* are binding and which do not bind?

A.   *The karmas that do not bind by consequences are referred to as Yajna. All the rest are bondage-producing ones.*

[Geetha Vahini, P 55]

Q 793. How is one to dedicate *Karmas*?

A.   *Lord Krishna said: "Have steady faith in the Atma; then dedicate all acts of yours to Me with no desire for the fruits thereof, no egoism and no sense of possession or pride.*

[Geetha Vahini, P 56]

Q 794. Is there no escape from *Karmas* for anyone?

A.   *"No. Consider this, O Arjuna. I have no need to do any karma; no! not anywhere in the three worlds. I am under no compulsion. Still I am ever engaged in karma. Think of this. If I desist, the world will be no more."*

If the wheel of creation is to move smooth, each one has to keep doing karma. Even he who has achieved the highest Jnana has to observe this rule. Eating and drinking, intake and release of breath – these too are karmas. So, there is no one who is karma-less.

[Geetha Vahini, P 56]

Q 795. But a *Jnani* (a realised soul) is said to have gone beyond *Karma*?

A.   *You may wonder why Jnanis should still do Karma. Well, people usually follow the ideal set by those in higher levels. Their acts form the basis of Dharma for all. If Jnanis are inactive, how are ordinary mortals to save themselves? They have no guide and so they lose themselves in the easy path of sensory pleasure. The duty of the wise is to foster the right and to practise it before others, so that they too may be prompted to follow. That is why the Jnani*

*has to be engaged in activity; he has to remove the sloth
and delusion of ordinary men.*

[Geetha V, P 57]

Q 796. What is the secret of *Karma*?

A.   *Karma (selfish karma) is the root cause of all evil. He who
is bound by Deha-Atma-Buddhi (the false idea that he is
just the body and nothing more) can never hope to conquer
karma. One must acquire the Brahma-Atma-Buddhi (the
awareness that one is Brahman and nothing less) in order
to be sure of victory. All acts must be performed in the
spirit of dedication to the Lord.*

[Geetha V, P 59]

Q 797. What is the final goal of *Karma*?

A.   *Jnana is the final goal and gain of karma. Jnana is the
treasure that is won by man's efforts to purify the mind
and to earn the Grace of God.*

[Geetha V, P 59]

Q 798. What is meant by *A-sahaja-karma* and *Sahaja-karma*?

A.   *Assumed karma is called A-sahaja karma, and karma that
is the expression of one's genuine self is Sahaja-karma.
Sahaja-karma will sit light and A-sahaja karma will
induce conceit, or the feeling of 'I am the doer'; so it will
result in elation, disgust or pride.*

[Geetha V, P 63]

Q 799. What is the distinction between *Karma*, *Vikarma* and *Akarma*?

A.   *Swa-dharma is Karma and all Karma done, not as dharma
is Vikarma. Akarma means action-lessness. To explain it
in simple language, understand that the activities of the
limbs, the senses, intelligence, the feelings, the emotions*

and mind are all Karmas. Now, Akarma means among other things, non-activity too. That is to say, it is the attribute of the Atma. So, Akarma means Atma-sthithi, the characteristic of the Atma.

[Geetha V, P 95-96]

Q 800. Can *Karma* be rendered ineffective?

A. *When the vision of Truth, samyak darshan is gained, all Karma becomes ineffective and harmless.* **The fire of Jnana has the power to consume and burn Karma.**

[Geetha V, P 97]

Q 801. Some people say that one must perforce suffer the consequences of *Prarabdha-kar.na*; he cannot escape from it. Is it so?

A. *This is a conclusion that other persons draw, not the experience of the Jnani himself. To those who watch him, he might appear to be reaping the fruit of the past Karma, but he is absolutely unaffected. Whoever is dependent on objects for happiness or pursues a sensory pleasure; whoever is motivated by impulses and desires, is bound by Karma. But those free from these cannot be affected by the temptations and attractions of the senses. Such is the true Sanyasin.* **The Jnani is supremely happy by himself, without the need to be dependent on other things. He finds Karma in Akarma and Akarma in Karma. He may be engaged in Karma, but he is not affected in the least.**

[Geetha V, P 97]

Q 802. Can we be completely saved from the consequences of *Karmas*?

A. *Grace takes away the malignity of the karma which you have to undergo. The effect of karma is rendered*

null, though the account of karma is there and has
to be rendered or the Lord can save a man completely
from the consequences, as was done by Me to the Bhakta
whose paralytic stroke and heart attacks I took over, some
months ago, in the Guru-poornima week!

[SSS Vol. 29, P 399]

Q 803. What are the surrendered *Karmas*?

A.   *Recognising the immanence of the Divine, one has to*
dedicate all acts to the Divine. What is the act (karma),
when you analyse it deeply? **It is the manipulation of**
the Divine by the Divine, for the sake of the Divine
through the skill endowed by the Divine. *There is no*
I or mine in it, except the Universal I and the Divine My.

[SSS Vol. 9, P 122]

Q 804. What are these four categories of *Karma*: *Karma-*
ateeta*, *Nishkama-karma*, *Sakama-karma* and
***Karma-bhrashta*?**

A.   ***Karma-ateeta: are the Jivanmuktas.*** *All their karmas*
have been burnt up by the fire of Jnana. Their impulses
for action have been scorched by the wisdom they have
gained. They have no further need for injunction and
prohibition (vidhi and nishedha). All that they do or feel
or think will be divine, holy, virtuous, and beneficial to
mankind. Every word they utter will be the word of God.
They have attained Kaivalya Mukti.

Nishkama-karma: *the second group is the adepts at*
Nishkama-karma. These are the Mumukshus, alert on the
path of liberation, who are intent on attaining it. So, they
do not look forward to the result. Their aim is Liberation
from the bondage. They win the Grace of the Lord in
proportion to their faith and practice.

Sakama-karma: Those who believe in Sakama-karma perform all acts through the desire for the fruit thereof. Since they have an eye on the fruit, they will not do any sinful act. Such men, when they depart from the world, will enter the Lokas they have sought and worked for and having stayed there as long as their merit entitles them, they have to return to earth.

Karma-bhrashta: They are not guided by any rule of conduct. They have no discrimination between virtue and vice, right and wrong. They have no horror of hell, no dread of devil, no reverence for God, no respect for the sastras. They are best pictured as beasts in human form. They strive for momentary pleasure and short-lived happiness.

[Geetha V, P 185-187]

Q 805. How does *Karma* affect the death and future birth of a person?

A. *Man by his karma in this life decides on his next birth, where and how it will be, even before leaving the world.* The new place is ready for him; his foreparts are already there. It is only after setting this that he relieves himself of the hold on this world. Men of this category move around in the wheel of birth and death.

[Geetha V, P 187]

Q 806. Should one aspire for good birth or good death?

A. *The sadhaka should not aspire for a good birth; he should seek a good death.* You may be born well, in a good family or with many favourable circumstances; but subsequent karma may not ensure a good death. So if a good death is aimed at, the trouble of being born and becoming once again subject to death can be avoided.

[Geetha Vahini, P 167]

Q 807. How do the Yogis who practise *Nishkama-karma* leave their bodies on death?

A.   *They pass away in Tejas during the day, while there is light, Sukla-paksha – in the bright half of the month and in the six month period of Uttarayana. Their path is known as Devayana.*

[Geetha V, P 188]

Q 808. How do the practitioners of *Sakama-karma* leave their bodies on death?

A.   *They pass away in Dhuma (smoke) at night, during the dark half of the month during the six months of Dakshinayana. They pass along Dhumadi Marg and reach Swarga (heaven) and there enjoy the pleasures they have yearned for. When the stock of merit is exhausted, they get born again.*

[Geetha V, P 189]

Q 809. Which is superior of the two – *Karma yoga* or *Karma sanyasa*?

A.   *Karma yoga is far superior to Karma-sanyasa. Well. Superior to both these is Dhyana yoga. Dhyana yoga needs the support of Karma yoga. Dhyana yoga is possible only on the basis of Nishkama Karma. If the mind is not under control it can become one's greatest foe. Those who renounce the fruits while actively engaged in Karma are the true Sanyasins, the real Renouncers.*

[Geetha V, P 112]

Q 810. If even after earning the highest heaven man has to be born again, where lies his salvation?

A.   *There is a state that knows no decline, beyond all these heavens. There are many roads by which that* *state can be won. There are four roads which are now used by mankind:*

(1) Karma-ateeta, beyond karma, unaffected by karma. (2) Nishkama-karma – karma without any desire for the fruit thereof. (3) Sakama-karma – that is, action with the desire to reap and enjoy its fruits. (4) Karma-bhrashta – karma that knows no control.

[Geetha V, P 185]

Q 811. **Who is the *Kartha* (the doer of Karma) and who is the *Bhoktha* (the recipient of the fruit of Karma)?**

A. *The Lord said: " I am the recipient of the sabda, sparsha, rupa, rasa and gandha. I am not only the Kartha, the entity responsible for the Karma; I am also the Bhoktha, the entity for which that Karma is gone through, the recipient of the fruits; I am the benefactor as well as the beneficiary."*

[Geetha V, P 161]

Q 812. **Do all *Karmas* have beginning and an end?**

A. *Every Karma has a beginning and an end. But Nishkama Karma (desire-less karma) has no such. That is the difference between the two. When karma is done with a view to the gain thereof, one has to suffer the loss, the pain, and even the punishment. But, Nishkama karma frees you from all these.*

[Geetha V, P 41]

Q 813. **Why is the mind of man restless and his heart tumultuous?**

A. *The reason for this can be traced to his Prarabdha-karma or the accumulated karma of his past lives.*

[Summer Showers 1979, P 108]

Q 814. **Can *Prarabdha-karma* be destroyed?**

A.   *Prarabdha-karma pursues man like the hound of
       hell. The accumulated dead weight of Prarabdha-
       karma can be destroyed only by sat-karma or good
       actions in the present life... Karma can be wiped
       out by karma alone.*

                                    [Summer Showers 1979, P 108]

Q 815. Is there any other easier course of *sadhana* for
        achieving oneness with God?

A.   *This blissful experience can also be gained by
       renouncing the desire for the fruits of karma.
       Nishkama karma creates a special bond of love
       between the creator and the jiva. One who performs
       action without desire for its results is alone dear to
       God...The renunciation however, must be total, not
       merely superficial.*

                                    [Summer Showers 1979, P 112]

Q 816. Do all our actions, good and bad, done unto others
        reach God?

A.   *Deho Devalaya Prokto Jeevo Devah Sanathanah
       (body is the temple and the indweller is God). Consider
       all bodies as temples of God and offer your salutations.
       Salute even your enemies.* **Sarva Jeeva Namaskaram
       Kesavam Pratigachchhati** *and likewise* **Sarva Jeeva
       Tiraskaram Keasavam Pratigachchhati** *(whomsoever
       you pay respect and homage, it reaches God and
       whomsoever you criticise, it also reaches God).*

                                    [SS Vol. 33, P 164-165 232]

Q 817. Does any balance of unresolved *Karmas* involve
        sure rebirth?

A.   *Any balance of Karma-consequences will involve
       some years of imprisonment in the body. The sastras*

advise man to wipe off four types of balances: by extinguishing all sparks from the fire; by getting rid of all sins, symptoms and causes of fever; by paying off all balance of debt; and by bearing all consequences of karmas. A spark may start another fire; a virus may multiply quickly and bring about relapse; a little unpaid debt will soon assume huge proportions through high rates of interest; a karma, however trite, done with intention to benefit by the fruit thereof will involve birth in order to eat the fruit.

[SSS. Vol. 6, P 153-154]

Q 818. **How to close the account of birth and death with nil balance?**

A. *So long as the consequence of Karma persists, man is bound to be reborn, to finish the consumption thereof. For, the slate of Karma has to be wiped clean so that the account of birth and death can be closed for nil balance.*

[SSS. Vol. 6, P 153]

Q 819. **Does it imply that God does not interfere in the fruits of *karma*?**

A. *The Lord is an impartial witness. He merely hands over the fruits of each one's actions. In case the consequence is unpleasant, God may interfere to get the pain reduced by proper propitiation. That authority He has.*

[SSS Vol. 28, P 52]

Q 820. **What is wrong in returning injury for injury?**

A. *Returning injury for injury, harm for harm or insult for insult only adds to the Karmic burden, which has to be endured and eliminated in future lives. This burden (of karma) is termed Agami or lineal...*

Paying evil for evil can never lighten the weight of Karma; it will become heavier.

[Sutra Vahini, P 16]

Q 821. Can rituals and *Karma* lead to liberation or Moksha?

A.   *The sacred activities (karma) like rituals and sacrifices laid down in the Vedas cannot confer liberation from bondage to birth and death, Moksha. They help only to cleanse the Consciousness. It is said that they raise man to heaven; but heaven too is but a bondage. It does not promise eternal freedom. The freedom which makes one aware of the Truth, of his own Truth, can be gained only through Sravana (listening to the guru), Manana (ruminating over what has been so listened to) and Nidhidhyasana (meditating on its validity and significance).*

[Sutra Vahini, P 14]

Q 822. Why can't *Karmas* liberate man?

A.   *Because objects and individuals, rites and activities are transitory. They suffer from decay and destruction. They can at best help the cleansing of the mind, that is all. Karma cannot liberate one from the basic ignorance, or award the awareness of the reality as Brahmam.*

[Sutra Vahini, P 20]

Q 823. How will the activity that binds stop?

A.   *Desire is the prompting behind all activity. Desire is the urge. No activity arises in those who have attained all desires, for they rest in the Atma, which has no desire.*

[SSS. Vol. 6, P 153]

12
JNANA YOGA

Q 824. What is true *Jnana*?

A.   *Jnana does not mean acquisition of textual knowledge. Adwaita Darsanam Jnanam (perception of non-duality is supreme wisdom).*

[SSS Vol. 35, P 246]

Q 825. What is the sign of a true *Jnani*?

A.   *A true Jnani is one who dedicates his body, mind and intellect to God. He thinks only of God and nothing else. He performs his activities with the sole purpose of pleasing God.*

[SSS Vol. 35, P 246]

Q 826. What disciplines are necessary to establish *Upanishadic Jnana* firmly in the heart?

A.   *To establish Jnana firmly in the heart, one-pointedness is essential and this can be gained by the body disciplines and Tapas. External control helps internal control.. To succeed in external controls is by comparison more difficult than to achieve success in controlling the internal!*

[Prema V, P 91]

Q 827. Which is the most powerful and effective spiritual sadhana?

A. *"Nahi Jnanena Sadrsam" – there is nothing to equal Jnana. And what is Jnana? That which makes you cross this sea of flux, this samsara.*

[Geetha Vahini, P 145]

Q 828. What is the secret of *Jnana*?

A. *You have to isolate and dismiss from the consciousness the impressions of the senses, the mind, the intelligence, etc. These have nothing to do with the Atma, which you really are. The Atma is unaffected by any subject or object. To know the Atma as such an entity, unaffected and unattached, is the secret of Jnana.*

[Geetha Vahini, P 60]

Q 829. What is the greatest sin?

A. *Isavasya Upanishad mentions that Ajnana (ignorance) is the greatest sin. The Kaarpanyadosha that the Geetha mentions is another name for the same Ajnana.*

[SSS Vol. 3, P 130]

Q 830. What has to be done by the seeker before *Jnana* dawns?

A. *There are three principles that have to be overcome before Jnana (knowledge) can dawn: the Physical (Deha-tattvam); the Sensory (Indriya-tattvam) and the Mental (Manas-tattvam). Even the mind has to be overcome before the One can be cognised; for, the mind seeks variety and change. It revels in the contact with the* *objective world called vrittis. The prevention of these vrittis in the mind...is the function of the science called Yoga.*

[SSS Vol. 5, P 104-105]

Q 831. How does *Jnana* take one to the goal of Liberation?

A. *Every single act of yours must be carried out with this jnana as its background that awareness of the Atma will guide you in the out-moving and the in-drawing paths, the Pravritti marga and the Nivritti marga. It will not block action but fill it with purpose and meaning. It will build up faith and moral life. It will take man to the realm of deliverance along the road of Nishkama Karma, the renunciation of the fruit of Karma, and not of Karma itself.*

[Geetha Vahini, P 60]

Q 832. What qualification is essential in a seeker to acquire the sacred spiritual *Jnana*?

A. ***Shraddha, steady faith in the Sastras and the Teachers, and in the acquisition of Jnana...****along with these, you must also be vigilant. Do not yield to sloth. Again, you may fall into company that is not congenial or encouraging. To escape the evil influence of such company and to strengthen your mind to avoid it, mastery over the senses is required.*

[Geetha Vahini, P 111]

Q 833. What should be the state of mind of a *Jnana yoga* sadhaka?

A. *The mind of the yoga adept should be like the steady upright unshaken flame of the lamp, kept in a windless windowsill.*

[Geetha Vahini, P 114-115]

Q 834. What is the basic requirement for success in *Dhyana yoga* and *Jnana yoga*?

A.   *Dhyana Yoga and Jnana Yoga both are inner disciplines;*
         they are based on Sadhana and Bhakti. Without these two,
         they are both unattainable; the pursuit itself is vain.

                                                          [Geetha V, P 116]

Q 835. What is meant by *Abheda-jnana*?

A.   *Jnana is of two kinds: the first is objective knowledge*
         (Vishayajnana) and the second, integral knowledge, or
         Abhedajnana. The first type is knowledge of the world;
         the second is the knowledge of the identity of Brahman
         and the individual Atma, which is called Abheda or
         undifferentiated Jnana. This Jnana is not a function of
         the intellect or buddhi; it is a feature of something beyond
         it, something that witnesses the activities of even the
         Buddhi.

                                                      [Geetha Vahini, P 145]

Q 836. How does *Abheda-jnana* lead man to the goal of
         life? What is the call of the Vedas in this respect?

A.   *It leads to Atma-samyama, the control of the senses,*
         detachment from the outer sensory world, the withdrawal
         of the mind from the outer world. This is the goal of all
         life; knowing the Paramatma, attaining Liberation...

         "Srunvantu Vishwe Amrutasya Puthraah!" is the
         call (of the Vedas), " Listen, O! Ye, children of
         Immortality, all over the world!" *That is the*
         invitation. The heritage of Immortality must be recognised
         and experienced.

                                                      [Geetha Vahini, P 146]

Q 837. How to ensure physical and spiritual health?

A.   *Earn the sword of jnana to cut asunder the veil of Maya.*
         Discriminate between the real and the unreal early
         enough, during the journey towards the Goal. If the eye

is not helping you to derive the unending joy of visualizing God in everything it brings before your mind, then it is far better to be blind; if your ears drag you into the realm of filthy cacophony, it is far better to be deaf. The senses must not plunge you into the sensual; they must serve your real interests and sublimate your desires and appetites. That is the only way to ensure health and happiness.

[SSS Vol. 8, P 189]

13
BUDDHI YOGA

Q 838. What is *Buddhi-yoga*?

A.   *When the desire to attain the fruit of action is renounced with full intellectual awareness, then, it is called what Krishna calls, Buddhi yoga.*

[Geetha Vahini, P 41]

Q 839. What is to be done to attain *Buddhi yoga*?

A.   *The intellect has to be purified and trained; otherwise it is impossible to give up attachment to the fruits of action and to continue* doing things as either duty or dedication. Such a purified intellect is named '*Yoga-buddhi*'.

[Geetha Vahini, P 41]

Q 840. Which faculty of man best reflects the attributes of Atma?

A.   *The senses control the body and the mind controls the senses. The mind, in turn, is controlled by the buddhi.* **Being closest to Atma, buddhi best reflects the attributes of Atma.** *The influence of the Atma directly falls upon the buddhi and, therefore, the buddhi functions as the presiding faculty in man.*

[Summer Showers 1979, P 74]

Q 841. How is one to lead the senses along the right path?

A. *Individuals often get upset and troubled by the desires that arise in their minds. The mind generates sankalpas (thoughts), which are checked by the intelligence. Intelligence alone has the power to make decisions and to discriminate between good and bad.* **Krishna advised Arjuna not to follow the mind, which, left to itself is prone to succumbing to the pulls of sensory pleasures, but instead, to subjugate it to the intelligence.**

[Summer Showers 1979, P 75]

Q 842. How does *buddhi* have the most important role to play in man's journey to life?

A. *For going about in a chariot, it is the charioteer who has the most important role to play. Lord Krishna said to Arjuna: "Arjuna! Your body is a chariot and your senses are the horses; your mind acts as the reins and your intelligence is the driver. If you let your intelligence guide your life's journey, you will reach your ultimate destination safely."*

[Summer Showers 1979, P 75]

Q 843. How is one to develop the inner vision?

A. **It is only when the mind follows the buddhi that the inner vision is developed. Inner vision leads to the experience of the Bliss of the Atma.** *External vision, however, subjects man to untold suffering.*

[Summer Showers 1979, P 77]

Q 844. How is one to invoke God for improvement of the faculty of Buddhi?

A. *"Aum bhurbhuvah suvah tat Savitur Varenyam Bhargo Devasya Dhimahi Dhiyo yo nah prachodayaat."*

So runs the sacred Gayatri Mantra, an invocation to the Sun for the improvement of the faculty of buddhi or intelligence. The darkness of ignorance is dispelled by the incandescence of the buddhi, which shines its light like the glorious sun. "Among the faculties, I am the buddhi", proclaims Krishna in the Vibhuti Yoga of the Bhagavad Gita.

[Summer Showers 1979, P.153]

14

RAJA YOGA, DHYANA YOGA (MEDITATION)

Q 845. What does Yoga mean?

A.   *Yoga is the unity of the individual with the Divine. Yoga means an end to dualism.* Yoga teaches that the Jiva (the individual soul) and Brahman are not separate but one.

This is the significance of the declaration in the Shruti (Vedas): "Ekam Sat Viprah bahudha Vadanti" (The Truth is one but the wise call it by many names).

[SSS Vol. 25, P 213]

Q 846. Which Yoga is recommended for merging the mind in the Atma?

A.   To merge the body, the mind, the intellect, the Will and the ego in the awareness of Aham (the 'I' or the Self) is Raja Yoga. The goal of life should be to become a Raja Yogi.

[SSS Vol. 25, P 220]

Q 847. It is said that Yoga has certain Angas or auxiliaries. How many are they and what are their names?

A.   *They are eight in all, Ashtanga, in fact – Yama, Niyama, Asana, Pranayama, Prathyahaara, Dhaarana, Dhyana, Samadhi – these are the names of the eight.*

[Prasnottara Vahini, P 81]

Q 848. It is said that Yoga helps man in going beyond birth and death. What is that Yoga?

A.   *Yoga Sastra declares that certain Asanas have to be utilised in order to remove the ever-widening circles of mental agitations and purify the mind; also to steady faith, to establish Jnana and arouse Kundalini Sakti latent in man.*

[Prasnottara Vahini, P 81]

Q 849. If Mukti is to be obtained, have all these to be practised to perfection, or is any one of them enough?

A.   *Oh, Mukti can be won if the first two, Yama and Niyama, are mastered.*

[Prasnottara Vahini, P 82]

Q 850. What is included under Yama?

A.   *Ahimsa, Sathya, Astheya, Brahmacharya, Daya, Aarjavam, Kshama, Dhrthi, Mithaahaaram, Soucham; all these ten are included in Yama.*

[Prasnottara Vahini, P 83]

Q 851. What are the characteristics of Niyama?

A.   *Tapas, Santosha, Aastikya-buddhi, Easwara-puja, Vedanta-vaakya-sravana, Lajja, Mati, Japam, Vrata, these ten form Niyama. These are the very foundations of the Mansion of Moksha; all Yogis must be well established in these; in Yama as well Niyama.*

[Prasnottara Vahini, P 89]

Q 852. What is Samadhi – the ultimate stage in Raja Yoga?

A.   *In the deep sleep state one is not aware of the names or forms or position or anything else. It is also described as the state of Samadhi. In that state names and forms do not exist. There is no consciousness of differences. There is no feeling of love or hatred. No likes and dislikes. Samadhi is not a state of unconsciousness. It is a transcendental state, in which all differences have ceased. This state is attained when the mind merges with the Atma.*

[SSS Vol. 25, P 208]

Q 853. Why is *Nidra* (sleep) said to be the nearest approximation to *Samadhi*?

A.   *You know from experience that deep sleep gives you maximum happiness. Think it over for a while; have you ever, in the waking stage, experienced that degree of calm, of quiet, of equanimity, of happiness? That is why Nidra is said to be the nearest approximation to Samadhi.*

[SSS Vol. 5, P 104]

Q 854. What promotes union with God?

A.   *There are two paths by which man can approach this: the inner and the outer. The outer Sadhana is "Nishkama Karma",engaging in activity without attachment towards the result of those activities as dedicated to the Lord. The inner sadhana is Dhyana and Samadhi. In Vedantic terminology, this is named Nidhidhyasana. Listen and meditate on what you have listened to – these two steps are the basis of Nidhidhyasana or inner Concentration. This leads to the control of senses, the withdrawal of the mind from the outer world and the goal of life, knowing the Paramatma, attaining Liberation.*

[Geetha Vahini, P 146]

■ Dhyana (Meditation)

Q 855. **What is the best time for** *dhyana* **and should one sit for dhyana only after taking bath?**

A. *Train yourself to wake up when Brahma-muhurtam begins; that is to say, at 3-00 a.m. You may require an alarm clock at first for the job; but soon, the urge for dhyana will rouse you. Do not take a bath before you sit for dhyana, for the ritual of the bath will arouse the senses and you will be too full of pulls in different directions for the process of dhyana to succeed. Regularity, sincerity, steadiness – these will reward you with success.*

[SSS. Vol. 7, P 24]

Q 856. **Is it enough to meditate on the declaration "***Aham Brahmasmi***"?**

A. *This may be done but when one meditates on the declaration "Aham Brahmasmi", one has to start with the understanding of the 'I'. This process of identification should not be an artificial exercise. It should come from the heart. Then, you will understand Brahman.*

[SSS Vol. 25, P 204]

Q 857. **Is it right for man to describe God as mother, father etc. and to meditate on that close-to-heart relationship?**

A. *There is a prayer addressed to God in which God is described as mother, father, brother, friend and everything*

else. This is not the right way to worship God. This kind
of prayer binds man to worldly relationships. Instead of
these multiple relationships, a simpler way of describing
*the relationship between man and God is to say: "**I am**
***you and you are me.**" The divinity inherent in man*
should be considered as one only, and not many.

[SSS Vol. 25, P 204]

Q 858. How to attain the status of a Witness?

A. *The sages have laid down methods by which man can*
attain the status of a witness. Dhyana (meditation) is the
most important of these. It is the penultimate of eight steps
(Ashtanga Yoga), the last one being Samadhi (Super-
conscious state of communion) and grants the wisdom to
be completely unaffected. The sixth stage is dharana
(concentration). Dharana is the stage when japa, prayer
and other practices are engaged in, in order to prepare
the concentration of mind for dhyana.

[SSS Vol. 14, P 167]

Q 859. What is the difference between meditation and concentration?

A. *Meditation is often misunderstood to be the same as*
concentration. Concentration is essential for ordinary
sensory perception...comes naturally to us in the process
of perceiving through the 5 senses and no particular
exertion or spiritual effort is required for it. It is incorrect,
therefore, to equate concentration with meditation at
which only the spiritual adepts excel.

Meditation is a process which occurs at a much
higher plane than human sensory perceptions. Being
a mental process that involves seeing through the
senses, concentration may be regarded as being

below or within the realm of the senses, while
meditation is beyond or above the world of the senses.

[Summer Showers 1979, P 81]

Q 860. **For the practice of *dhyana* or meditation what**
should be taken as *dhyeya* or object of meditation?

A.   *For one who desires to practise dhyana or*
meditation, it is advisable that 'jyoti' (light) is taken
as the dhyeya or object of meditation and not a form
of divinity such as that of Rama, Krishna or Easwara, for
these forms too are subject to change and ultimately perish.
Light does not perish or change. Moreover, a flame can
kindle a million others without getting extinguished and
is therefore inexhaustible.

[Summer Showers 1979, P 82]

Q 861. How is one to proceed in meditation with 'Jyoti dhyana'?

A.   *In the process of meditation on light, the progression must*
be from restlessness to tranquility and from the tranquility
to Divine Effulgence. One should sit cross-legged and
erect to ensure an easy flow of the divine force from the
mooladhara chakra to the sahasrara chakra through the
sushumna naadi. The aspirant should fix his gaze on the
flame and gradually close his eyes, mentally transferring
or absorbing the flame into his heart as it were.

The lotus of spiritual heart should then be imagined
as blossoming in the effulgent beauty dispelling with
its radiance the dark forces of life. One should then
imagine that out of the heart so illumined, rays of
light proceed gradually to all parts of the body,
suffusing everything with light and imbuing it with
sacredness and purity all over.

As the light has reached the hands, the individual ought not to do any wrongful act; since the flame shines in his eyes, he cannot look at undesirable sights. So also, since the jyoti has permeated his ears, he should not listen to wild talk. His feet too, since they have been filled with light, should not tread upon unholy path. Thus, this type of meditation ennobles man and helps him scale great spiritual heights very steadily.

If we keep the mind busy, in this manner, with the task of carrying light to all parts the body; it will not wander and will remain steady. The whole process takes about 20 or 30 minutes to complete. This kind of meditation should not be regarded as an exercise in fantasy. No doubt, in the beginning, imagination will be involved but by constant practice, it will be transformed into a powerful thought-wave, creating an indelible impression on the heart leading to union with God.

The meditation should not end with the individual visualizing the light in himself. He should see it in his friends and relatives, and even in his enemies. He should see the whole creation bathed in the resplendent light of the Divinity. This would make him live a life full of love and happiness.

[Summer Showers 1979, P 82-83]

Q 862. Can we picture the form of God within the light?

A. *If you so desire you may in the initial stages, picture the form of God, which is dear to you within the flame on which you meditate; you must however realise that the form has got to dissolve in the light, sooner or later. You must not try to confine Divinity to any one particular*

*form; you must see God in His all-pervasive-form, as One
who resides in the hearts of all beings.*

[Summer Showers 1979, P 83]

Q 863. How long should one sit in meditation?

A.   *In real dhyana, you soon get over the consciousness that
you are doing dhyana; in fact, every moment in life must
be utilized for dhyana. That is the best way of life. When
you sweep your rooms clean, tell yourself that your hearts
too have to be swept likewise. When you cut vegetables,
feel that lust and greed too have to be cut into pieces. When
you press chapattis wider and wider, desire in addition
that your love may expand in wider and wider circles,
and expand even into the region of strangers and foes.
These are the means by which you can make your routine
of living into a route to Liberation.*

[SSS Vol. 8, P 206]

Q 864. What is real meditation?

A.   *Real meditation is getting absorbed in God as the
only thought, the only goal. God only, only God.
Think God, breathe God, love God...As long one
thinks "I am meditating" that is the mind and is
not meditation. As long as one knows he is
meditating, he is not meditating. In that absorption
in God, one puts aside every form and merges into God.
In that process the mind naturally stops.*

[Conversations, P 145-146]

Q 865. Are time and place important factors in *dhyana* and yogic practice?

A.   *We should perform dhyana in an unostentatious manner,
unobserved by others. Fish are sold in heaps at the fish
market but diamonds are carefully preserved at the*

jeweller's shop and displayed only to worthy customers. Likewise, if we sit for meditation at all places indiscriminately, inviting public attention, we would be reducing dhyana to cheap exhibitionism.

[SS 1979, P 84]

For meditation to be most effective it should be performed at a fixed time and at a fixed place every day…The ideal time is Brahmamuhurtam, that is, the period commencing at 3 a.m. and ending with 6 a.m. early in the morning.

[Summer Showers 1979, P 111]

Q 866. Does *dhyana* lead to *Jnana*?

A. *Dhyana endows man with jnana or Supreme wisdom. Jnana is not mere intellectual gymnastics. It is not a flight of imagination. Neither is it a mental concoction. It is a continual experience of the reality of the Atma.* **"Only one in a million makes an attempt to realize the Atma. Even among them only one in a thousand understands the process of realizing the Atma. Among the thousands of such people only one reaches Me. Those who have achieved self-realization and merged in Me are very few indeed", said Krishna to Arjuna.**

[Summer Showers 1979, P 104]

Q 867. Does *dhyana* lead to winning the grace of God?

A. *The Gita describes genuine dhyana as "Ananyaaschinta-yantho mam ye janah paryupaasathe" (adoring Me without any other thought or feeling). Krishna has assured such persons that He would Himself carry their burden and be by their side, guiding and guarding (Yoga Kshema).* Persons adept *in this dhyana are very rare; most people go through the external exercises only. So they are unable to win Grace.*

[SSS Vol. 14, P 167-168]

Q 868. How does *dhyana* help in cognizing the immanence of Brahman?

A.   *It is Brahman that has manifested itself in all this infinitude. Krishna exhorted Arjuna to ignore the diversity in unity and discern the unity in diversity. We have to comprehend the non-dual Atmic nature of this world of multiplicity.*

[Summer Showers 1979, P 111]

Q 869. What are the benefits of *dhyana*?

A.   *Dhyana is an infallible aid to spiritual progress. **Freedom from the consequence of karma can be attained through dhyana.** This freedom enables the sadhaka to acquire inner tranquility.*

[Summer Showers 1979, P 108]

Q 870. Does abstinence from food help in undertaking *dhyana*?

A.   *For meditation, Krishna lays down two important injunctions: a moderate diet and a regulated conduct of life. "Yuktahara Viharasya" said Krishna. Yuktahara does not mean complete abstinence from food, as this would lead to physical emaciation and mental fatigue…Thus, food in the right quantities and of the proper type is necessary if an individual is to meditate effectively.*

[Summer Showers 1979, P 86]

Q 871. How to establish in perfect equanimity in *dhyana*?

A.   *Desire is a storm; greed is a whirlpool; pride is a precipice; attachment is an avalanche; egoism is a* *volcano. Keep these things away, so that when you do japa or dhyana, they do not disturb the equanimity.*

[SSS Vol. 9, P 31]

Q 872. How one can drive out traces of all evil from the mind?

A. *The power of dharana (concentration and determination) enables the sadhaka to banish all evil from his heart and enthrone virtue in its place. Dharana leads to dhyana.* In other words, concentration leads to contemplation and assimilation, and these, in turn, lead to meditation.

[Summer Showers 1979, P 109]

Q 873. What comes in the way of progress in *dhyana*?

A. *Dhyana is of no avail if attachment to body and kith and kin continues to linger.* The physical body has to be dedicated to the performance of Nishkama-karma for the benefit of others.

[Summer Showers 1979, P 113]

Q 874. Does meditation lead to oneness with the object of meditation?

A. *You have to try and experience in meditation the oneness of the Sarvatma (Cosmic Soul) and the Ekatma (individual soul). Ekagrata (one-pointedness) for a single moment does not amount to dhyana (meditation). Meditation is sustained concentration and identification with the 'dhyeya' (the object of meditation).*

[Summer Showers 1979, P 113]

Q 875. Is there any specific rule for sitting in meditation?

A. *Adopting a comfortable posture, you have to sit*

straight so that Kundalini power is afforded unhampered movement. The Kundalini power is present in man in the Mooladhara Chakra as a divinely radiant power. Its upward flow to the Sahasrara Chakra or the thousand-petalled lotus through the intermediary centres called the Swadhisthana, Manipura, Anahata, Vishuddha and Ajna Chakras takes man to various levels of consciousness and spiritual awakening.

[Summer Showers 1979, P 111]

Krishna told Arjuna that one should be alone while meditating. The body should not touch the earth or another body. This is because contact with the earth makes the individual lose the divine current generated in him during meditation. Regularity of time is an important factor in dhyana. One should stick to the same time every day.

[Summer Showers 1979, P 84]

Q 876. Is a fixed routine essential for meditation?

A.   *For meditation to be most effective, it should be performed at a fixed time and at a fixed place everyday* and according to a well-regulated procedure. Sometimes the routine may be upset, as, for example, you have to go on a journey – it may not be possible to perform meditation at the usual place or according to the normal procedure. Nevertheless, one must ensure that at the usual appointed hour every day, the meditation is performed steadfastly.

[Summer Showers 1979, P111]

Q 877. Should *dhyana* always be done individually?

A.   *Apart from the dhyana that you do individually, it is good for you to sit for ten or fifteen minutes, at the place where you did bhajan, and after Omkar, collect your thoughts and meditate on the God whom you adored so long. The group dhyana after bhajan will prepare the ground for individual dhyana. The taste will grow; the duration will become longer, the peace will become deeper.*

[SSS Vol. 8, P 110]

Q 878. What other instructions are to be followed for a successful *Dhyana?*

A. *During meditation the sadhaka should neither shut the eyes completely nor open them wide. He should gaze at the tip of his nose with half-closed eyes and concentrate on the divine radiant power at the Ajna chakra.*

[Summer Showers 1979, P 112]

Q 879. Where should hands be kept during *dhyana?*

A. **In this blissful mood one has to keep his hands in the chin-mudra, with the thumb and index fingers of both the hands kept apart. The thumb represents Brahman. The forefinger represents the jiva. The jiva in combination with its gunas is conditioned by time. God, however, is beyond time and, therefore, all gunas vanish when the jiva and God become one.**

[Summer Showers 1979, P 112]

Q 880. What is the essence of *Dhyana?*

A. *There are three gunas: sathwa, rajas and tamas. There are three eyes: the two physical eyes and the invisible spiritual eye. There are three times: the past, the present and the future. And there are the three worlds. The unity of these triads is vouchsafed to the spiritual aspirant during his transcendental state of meditation. Then sin and sorrow are annihilated. Sat-Chit-Ananda (Existence-*

Consciousness-Bliss) is experienced through meditation and complete surrender. This is the essence of dhyana.

[Summer Showers 1979, P 97]

Q 881. Is it all right for devotees to start meditating in the Prasanthi Mandir while Bhagawan is giving darshan?

A.   *You know why God has given you the eyes? Is it to see everything that comes your way? No, no. The eyes are given to see God. But there are some people who close their eyes and start meditating even while sitting in front of Swami. Such meditation is false piety. People who close their eyes in front of God might have been blind in their previous births. It is an unhealthy and unholy practice to close your eyes in front of God. Open your eyes and see Him. Open not only the physical eyes, but also the eye of wisdom.*

[SSS Vol. 34, P 283]

✳✳✳

15
AUM – PRANAVA

Q 882. What does the word Gita mean?

A. *Literally the word Gita means a 'song'. Since God is omnipresent, the song of God too must be omnipresent. So, in reality, **Pranava or Om is the Gita of God.***
[SSS Vol. 14, P 63]

Q 883. How can we hear *Om*, the song of the Lord that wells up from the heart?

A. *Our Self is resonant with Pranava, but amid the clamour of the world our little selves are not able to hear it. Our own senses lay claim to our attention. Our minds crave for being let free among the pleasures of the world. Obviously our passions and prejudices have to be calmed before we can hear Om, the song of the Lord that wells up from the heart.*
[SSS Vol. 14, P 63]

Q 884. How is one to achieve the state so as to be able to hear the universal sound of Om?

A. *March on with your eyes on the goal. Do not worry about the past, its mistakes and its failures. Do not follow the whims and fancies of the mind any longer. Follow the call of the Divine arising from the hearts of fellowmen. Serve them in an attitude of worship. Do not expect anything in return, not even gratitude, for, you have dedicated the act to the indwelling God. This will purify you so much that you will then be able to listen to the 'Soham' that your breath repeats every moment.* **Soham transmutes itself into Om when the distinction between He and I has dissolved in the process of Samadhi.**

[SSS Vol. 14, P 64]

Q 885. What does Om represent?

A.   *Om is identical with Brahman. The sound Om, the 'Pranava' represents the entire content of the Brahman.*
[Summer Showers 1972, P 85]

Q 886. Is it true that a man who is able to repeat the *Pranava* **with the last breath attains the Indestructible (akshara) Brahman and becomes immortal?**

A.   *The scriptures assert that a man who is able to repeat the Pranava during his last breath attains the Indestructible (akshara) state of immortality. The whole cosmos is permeated with Pranava. Pranava is the manifestation of God. A, U, M are the three primary sounds that constitute Pranava. The physical world called Bhu Loka, the higher astral world of Bhuvar Loka and the highest world of Suvar Loka – these three worlds are pervaded by Pranava. The Rig, Yajur and Sama Vedas are also contained within the Pranava.*
[Summer Showers 1991, P 92]

Q 887. What merit accrues to the seeker when the three *matras* **of AUM are employed separately for meditation?**

A. *Note the triples. Bhu-Bhuvah-Suvah are the three worlds. Rig-Yajur-Sama are the three Vedas. A-U-M are the three primary sounds (matras). The Pranava alone pervades the three worlds, the three Vedas. All the sounds in this world are born from Om alone. Those who deem Om to be just a sound, those who do not go beyond its mechanical recitation (those who do not meditate on all the three matras combined), receive only worldly benefits from the repetition.*
[Summer Showers 1991, P 92-93]

Q 888. What benefits does one attain by meditating on AUM with three matras?

A. *Those who contemplate on the significance of Om while chanting it with concentration (meditating on the three matras) are eligible to live in the pleasure filled world (Chandra Loka) lunar world after death, so say the scriptures.*
[Summer Showers 1991, P 93]

889. Do the Chandra and Surya Lokas mean the physical moon and sun?

A. *Chandra Loka is not to be confused with the Physical Moon. "Chandrama Manaso Jaatah, Chakshooh Soorya Ajaayata" – From His mind emerged the Moon and from His eyes, the Sun. When I speak of Chandra (moon) and Surya (Sun) principles, students should not confuse them with the physical Sun and Moon. The moon is representation of mind. Meaning, with thoughts pertaining to the world, man attains the Chandraloka – means he attains a plane of existence where mental delights are experienced. The Sun represents the light of the eyes. When our vision (drishti) is merged with creation (srishti), we perceive the truth of the scriptures.*
[Summer showers 1991, P 93]

Q 890. Besides three *matras*, A, U, M – AUM (Om) also has a *bindu*. What do they signify? What are *Naada*, *Bindu* and *Kalaa*?

A. *Omkaara has three constituents. A-kaara, U-kaara and M-kaara (the three syllables – A, U, M). A-kaara represents the vital principle Praana-tattva. U-kaara represents the Mind. M-kaara represents the body. Omkaara is thus the unified expression of the Atma, the mind and the body.*

[SSS Vol. 25, P 335]

The cosmos emerged from A-kaara. It is the Praana (life force). The Mind principle came from U-kaara. The Body emerged from M-kaara. The Atma, the Mind and the Body, which emanated from the three syllables "A", "U" and "M", permeate the sun, the firmament and the entire creation. Omkaara is the essential basis for the entire creation

The Omkaara principle has three forms: Naada, Bindu and Kalaa. Naada is the sound that comes from the life-breath...Bindu is unified form of the Atma, the Mind and the Body. Kalaa is the reflected image of the Paramatma (Omniself) through the Buddhi (intellect).

[SSS Vol. 25, P 336]

Q 891. How is OM to be recited?

A. *The uttering of Omkaara (AUM) should be done in a sweet and smoothly progreesive way starting with the sound of "A" which sound should come from the navel, and then the sound "U" from the throat, and finally conclude with "M" from the lips. It should resemble the sound of an aeroplane when it is far off, gradually increasing in volume as it approaches*

the aerodrome and finally subsiding after landing.
The Veda teaches this very clearly.

[SSS Vol. 26, P 352]

Q 892. With Om prefixed does a *mantra* get energized?

A.   *Sadhakas would be benefited more if they repeat the*
           Panchakshri or Ashtakshari with the Pranava
           added in the beginning. When they have proceeded
           some distance thus, they can give up even the words
           and concentrate on the Form depicted through the
           sound and transform the mantra into the Devata
           Himself. That is why the Sruthi says, "Nissabdo
           Brahma Uchyathe" – Brahma is Silence, absence of
           Sound.

[Prasnottara Vahini, P 68]

Q 893. Lord Krishna said: " I am the *Pranava* in the
Vedas." What does this mean?

A.   *Brahman fills everything. The Five Elements are its*
           manifestation. It is Inner Motivator, unseen by those who
           look only at the surface. It is the Antharyamin in other
           *words. That is why **Krishna said: "I am Rasa in Water;***
           I am Effulgence , Prabha in the Sun and Moon; I am
           the Pranava in the Vedas; I am Sound in the Akasha;
           I am Pourushham (Heroism, Adventure and
           ***Aspiration)in man...**The Vedas are reputedly 'An-aadi'*
           or 'Beginning-less'. Pranava is spoken of as the very life–
           breath of Vedas, which are themselves beyond all beginning.
           Take it that the Pranava is the subtle essence, the underlying
           Form of every particle and substance in the Universe.

[Geetha Vahini, P 123-124]

Q 894. How can the goal be reached through the Upasana
of Pranava?

A.   *Pranava is the bow; the Atma is the arrow; Para Brahman is the target. So, the sadhaka must, like the practitioner of the art of archery, be unaffected by the things that agitate the mind. He should pay one-pointed attention to the target.*

[Prasnottara Vahini, P 71]

Q 895. How should the mind be merged in the *Pranava*?

A.   *The mind has an innate tendency to merge in whatever it contacts. It craves for this. So, it is ever agitated and restless.* **But by constant practice and training, the mind can be directed towards the Pranava and taught to merge with it. It is naturally drawn towards Sound…By practice, man can merge himself into the Bliss of Pranava. This Shabadopasana is a principal means of realising the Paramatma.**

[Geetha Vahini, P 126]

Q 896. What merit does one attain by meditation on *Pranava* or Om?

A.   **Pranava, when pronounced at the moment of death awards merger with the Akshara-Param-Brahman Itself.**

[Geetha Vahini, P 162]

Q 897. What does 'moment of death' mean?

A.   *'The moment of death' does not mean 'some future point of time'. It means, 'this very moment!' Any moment might turn out to be the 'moment of death'. So, every moment is the last. Every moment must be filled with Pranava.*

[Geetha Vahini, P 162]

Q 898. What determines the fate of man after death?

A.   *The fate of man after death is moulded by the thought that predominated in him at the moment* *of death. The thought is the foundation on which the next birth is built. "Whoever at that time remembers Me attains My Glory, reaches Me in fact," declares Krishna. So each Karma of man, every striving of his, every sadhana, should be aimed at sanctifying that fateful moment. The years of life must be devoted to the discipline that will bring up at that moment the thought of Pranava.*

[Geetha Vahini, P 162]

Q 899. If one wishes to get holy thoughts at the last moment of life, has one to strive for it from now on? Cannot one get fixed in the holy thoughts at the moment of death?

A. *Krishna said: "Arjuna! the mind has to be educated into the habit, through what is called Abhyasa-yoga, the discipline of constant practice. It has to be trained to avoid other thoughts and concentrate on the Lord only. Then only can you reach Parama Purusha. Unless you systematically teach it and train it, you will not remember the Parama Purusha at the moment of death".*

[Geetha Vahini, P 164]

Q 900. Should Om be recited vocally or mentally?

A. *Om has to be pronounced in the mind, not through the mouth as the sensory organ.*

[Geetha Vahini, P 176]

Q 901. '*Japathonaasthi Paathakam*' – he who does *Japam* has no sin. If *Japam* cures one from sin, does it mean that it leads to Liberation or Moksha?

A. *Evidently Japam is powerless to bring that about. Japam will not enable one to concretise the Lord.*

[Geetha Vahini, P 176]

Q 902. If *Japam* does not lead to *Moksha*, how else to seek *Moksha* then?

A.   *"Moksha need not be sought after separately, apart from other objectives. If Om is recited and the significance of the Om, that is to say, the Lord is meditated upon, then the Lord is attained by you. In other words, you are liberated...Abhyasa-yoga (steady practice), will ensure you both results, freedom from sin and Liberation".*

[Geetha Vahini, P 177]

Q 903. The Gita says that those who repeat *Pranava* with their last breath, attain the Lord. But what about those who do not? Their number is certainly much larger. Have they no chance of release from the cycle of birth and death?

A.   *All those who yearn for the presence of the Lord, all who desire to enter the Darbar of the Lord, all have admission there. It is not every one that can repeat the Pranava at the last moment. That is why constant remembrance of the Lord is said to have the power of inducing the Lord to bear the burden of your Yoga-Kshema, happiness here and hereafter. Sadhana gains everything, sadhana, steady and strong.*

[Geetha Vahini, P 178]

Q 904. What is the relation between the three primal sounds of Omkara and three states of consciousness?

A.   *Omkar is the fusion of three primal sounds A, U and M. These three letters represent respectively the jagrat (waking), the swapna (dream) and the sushupti (deep sleep) states of consciousness. They also symbolize*

> *Brahma, Vishnu and Maheshwara. **This trinity represents the three personified realities corresponding to the afore-mentioned three states of consciousness.***
>
> [Summer Showers 1979, P 100]

Q 905. What is Primordial sound?

A. *The sound that emanated when the big bang took place, is Pranava. That is Omkara, the primordial sound. This sound of Pranava is all-pervasive.*

[SS Vol. 35, P 190]

Q 906. How did Pranava originate?

A. *It originated from Paramaanu (atom). In fact, there is nothing else than atoms in this universe.*

[SSS Vol. 35, P 190]

Q 907. How can one understand and realise this truth of Pranava?

A. *This was the enquiry of sage Kanada. Ultimately, he realised the principle of Pranava. **This primordial sound has to be contemplated upon by man for attaining liberation.***

> *The primordial sound 'Pranava' is verily the Divinity which is subtler than the subtlest and vaster than the vastest. It is all-pervasive and stands as the eternal witness.*

[SSS Vol. 35, P 190]

■ Soham

Q 908. What does Soham mean? How does it merge into Aum during meditation?

A.   *With each breath, you are averring 'Soham', I am*
      He. Not only you, every being avers it. It is a fact
      which you have ignored so long. Believe it now.
      When you watch your breath and meditate on that
      Grand Truth, slowly the 'I' and the 'He' will merge
      and there will no more be two, for Soham will
      become transformed into Om, the Primal Sound,
      Pranava, which the Vedas proclaim as the symbol
      of the Nirakara Parabrahma.

                                                        [SSS Vol. 14, P 283]

Q 909. What are the essential pre-requisites for a good
       dhyana?

A.   *Before you start dhyana, your meditation session,*
      chant Soham, inhaling 'So' and exhaling 'Ham'.
      Soham means 'He is I', it identifies you with the
      Infinite and expands your Consciousness. Harmonise
      the breath and the thought. Breathe gently, naturally; do
      not make it artificial and laboured. It must flow in and out,
      soft and silent; if you have some flour on your palm and
      hold it near the nostrils, it should not get fluttered the least.
      The breath has to be soft as that! The faster the breath, the
      sooner you are burnt up, the shorter becomes your life span!
      Slow breath quietens and calms the emotions. The mood of
      relaxation produced by the Soham recital is a pre-condition
      for a profitable session of meditation.

                                                         [SSS Vol. 9, P 30]

■ Gayatri

Q 910. What does Gayatri signify?

A.   *Gayatri signifies the mastery over the senses.*

                                                        [SSS Vol. 26, P 172]

Q 911. What are the two other names of Gayatri?

A.   *Gayatri has two other names – Savitri and Saraswathi. Savitri is the master of life. Saraswathi is the presiding deity for Vaak (speech).*

[SSS Vol. 26, P 172]

Q 912. What does Gayatri *mantra* refer to?

A.   *The Gayatri mantra "Bhur-Bhuvah-Suvah" refers to the body, life and awareness. "Bhur-Bhuvah-Suvah" does not refer to the three worlds outside man. All the three are in him. Hence man is not an ordinary being. He is Chaiyanya-Swarupa (the embodiment of the Cosmic Divine Consciousness).*

[SSS Vol. 26, P 172]

Q 913. What is *Hamsa Gayatri* and what benefits it gives?

A.   *"SOHAM" is also known as Hamsa Gayatri. Hamsa (the swan) is credited with the capacity to separate the milk from the water with which it is mixed. Hamsa Gayatri is recited to separate the body-consciousness from the Atma.*

[SSS Vol. 26, P 172]

Q 914. Who is Gayatri? Is Gayatri a goddess?

A.   *Gayatri is not a goddess. Gayatri is the mother of the Vedas (Gayatrim Chandasaam Mataa). "Gaayantam traayate iti Gayatri" (Gayatri is that which redeems the chanter of the mantra). Gayatri is present whenever the name is chanted.*

[SSS Vol. 28, P 239]

Q 915. What is the inner significance of *"Bhur-Bhuvah-Suvah"* in the Gayatri *mantra*?

A.   *These represent the three worlds, which are in the body itself. Bhu represents Prakriti (Earth), which is the physical body. Mind is Bhuvarloka. Prajnaana (spiritual awareness) is Suvarloka. Body represents materialisation, as it is made up of the five physical elements. The mind is Vibration and Prajnaana is Radiation. If you enquire into their inner significance, all the three are in your body itself.*

[SSS Vol. 27, P 229]

16
GURU, SAINTS AND SAGES

Q 916. What is the role of a Guru?

A.   *Guru dispels the darkness of ignorance.* '*Gu*' *stands for Gunateeta (attributeless).* '*Ru*' *signifies Rupavarjita (formless). There is another interpretation of the word Guru. "Gu" signifies darkness and "Ru" denotes that which dispels darkness). So, God, who is attributeless and formless, is the true Guru.*

[SSS Vol. 33, P 162]

Q 917. What is the role of a Guru?

A.   *Shakthipata means that the guru hands over in one shower all the capabilities to the disciple. This, however, is not the correct meaning. Shakthipata is something that is given only when there is deservedness. It is not given where there is no deservedness. In all individuals this Shakthi is present in a hidden manner and is in a latent form.*

   What the guru does is simply to remove the veil of ignorance, which is hiding the power that is intrinsically present. The guru, therefore, simply uncovers that which is already present. *He does not* *hand in anything new. The aspect of Brahman is not something, which can be given by one to another.*

[Summer Showers 1974, P 44]

Q 918. Can *guru-mantra* help in achieving this goal of unification with the Divine?

A.   *The Guru must exhort the individual self to realise the universal Self. There are in the world many other types also. There is the Guru who gives you a mantra (sacred formula), tells you its potentialities, and directs you to repeat it sincerely and steadily. He is the deeksha-guru. He assures that his duty ends with the gift of the mantra and the command to use it with conviction and care. He does not direct the pupil to master his senses or guide him to march forward to attain victory. For the pupil, the mantra is a formula to be repeated in a parrot-like way. He might even know that it is a precious gift, but without the sadhana (spiritual discipline) of self-improvement, the gift has no value at all!*

[SSS Vol. 14, P 163-164]

Q 919. Can service of the Guru in total submission compensate for the pupil's deficiency and earn Guru's grace?

A.   *Sankara, the great Acharya, had four chief disciples Totaka, Hastamalaka, Sureswara and Padmapada. Of these, Padmapada was intent only on service to the Guru. He could not pay attention to the lessons. The others used to sneer at him for his backwardness in studies. But, his deep reverence for the Guru made up for it. One day, he washed the clothes of his Guru and dried them on a rock in the middle of the river; but, even as he was folding them, the river rose fast in a swirling flood; and he had scarce a*

*foothold on the top of the rock. It was getting late. The
Guru would need the washed clothes soon. So, Padmapada
resolved to walk across, over the raging waters. He knew
that the blessing of his Guru would save him. And it did.
Wherever his foot was planted, a sturdy lotus bloomed
and bore it on its petals. That is why he came to be called,
Lotus-footed. Padma-pada! The grace of the Guru enabled
him to master all knowledge and shine as a brilliant
exponent of the ancient wisdom.*

[SSS Vol. 7, P 27]

**Q 920. To acquire *Brahma-jnana*, should one see a guru?
What are the qualifications of a guru and the pupil?**

A. *The great one who has the Atmic truth imprinted on the
heart is alone to be accepted as the guru. The individual
who can welcome this Truth and is eager to know it, he
alone is to be accepted as the pupil. The seed must have
the life principle latent in it. The field must be ploughed
and made fit for sowing. The spiritual harvest will be
plentiful if both these conditions are fulfilled. The listener
has to possess a clear receptive intellect or else the
philosophical principles that form the basis of Jnana will
not be comprehended. The guru and the pupil both have
to be of this stature.*

[Vidya Vahini, P 31-32]

Q 921. Who is the Guru of all gurus?

A. **They are the Avatars, the Human Incarnations of
God. They confer, by mere willing, the blessing of
spiritual strength. They command and by the very
force of that command, the lowest of the low rises
to the status of One who has attained the goal of
spiritual sadhana (Siddha purusha). Such persons**

are the Gurus of all gurus. They are the highest manifestations of God in the human form.

[Vidya Vahini, P 32]

Q 922. What is the exact role of a Guru?

A.   *The guru warns and wakens. He reveals the Truth and encourages you to progress towards it. Unless you have the yearning, the questioning heart, the seeking intelligence, he cannot do much.* The hungry can be fed; he who has no hunger will discard food as an infliction. *The guru is a gardener, who will tend the plant; but, the sapling must have sprouted before he can take charge. He does not add anything new to the plant; he only helps it to grow according to its own destiny, quicker perhaps.* He removes poverty by pointing to the treasure that lies buried in the very habitation of man; he advises the method of recovering it, the vigilance needed to use it to the best advantage.

[SSS Vol.5, P 195]

Q 923. The scriptures say that one should try to sublimate one's life by seeking a Guru and acting according to his injunctions. How many types of Gurus are there?

A.   *There are 8 types of Gurus:*

   *(1) The **Bodha Guru** – he teaches Sastras and encourages the pupil to act upon Sastraic injunctions.*

   *(2) The **Veda Guru** – imparts inner messages of the Vedas, establishes the pupil in spiritual truths and turns his mind towards God.*

   *(3) The **Nishiddha Guru** – imparts knowledge about rights and duties.*

   *(4) The **Kaamya Guru** – makes one engage himself in*

Punya (meritorious) karmas to secure happiness in both the worlds.

(5) *The **Vaachaka Guru** – imparts knowledge of Yoga and prepares the pupil for the spiritual life.*

(6) *The **Soochaka Guru** – teaches how the senses are to be controlled through various types of disciplines.*

(7) *The **Kaarana Guru** – reveals the unity of the jivi and the Atma.*

(8) *The **Vihita Guru** – clears all doubts, purifies the mind and shows how self-realisation can be attained.*

[SSS Vol. 19, P 113]

Q 924. Who is the foremost in these Gurus?

A. *Kaarana Guru is the foremost. Through his teachings and practices he helps the disciple to progress from the human to the divine Consciousness. Only the divine can act as such a teacher. All other Gurus can be helpful only to a limited extent.*

[SSS Vol. 19, P 113]

Q 925. What is the inner meaning of the word *Rishi* and who was the first *Rishi*?

A. *One who can explain and expound the essential form of the Veda can be called a Rishi. Our Puranas have been telling us that Vasishta was the first Rishi. **Vasishta had the aspect of Brahman in him and he was called Brahma-rishi.***

[Summer Showers 1974, P 43]

Q 926. What are the qualities and qualifications of a Brahma-rishi?

A. *One would truly become a Brahma-rishi only when one has directly experienced the Omkara and the Vashatkara which the Veda has explained, and grasped fully the* *meaning of the sound Om and of Veda…It is quite easy to call oneself by the name Brahma-rishi but it is difficult to get the qualities of a Brahma-rishi. If one wants to acquire the aspect of Brahma-rishi, one should merge in the Brahman and become identical with the Brahman.*

[Summer Showers 1974, P 43-44]

Q 927. **How did Viswamitra come to acquire the title of Brahmarishi?**

A.   *Vasishta had the aspect of Brahman in him and he was called the Brahmarishi. Viswamitra also wanted to acquire this name of a Brahmarishi and he himself undertook great penance and then acquired the aspect of Brahman. As soon as he had the vision of Brahman, he was addressed as Brahmarishi by Brahman Himself…Because Viswamitra had surrendered everything to Brahman, these aspects were taught to Viswamitra by Brahman Himself. If one is able to get the grace of Brahman, then everything will be under control.*

[Summer Showers 1974, P 43-44]

Q 928. **What did the ancient sages declare after their God-experience?**

A.   *The sages declared: "Witness the Divine effulgence for yourselves. We have seen Him. Where? Antar Bahischa Thath Sarvam Vyaapya Narayana Sthitaha – God is present inside, outside, everywhere".*

[Summer Showers 1991, P 19]

Q 929. **How does God look like?**

A.   *The sages said: "Do you know how he looks? Vedaaha-*

*metham Purusham Mahaantam, Aditya Varnam
Tamasah Parastaat"* – *It is impossible to describe
that Great Person, brilliant like the Sun. He is
present beyond darkness (tamas). Unless we
transcend the darkness of ignorance, we cannot
experience Him.."*

[Summer Showers 1991, P 19]

Q 930. What was the great service of sage Vyasa to the mankind?

A. *Vyasa collated the Vedic Texts and composed the Brahma-sutras, stringing together in epigrammatic form the essential teachings of Veda and Vedanta. He also placed humanity under a deep debt of gratitude by elaborating the moral and spiritual lessons of Vedanta and Veda in the magnificent poetic philosophical epic, Mahabharata and in the sweet Bhakti saturated collections of Divine stories called Bhagavata. Each of these can by itself effect the liberation of Man, provided he imbibes the lessons and practises them.*

[SSS Vol. 6, P 88]

Q 931. Who was Ratnakara and how did he become a great Rishi?

A. *Valmiki, before he became a great sage was known as Ratnakara. He was a hunter and used to rob the wayfarers of their belongings. One day, he came across the Saptha Rishis, who took pity on him and wanted to light the lamp of wisdom in him. They urged him to give up his wicked actions. Ratnakara said he could not do so, as it was the only way to feed his wife and children. The Saptha Rishis asked Ratnakara to find out whether they were prepared to share the sin he committed for their sake. Ratnakara went home and asked his wife and children, "Are you prepared to share my sin just as you share my booty every day?" They replied in the negative. His wife said that she was not responsible for the merit or sin he committed. The incident opened his eye. He went back to the Saptha Rishis, fell at their feet and prayed for guidance. They told him to contemplate on Lord Rama and chant His Name incessantly. Ratnakara did accordingly, and consequently, his face shone with the divine effulgence of Lord Rama.*

[SSS Vol. 32 Part - 2, P 118]

Q 932. Who was Sukracharya?

A.   *Sukracharya was the preceptor of the Asuras (demons).*

[SSS Vol. 27, P 228]

✳✳✳

17
SELF-REALISATION

■ Self-Realisation

Q 933. Is it possible to realise God here and now? Why is the realisation of the purpose of life – the realisation of the Higher Self so difficult?

A. *Paramatma alone is real. Paramatma is Truth. Paramatma is love. Meditate on Him as Truth, as Love. It is possible to realise Him, in whatever form you meditate upon. Be always in the company of His devotees. Through this satsanga, viveka and vairagya will be implanted and increased. This will strengthen the spirit. Your mind will then merge in Paramatma.*

[Prema V, P 21]

Man commits the great fault in identifying himself with the body. He has accumulated a variety of things for the upkeep and comfort of the body. Even when the body becomes weak and decrepit with age, he attempts to bolster it up by some means or the other. But, how long can death be postponed? When Yama's warrant comes, each has to depart. Before death, position, pride, power, all vanish. **Realising this, strive day and night with purity of body, mind and spirit, to realise the Higher Self.** *Remember that you are not this body. Tat Twam Asi. Thou art That. This is the highest and the holiest Mahavakya.*

[Prema V, P 9]

Q 934. What is indispensable for realising the Truth?

A.   *For attaining this stage, an ethical life is the foundation. This ethical life is based upon discrimination between Truth and Falsehood – Viveka. Then again, individual effort and Divine Grace should both be existent. One should also practise the great lesson that the body and the Atma are separate. Such viveka or discrimination is necessary. It is indispensable for realising the Truth which is God Himself.*

[Prema V, P 19]

Q 935. How should one proceed to realise God?

A.   **When we try to understand the inner meaning of concentrating on the mid eyebrows, we come to the conclusion that God can be realised only in a quiet, serene and pure place. Such place does not exist outside you. It is present in your own internal self.** *From times, immemorial, Maha Rishis have searched for such a place and they came to the conclusion that they should turn their vision and thoughts inward to find such a place and by this process they could get a glimpse of God and enjoy the Divine Bliss. We should make an attempt to develop an inner vision to realise the Divine that is omnipresent and we can find Him within our own self.*

[Summer Showers 1974]

Q 936. Who is it that 'sees' Atma in the Samadhi state? What is the secret of success of realisation of Atma?

A. *In the state of Samadhi, Atma is the 'seer' and intellect, 'the seen'. There is nothing that can see the Atma. Hence, it is always the 'seer and never the 'seen'…the body which is of the nature of 'Mrinmaya' (full of dirt) harbours in itself the Atma which is of the nature of 'Chinmaya' (full of pure consciousness). The secret of man's success lies in the thorough understanding and unraveling of this 'Chinmaya tathwa' (principle of pure consciousness).*

[SS Vol. 24, P 118, 119]

Q 937. When and where is the *Paramjyoti*, the Divine light seen during *sadhana* by a seeker?

A. *Of those who have become sadhakas, the Manas (mind) is Mathura, the Hridyam (heart) is Dwakra, and the deha (body) is Kashi. At the seat of the tenth gate (dashama dwara) it is possible to realize the Paramjyoti, the Supreme Effulgence. All efforts are of no avail if the heart is not pure. The vasana of man will not disappear even if he is immersed in many heart purifying sadhanas, so long as the heart is full of illusion of egoism. Such a man, if he is desirous of getting rid of the feeling of 'I' and 'Mine', must worship God. He must become a sadhaka without likes and dislikes.*

[Prema V, P 73]

Q 938. What is the most important basis of sadhana for self-realisation?

A. *In this Kali age, owing to the perversions of time, place and circumstances, you are prone to ignore the promptings of the inner conscience and act in response to the external impressions.* **You must develop the inner vision. If you keep your hearts pure, you can cleanse**

these impurities. Develop Self-confidence for this purpose. The rest will follow – Self-satisfaction, Self-sacrifice and Self-realisation. At the basis of all these is the awareness of the Self, the Atma-principle.

[SSS Vol. 24, P 134]

Q 939. Is spiritual practice needed even after realising one's divinity?

A.   *Just as fire is needed till the rice is cooked, so also the spiritual practices are needed till you realise the innate divinity.*

[SSS Vol. 32 Part 2, P 189]

Q 940. How is one to distinguish between reflection and the inner reality? What is *Saakshatkara*?

A.   *The world is like a mirror. All that you find in this mirror is only the reflection, not the reality. Your right eye appears as left eye in the mirror. Then how can you consider it as reality? When the mirror is removed, the reflection also disappears and the reality remains. Consider yourself as embodiment of divinity. Experience your nature of love. This is **Saakshatkara** (vision of the Self). Some people claim to have the vision of the Self in meditation, but the vision of your reality is true **Saakshatkara**.*

[SSS Vol. 33, P 160]

People talk about Saakshatkara. What is it? It is not something external. Saakshatkara is contemplation of the Divine at all times and in all states within one's self. "Sarvadaa, sarvakaaleshu sarvatra Hari Chintanam" (thinking of God at all times, in all places continuously).

[SSS Vol. 26, P 322]

■ Liberation (Mukti, Moksha)

Q 941. What does *Moksha* mean?

A. *The word Moksha does not represent something which is exhaustible and which you can purchase from a shop. Moksha is regarded as a limitless entity. So long as there is attachment in you, the world will appear permanent. On the lotus of your heart, this attachment always moves like mercury. This kind of mercurial lust which is continually moving from place to place should be removed and this process of* **Moha-kshaya is Moksha. Once this attachment goes, what remains is simply Ananda.** *To convert our lives to some extent in this manner is the path of Brahman.*

[Summer Showers 1974, P 63]

Q 942. What should be the priority-pursuit for the one aspiring for liberation?

A. **Whatever activity a person may be engaged in, he must, as automatically as he takes in breath, be contemplating on these lines and should always be aware of this: " I am born to serve God and to realise my true self."** *All acts – wearing, eating, walking, studying, serving, moving, - should be performed in the belief that they take one into the Presence (of God). Everything should be done in the spirit of dedication to the Lord.*

[Prema V, P 65]

Q 943. What is Moksha?

A. *Liberation (Moksha) cannot be attained by the study of texts. It cannot be attained by listening to the teachings* *of others. **Moha Kshaya is Moksha (annihilation of desire is liberation).***

[SS – June 2000, P 182 (Buddha Purnima
Discourse at Brindavan on 21-5-2000)]

Q 944. What guarantees attainment of Moksha?

A.   *An aspirant eager to attain the Mansion of Moksha, the Abode of Freedom, needs renunciaton and Wisdom, renunciation of worldly desires and wisdom to become aware of the Atma.*

[Sutra Vahini, P 23]

Q 945. What kind of renunciation is required for attaining Moksha?

A.   *The sense of 'mine' is the bond of deluding attachment. How long can one cling to what he fondles as mine? Some day he has to give up all he has and leave alone and empty handed. This is the inescapable destiny.*

One has to give up such assumed relationships and artificial attachments through rigorous analysis of their nature and give them up as quickly as possible. This is what the world teaches as the lesson of renunciation.

[Sutra Vahini, P 23]

Q 946. What are the four stages of the life-divine achieved through *dhyana*?

A.   *The four phases of spiritual advancement are: 'salokya', 'sameepya', 'sarupya' and 'sayujya'.*

Salokya is the entrance to the field of theocentric reality. Sameepya is proximity to the fundamental spiritual substance of the universe. Sarupya is the assimilation of the form of the deity. Sayujya is liberation and ultimate union with the Godhead.

[Summer Showers 1979, P 93]

Q 947. What do the stages *Salokyam, Sameepyam, Sarupyam* and *Sayujyam* mean?

A. *Salokyam is entering the world of God. Sameepyam is going nearer to God. Sarupyam is acquiring the feeling that you are part of God and Sayujyam is final merging with God.*

[SS Vol. 26, P 134]

Q 948. The Upanishads say that those who reach Brahmaloka heaven need not be born again. Are they free from the cycle of birth and death?

A. *"There are two types of liberation mentioned in the Upanishads, Sadyomukti and Krama-mukti. Sadyomukti is also referred to as Kaivalya-mukti. For earning this, no one need aspire for any heaven. They get this on the spot, and not by stages, step by step. Liberation secured thus is a possession forever. The rest are liable to change. When the effect of the merit acquired wears out, heaven has to be given up, and life on earth starts anew. Such souls know no merging. Only those who attain Kaivalya, merge and become One with the Eternal, the Universal."*

[Geetha Vahini, P 184]

Q 949. Does it mean, "the souls that attain *Kaivalya* are destroyed? Or is there any difference between merging and destruction, *Layam* and *Naasam*?" What is the concept of mergence in the Lord?

A. *"No! Layam is not Naasam. Merging is not destruction. Laya happens when it becomes invisible. Just because a* *thing has gone out of sight, how can you pronounce it 'destroyed'?*

Lump of sugar or salt placed in water disappears. You can see it no more. Can you say it has been destroyed? No. It has merged. It is there, the taste declares. It has lost the form, but it is present in its quality, its guna. The jiva also merges like this in Brahmam. It is not destroyed at all. *When the jiva is not merged like this, it can at best only wander between heaven and earth, deserving life in heaven for some time and descending again to earth for further efforts towards salvation."*

[Geetha Vahini, P 184]

Q 950. Through what different stages does Bhakti pass on way to Moksha?

A.   *When karma is prompted by Bhakti, it is Samsara Bhakti; when Jnana also blossoms a little, it is Vanaprastha Bhakti; when Bhakti fructifies into Jnana, then it is Sanyasa Bhakti or Moksha itself.*

[SSS Vol. 4, P 194-195]

Q 951. What is the means of gaining Moksha?

A.   *Vijnana is the means.*   .

[Prasnottara Vahini, P 42]

Q 952. Some say that Yoga is the means. Is that true?

A.   *That is also true. There can be two roads to a place, isn't it?*

[Prasnottara Vahini, P 42]

Q 953. Which is the better road?

A.   *Both are good and important. Both take you to the same goal, only, you cannot travel on both at the same time. People can choose the road that suits their inner promptings and do the sadhana of that path. Both release the sadhaka from bondage.*

[Prasnottara Vahini, P 42]

Q 954. Should the desire for Moksha be also given up by the *sadhaka* at some stage?

A. *The Lord, who incarnates to restore Dharma, Himself advises the renouncing of all Dharma for the sake of the ultimate Liberation or Moksha and in the same Bhagavad Gita* **He recommends in the last chapter the giving up of even the craving for Moksha or Liberation, for there is in reality, "no bondage and release." It is only a delusion born of ignorance, which disappears when the Light of knowledge is allowed to illumine the place where darkness prevailed.**

[SSS Vol. 7, P 114]

Q 955. How does a seeker travel from Bhakti to Mukti (liberation)?

A. **From Bhakti you get Shakti (power, energy) for the body, mind and spirit. Through this Bhakti and Shakti, you get immersed in Rakti (attachment) towards God and develop Virakti (detachment) from the world. Then God confers on you Bhukti (food) and also Mukti (liberation).**

[SSS Vol. 32 Part 2, P 142]

Q 956. What is the concept of mergence in God?

A. *Parvathi underwent extreme austerities and subjected herself (that is to say, her ego-consciousness) to sun and rain, cold and hunger and thus transformed herself. Finally Easwara (Siva) accepted her as half of Himself.* **This is a stage in spiritual advancement called**

Sayujya (merger). This is the same as Moksha and Mukti, liberation and release.

[Vidya Vahini, P 21]

Q 957. What qualification is required for attaining this state of mergence or Moksha?

A. *Moksha means liberation. All embodied beings long for liberation from the limitation the embodiment connotes. Every living being is perforce a Mumukshu – an aspirant for Moksha. One has to be a tyagi, well-versed in detachment. This is the final Truth.*

[Vidya Vahini, P 21]

Q 958. What is the Vedic Sutra of Oneness?

A. *The Vedic Sutra is: "Ekoham bahusyam" (I am One, I shall be many). It is the one that pretends to be many. So one has to feel the impact of the One, rather than of the many, while moving in the world.*

[SSS Vol. 14, P 99]

■ Jivanmukti

Q 959. How is the stage of *Jivanmukti* reached?

A. *The contemplation of the Godhead as 'above and beyond all attributes' is necessary for the attainment of Jivanmukti.*

[Geetha Vahini, P 224]

Q 960. What is the state of liberation?

A. *Liberation is just the awareness of Truth, the falling off of the scales of delusion from the eye. It is not a special suburb of select Souls; it is not a closed monopoly of expert sadhakas. Like the Godavari losing its form, its name* *and its taste in the sea, liberation dissolves the name and form, aptitudes and attitudes. You are no more a separate, particular individual. The raindrop has merged in the sea, from where the drop arose.* Of course, there was no bondage at any time, and no prison; there was only a fixation in the mind that one was bound, that one was in prison, that one was limited and finite!

[SSS Vol. 5, P 61-62]

Q 961. What is the state of *Nirvana?*

A. *Man aspires for Mukti (liberation)? What is Mukti? It is not the attainment of a heavenly abode. Mukti means freedom from suffering. You need to have Mukti at three levels. – body, mind and soul. For example, you are hungry. When you eat food, your hunger is satiated. This is also a kind of Mukti. You are suffering from a disease. You take a medicine and get cured. This is also Mukti. All this is related to the body. At the mental level, Mukti means controlling the vagaries of the mind. But true liberation lies in understanding the principle of the Atma which neither comes nor goes. His is termed as Nirvana.*

[SSS Vol. 34, P 132-133]

Q 962. What is it that man must do to reach that state of Bliss known as *Nirvana?*

A. *To reach this stage of Bliss, man must live a life of sadhana. If you take one step after another, however short the step, you can walk even a hundred miles. **The Ichcha-sakti (Will Power) has to be sharpened and shaped as an instrument for progress.***

[SSS Vol. 9, P 181]

963. What *sadhana* path is to be followed for attaining *Jivanmukti* ?

A.   *Concentration on God with a fragmented mind is an exercise in futility. Single-minded devotion is the easiest path to salvation. In fact, an Ananya Bhakta becomes a Jivanmukta (one liberated during life).*

[Summer Showers 1979, P 151]

Q 964. What is the state of the self-realised liberated sages, the Jivanmuktas?

A.   *"All their Karmas have been burnt up by the Fire of Jnana; their impulses for action have been scorched by the Wisdom they have gained. They have no further need for injunction and prohibition, (Vidhi and Nishedha).* They need no sadhana like Dana (charity), Dharma (virtuous living), Tapas (austerity). All they do or feel or think will be divine, holy, virtuous, beneficial to mankind. The very earth they tread on is sacrosanct; every word they utter will be the word of God.; their breath need not take them, on death, to realms that are heavenly; they merge, on the falling away of bodily raiment, without delay, in Brahman. Such are the Jivis who were described by Me now as having Kaivalyamukti, Brahma-praapthi or Sadyomukthi."*

[Geetha Vahini, P 186]

✳✳✳

18
AVATAR

■ **Avatar**

Q 965. What is the criterion for the advent of an Avatar?

A. *The Avatar comes when there is yet a remnant of good men, yet a trace of Dharma; for what is the use of a doctor when the patient has collapsed? When a large number of good men are afflicted with the fear for the survival of goodness, then the Lord incarnates to feed their drooping spirits and revive faith and courage. "* **Paritranaya Sadhoonam"** *in the Geetha does not mean the "protection of sadhus or ascetics". It means the "protection of all who have sadhu virtues". 'Sadhu' means 'good'. Sadhu virtues might be found even in animals and insects and worms. He will guard and guide even such. He comes to promote Dharma and Virtue. Virtue is the foundation of Dharma.*

[SSS Vol. 2, P 154]

Q 966. Is granting fulfilment of realisation of goal to the seekers also one of the missions of the Avatar? How can man get such help from the Avatar?

A.   *To confer on man Jnana, God in His infinite mercy comes down as man; or else, man will degrade himself to the level of beasts. **Unless he learns to surrender his ego in complete sincerity, with no reservations to the Lord, he cannot realise Him, though He is resident in his own heart.** The anguish that fills the penitent seeker will move the Lord to manifest Himself. In the ecstasy of that moment, man will experience: I am Thou; Thou Art I.*

[Sanathana Sarathi – Nov. 2000, P 357]

Q 967. Do Avatars possess special power and strength?

A.   *Nobody knows My power and strength. But I use them according to the need and the situation. I use My power discreetly. Speed breakers are meant to control speed. They are necessary and they ensure safety. Likewise, sometimes I control My power. These are all signs of My Divinity. **You will know My Divine Glory slowly and steadily in course of time.***

[Sanathana Sarathi – Oct. 2002, P 320 (Summer Course Discourse No. 3 on 17-5-2002)]

Q 968. Are Avatars in human body beyond attachment?

A.   *Though I have a human body, I am free from human attachment. **Though the body is human, I am entirely Divine.***

[Sanathana Sarathi– Oct. 2002, P 320 (Summer Course Discourse No. 3 on 17-5-2002)]

Q 969. Do the divine incarnations leave their bodies at will or like all other mortal forms?

A.   *As Rama and Krishna were born with human bodies people entertained the wrong notion that they died in an ordinary way. Rama and Krishna did not shed their bodies* *like ordinary mortals. Rama stepped into the Sarayu river and reached His celestial abode. Similarly, Krishna was seen lying under a tree in a forest and then ascended to heaven. The bodies of divine incarnations do not fall in the hands of mortals. You must have the capacity to understand Divinity.*

[Sanathana Sarathi – Oct. 2002, P 320 (Summer Course Discourse No.3 on 17-5-2002)]

Q 970. Why is it difficult for most people to believe in the divinity of the Avatars in their lifetime?

A. *Since I eat like you, talk like you and sing like you, you are deluded into thinking that I am also a human being like you. It is sheer ignorance to think about Me in that way.*

[Sanathana Sarathi – Oct. 2002, P 320 (Summer Course Discourse No. 3 on 17-5-2002)]

Q 971. Why is it not possible to understand the *Leelas* of the Avatars?

A. *Such is the nature of the marvellous acts of the Avatar. Their significance is wonderous and is beyond the grasp of human mind. As the Upanishads say, "Yatho Vacho Nivarthanthe Aprapya Manasa Saha" (these are of a nature where the words and thoughts rebound in futility without comprehending them).*

[SSS Vol. 34, P 216]

Q 972. Do all Avatars manifest wonders and miracles?

A. *The Divine has to reveal itself through these manifestations, largely shaped and modified by the nature of the times, the region and the cultural environment. The signs and wonders that I manifest are given names that do not connote the purpose or* *effect. They can be called chamatkara, that lead on to samskara, which in turn urge one on towards paropkara and finally result in sakshatkara. Chamatkara is any act, which attracts on account of its inexplicability. This aspect of attraction is inherent in the Avatar (divine incarnation)...This attribute of attraction is a characteristic of Divinity.*

[SSS Vol. 13, P 164-165]

Q 973. **Krishna Avatar has been described as a *Purna Avatar*. Do different Avatars of God incarnate with different potencies?**

A. *All Avatars are equally divine and it is pointless to describe one incarnation as partial and another full. The form and role of each Avatar are dependent on the circumstances and the needs, which led to the advent.* Avatars are not to be judged in quantitative terms. Qualitatively they are all essentially one. *All Avatars are "full" in fact.* Only their forms and names differ according to the circumstances in which they appeared.

[SSS Vol. 19, P 145]

Q 974. **What is the significance of the other meanings of the name "Krishna" Avatar?**

A. *"Ka" symbolises the sun principle also. "Ra" represents the principle of delight. "Sha" represents Vishnu, the source of all wealth and prosperity. "Na" signifies the Narasimha Avatara, the combination of man and animal in an integral unity. "A" reveals the Akshara Swarupa of the Lord, His imperishable and eternal quality.*

[SSS Vol. 19, P 145]

■ Divinity Of Bhagawan Sri Sathya Sai Baba

Q 975. What are Swami's instructions to the devotees coming to listen to Swami's discourses?

A. *You must try and digest at least a small portion and after digesting, you must get the strength therefrom into your body and put it into practice.* After listening to these discourses here, when you go back to your lodging, you should not spend your time in unnecessary conversation. You should recapitulate and recollect what you have listened to.

[Summer Showers 1977, P 158]

Q 976. Equipped with what potencies (*Sakthis*) the Lord incarnates in human form?

A. *In each Yuga, you have the Avatar of the Lord come to redeem, revive and re-build. At the present time, Maha Sakthi (Super Power), Maya Sakthi (Power of Illusion) and Yoga Sakthi (Power of Vision with God) have come, all together, in one Human Form. Your endeavour should be to draw near and earn Grace therefrom.*

[SSS Vol. 7, P 142]

Q 977. Who are *Ansha-avatars*?

A. *God or divinely inspired saint or messiah makes His advent on earth to reform the wicked and restore the reign of Dharma. Such incarnations are known as Archana-naama forms of the Divine. In this Archana-naama form, the manifestations are regarded as Ansha-avatars - manifestations of aspects of the Divine.*

[SSS Vol. 29, P 304]

Q 978. Who are *Poorna Avatars*?

A.   *The Vibhava-avatars (like Rama and Krishna) are*
         Poorna-avatars (total manifestations of the Divine).
         The Archana-avatars are Ansha-avatars (partial
         manifestations). Such Avatars incarnate from time
         to time, not only in India but in all countries.

[SSS Vol. 29, P 305]

Q 979. Who are the messengers of God? To which category Jesus Christ belonged?

A.   *Jesus declared at first that He was "a messenger of God."*
         Who are the messengers? They are of two kinds.
         Yamadootas and Avadootas. Yamadootas are
         messengers who inflict harm on people. Avadootas
         are messengers who protect. Jesus belonged to the
         second category. In due course, he recognised his own
         inner divinity. Then he declared: "I am the Son of God."
         Thereby he proclaimed his right to a share in all the
         qualities of God. When he acquired all the qualities of the
         Divine, he announced: "I and my Father are one."

[SS Vol. 29, P 305]

Q 980. To which category did Zoroaster belong?

A.   *The same threefold progress can be seen in the*
         pronouncements of Zoroaster. First he declared: "I am in
         the light." Then he said: "The light is in me." Finally he
         declared: "I am the light." These declarations can be
         compared to the three systems of Indian philosophy:
         Dualism, Qualified Non-dualism and Non-dualism.

[SSS Vol. 29, P 305]

Q 981. What was the status of Sri Shankaracharya?

A.   *Shankara considered himself a servant of God. He*
         propagated the Advaitik doctrine. He declared: "The
         bodies are different, the forms are different, but the inner Self

is one alone. "**Ekam eva Adviteeyam**" (**The Self is one only; there is no second**). *God is one and the goal is one.*

[SSS Vol. 29, P 305, 307]

Q 982. Is Sai-Principle omnipotent?

A. *The Suddha Sathwa, which constitutes the Sai Principle, is omnipotent. There is nothing that is beyond its power. It is the embodiment of all powers. It should be everyone's aim to strive to recognise this Supreme Principle.*

[SSS Vol. 21, P 44]

Q 983. CAN WE ENVISION THE REALITY OF BHAGAWAN SRI SATHYA SAI BABA?

A. *"THIS IS A HUMAN FORM IN WHICH EVERY DIVINE ENTITY, EVERY DIVINE PRINCIPLE, THAT IS TO SAY, ALL THE NAMES AND FORMS ASCRIBED BY MAN TO GOD, ARE MANIFEST" – "Sarvadaivatwa sarvaroopaalanu dharin-china maanavaakaarame ee aakaaram." Do not allow doubt to distract you; IF YOU ONLY INSTALL, IN THE ALTAR OF YOUR HEART, STEADY FAITH IN MY DIVINITY, YOU CAN WIN A VISION OF MY REALITY. Instead, if you swing like a pendulum of a clock, you can never succeed in comprehending the Truth and win that Bliss. You are very fortunate that you have a chance to experience the bliss of the vision of the sarvadaivatwa swarupam (the Form, which is all Forms of all Gods) now, in this life itself.*

[SSS Vol. 8, P 99-100]

Q 984. Why most people fail to understand the reality of the Avatar?

A. *In truth, you cannot understand the nature of My*

Reality either today, or even after a thousand years of steady austerity or ardent inquiry even if all mankind joins in the effort. But, in a short time, you will become cognizant of the Bliss showered by the Divine Principle, which has taken upon itself this sacred body and this sacred Name. Your good fortune which will provide you this chance is greater than what was available for anchorites, monks, sages, saints and even personalities embodying facets of Divine Glory!

[SSS Vol. 8, P 99]

Q 985. How to benefit from the Avatar?

A.   *Any moment, My Divinity may be revealed to you; you have to be ready, prepared for that moment. Since Divinity is enveloped by humanness, you must endeavour to overcome the Maya (delusion) that hides it from your eyes.*

[SSS Vol. 8, P 99]

Q 986. What is the goal of this Sai Avatar?

A.   *In each Yuga, the Divine has incarnated itself as an Avatar for some particular task. This Incarnation is different in that It has to deal with the crisis which is world-wide and world-shaking. Immorality has put on the garb of morality and is enticing man into the morass of sin. Truth is condemned as a trap; justice is jeered at; saints are harassed as social enemies. Hence, this Incarnation has come to uphold the True and suppress the False.*

[SSS Vol. 8, P 157]

Q 987. Is the task of the Avatar to liberate only those souls who are ready for deliverance?

A.   *The airoplane has to land at certain places in order to take in those who have won the right to fly by the tickets they have purchased. So, too, the Lord has to come down so that those who have won the right to be liberated may be saved; incidentally, others too will know the Lord, of His grace, of ways of winning it, of the joy of liberation.*

[SSS Vol. 3, P 30]

Q 988. Swami, what is your advice to the devotees who throng Prasanthi Nilayam by the thousands drawn by diverse needs or a taste for spiritual matters or love or reverence for this Divine Form?

A. *Do not delay any more; take hold of this unique chance, even while you can. Ask Me about the sadhana you should adopt for your liberation; begin practising from this day. Later, it may be difficult to approach Me and ask Me. For, people are coming towards Me in full unending streams, and you may have to take Darshan of Me from miles away! This is bound to grow into a Vishwa-vriksha (a World-tree), that provides shade and shelter for all. This has come down in this Form with that very purpose. It knows no halting, no hesitation. My name is Sathya, Truth. My teaching is Truth. My path is Truth. I am Truth.*

[SSS Vol. 8, P 157]

Q 989. Why is it so difficult to cognise the Divine Reality in Sai Form?

A. *Since I move about with you, eat like you, and talk with you, you are deluded into the belief that this is but an instance of common humanity. Be warned against this mistake. I am also deluding you by My singing with you, talking with you, and engaging Myself in activities with you. But, any moment, My*

Divinity may be revealed to you; you have to be ready, prepared for the moment. Since Divinity is enveloped by human-ness, you must endeavour to overcome the Maya (delusion) that hides it from your eyes.
[SSS Vol. 8, P 99]

Q 990. How can a devotee benefit from this Yuga Avatar?

A. *Utilise the chance of association with Me as much as possible, and endeavour as quickly and as best as you can, to follow the directions that I have been giving. Obeying My instructions is enough; it will benefit you more than the most rigorous asceticism. Practise Sathya (truth), Dharma (righteousness), Santhi (peace) and Prema (love), which are dear to Me. Resolve to keep those ideals before you ever, in all your thoughts, words, deeds. That can confer on you the summum bonum of Mergence in the Supreme Substance of Divinity.*

[SSS Vol. 8, P 101]

Q 991. Is it right to address God and seek His guidance for worldly matters?

A. *It is always preferable to approach God for the fulfilment of wants, rather than cringe before men, who themselves are but tools in the hands of God. In His own silent way, God will transform the mind and turn it towards sadhana and successful spiritual pilgrimage. He cannot allow His children to lose their way and suffer in the jungle. When you approach God and seek His help and guidance, you have taken the first step to save yourself. You are then led to accept His Will as your own.*

[SSS Vol. 5, P 239]

Q 992. How should we approach Swami?

A. *You know there is a rule here that you should come with empty hands, without even the traditional offerings of patram, pushpam, phalam and toyam (leaf, flower, fruit and water). Come with clean hands, hands that supplicate, not supply; hands that proclaim that they have renounced attachment to riches; then, I fill them with Grace.* I must say that I demand and take Sathya, Dharma, Shanthi and Prema...

[SSS Vol. 5, P 239]

When you demand a thing, you must be prepared to pay the price, the price equal to its value. Give something divine if you want the Divine. Do not try to get it for a flower that fades, a fruit that rots, a leaf that dries, or water that evaporates.

[SSS Vol. 5, P 234]

Q 993. How to win a glimpse of the Truth of Sai?

A. *About Me, there are some who have had a glimpse of the Truth; there are others who have not been able to achieve even that. But, My Prema is showered equally on all; I do not reveal or refuse; it is for you to discover and decide, derive Ananda by diving into the depths. How can an ant calculate the depth of the sea? How can a man on the ground describe the features of the pilot of a plane in the sky? Unless you rise to the heights, by following certain disciplines, you cannot experience Godhead.*

[SSS Vol. 5, P 238]

Q 994. Can the departed souls communicate with Swami?

A. *On occasions, departed souls come to have Swami's Darshan both during the day as well as night. Those who left their bodies 50 to 60 years ago also come to visit Swami. One morning, Swami returned to the Auditorium as usual after morning Bhajans. It was around 10 o'clock, and Swami went upstairs. Sitting there in the chamber was Easwaramma, the mother of Swami's body. Swami asked her, "Why do you come like this? What would people say? Don't come like this." She replied, "Swami, I am Your mother. What do You know about the love of a mother? Only a mother can understand my feelings. I am a mother and You are God full of love for all. A mother cannot understand God's love and God cannot understand a mother's love! I have come here in order to tell you something..."*

[Sanathana Sarathi – Nov. 2000, P 350-351
(Discourse on 18-5-2000 at Brindavan)]

Q 995. Does Swami also get angry at times?

A.   *Swami is very patient. Mountains may move but Swami's heart is ever unruffled and peaceful. However, at times, Swami may pretend to be angry. This tactic is used solely to improve and correct the people who are going astray. Such methods become necessary because people do not always respond to nice words of advice! When Swami gently asks people to sit down, they do not listen but when He raises His voice, there is instant obedience!*

[Sanathana Sarathi – Nov. 2000, P 354
(Discourse on 18-5-2000 at Brindavan)]

Q 996. Does an Avatar choose His parents to come on earth in human form?

A.   *The parents of this body were chosen by Me...Their lives were sanctified as they were selected by Swami.*

[SSS Vol. 35, P 265, 266]

997. What is Swami' message to the *devotees?*

A. Strengthened by Swami's Grace, encouraged by Swami's Blessings, engage in Sadhana (spiritual practice) and achieve success by realising the Goal of Life.

[SSS. Vol. 9, P 87]

Q 998. Swami! how is it that You refrain from talking to some people?

A. *I have got principles. My word is very precious. Even if you don't give value to My word, I attach great importance and value to My word. If somebody does not heed My word, I don't like to waste My words by speaking to him. Hence in order to save the value of My words, I stop talking to such persons.*

[Summer Showers 1990, P 144]

Q 999. What should be the ideal relationship of a devotee with Swami?

A. *You should become fruits which have to be offered to Swami. You should become the offering (Naivedya). You should become Swami's instrument. You should become the beloved of Swami. You should take each step in keeping with Swami's step. You should stand by Swami as His companion, like His shadow. I am in need of such persons. They are the very embodiments of my love. "They are I". "I am they".*

[Sanathana Sarathi - Nov.1995, P 329]

Q 1000. What are the four F's that constitute Swami's command?

A. *There are four F's that you will have to fix before your attention.*

1. Follow the master 2. Face the Devil 3. Fight to the End 4. Finish the Game

Follow the Master means, observe Dharma. Face the Devil means; overcome the temptations that beset you when you try to earn artha (wealth or the wherewithal to live in comfort). Fight to the End means, struggle ceaselessly; wage war against the six enemies that are led by kama (lust). And finally, Finish at the Goal means, do not stop until the goal of Moksha (Liberation from the ignorance and delusion) is reached.

[SSS. Vol. 13, P 82]

Q 1001. **What was the first lesson given by this Avatar?**

A. *The very first lesson I gave when I declared My Identity at Uravakonda was: "Manasa Bhajare Gurucharanam, Dustara Bhavasagara Taranam."*

That is to say: First know that you are in this cycle of birth and death, the ocean of worldly life (Bhavasagara); then, resolve on crossing it (taranam); then fix on a Guru or the Name and Form of God which appeals to you; lastly, dwell on His Glory, do bhajan, but do it with all your mind. He, who is deluded by this relative reality is the worldly person (samsara); he who is aware that it is only relatively real is the spiritual practitioner (sadhaka).

[SSS Vol. 4, P 11]

***

BIBLIOGRAPHY

1. Summer Showers in Brindavan 1972, 1974, 1977, 1979, 1990, 1991, 1993, 1996, 1997

2. Sathya Sai Speaks Vol. 1, 2, 3, 4, 5, 6, 7, 8, 9, 10, 11, 12, 13, 14, 15, 16, 17, 18, 19, 20, 21, 22, 23, 24, 25, 26, 27, 28, 29, 30, 31, 32, 33, 34, 35

3. Geetha Vahini

4. Prema Vahini

5. Prasanthi Vahini

6. Sutra Vahini

7. Vidya Vahini

8. Prasnottara Vahini

9. Conversations - with Bhagavan Sri Sathya Sai Baba

10. Sadhana – The Inward Path by Sri N. Kasturi

11. Sanathana Sarathi:

   Aug.1983, Oct.1983, Oct.1994, Jan. 1995, April 1995, Sept.1995, Nov.1995, Nov.1999, Dec.1999, May 2000, June 2000, Aug. 2000, Jan.2001, May 2001, July 2001, Sept. 2001, Nov 2001, June 2002, Aug. 2002, Oct. 2002, Nov. 2002, Dec. 2002, Jan. 2003, Feb. 2003, May 2003

SRI SATHYA SAI BOOKS AND PUBLICATIONS TRUST
PRASANTHI NILAYAM

PIN 515 134, ANANTAPUR DISTRICT, ANDHRA PRADESH, INDIA
IMPORTER / EXPORTER CODE NO. 0990001032
RESERVE BANK OF INDIA EXPORTER CODE NO. HS-2001198

	Price Rs.	Wt. in Gms. approx.
THE VAHINI SERIES : (BOOKS WRITTEN BY BHAGAWAN SRI SATHYA SAI BABA)		
Bhagavatha Vahini	42.00	490
(The story of the Glory of the Lord)		
Dharma Vahini (Stream of Righteousness)	19.00	230
Dhyana Vahini (Stream of Meditation)	19.00	210
Geetha Vahini (The Divine Gospel)	32.00	415
Jnana Vahini (The Stream of Eternal Wisdom)	16.00	165
Leela Kaivalya Vahini (The Cosmic Play of God)	8.00	75
Prasanthi Vahini (The Supreme Bliss of Divine)	14.00	140
Prasnottara Vahini (Answers to Spiritual Questions)	15.00	95
Prema Vahini (The Stream of Divine Love)	20.00	125
Rama Katha Rasa Vahini Part-I (The Sweet Story of Rama's Glory)	48.00	705
Rama Katha Rasa Vahini Part-II (The Sweet Story of Rama's Glory)	36.00	460
Sandeha Nivarini (Clearance of Spiritual Doubts)	18.00	230
Sathya Sai Vahini (Spiritual Message of Sri Sathya Sai)	34.00	406
Sutra Vahini (Stream of Aphorisms on Brahman)	19.00	110
Upanishad Vahini (Essence of Vedic Knowledge)	18.00	225
Vidya Vahini (Flow of Spiritual Education)	17.00	210
SATHYA SAI SPEAKS SERIES:		
(DISCOURSES BY BHAGAWAN SRI SATHYA SAI BABA) (REVISED & ENLARGED EDITIONS)		
Sathya Sai Speaks Vol. I (Years 1953 to 1960)	34.00	390
Sathya Sai Speaks Vol. II (Years 1961 to 1962)	39.00	490
Sathya Sai Speaks Vol. III (Year 1963)	38.00	420
Sathya Sai Speaks Vol. IV (Year 1964)	39.00	510
Sathya Sai Speaks Vol. V (Year 1965)	43.00	535
Sathya Sai Speaks Vol. VI (Year 1966)	40.00	405
Sathya Sai Speaks Vol. VII (Year 1967)	40.00	410
Sathya Sai Speaks Vol. VIII (Year 1968)	39.00	425
Sathya Sai Speaks Vol. IX (Year 1969)	30.00	345
Sathya Sai Speaks Vol. X (Year 1970)	35.00	450
Sathya Sai Speaks Vol. XI (Years 1971 to 1972)	45.00	565
Sathya Sai Speaks Vol. XII (Years 1973 to 1974)	42.00	535
Sathya Sai Speaks Vol. XIII (Years 1975 to 1977)	30.00	445
Sathya Sai Speaks Vol. XIV (Years 1978 to 1980)	40.00	625
Sathya Sai Speaks Vol. XV (Years 1981 to 1982)	40.00	550
Sathya Sai Speaks Vol.XVI (Year 1983)	30.00	330
Sathya Sai Speaks Vol. XVII (Year 1984)	31.00	360
Sathya Sai Speaks Vol. XVIII (Year 1985)	25.00	365
Sathya Sai Speaks Vol. XIX (Year 1986)	30.00	405
Sathya Sai Speaks Vol. XX (Year 1987)	39.00	460
Sathya Sai Speaks Vol. XXI (Year 1988)	35.00	455
Sathya Sai Speaks Vol. XXII (Year 1989)	35.00	475
Sathya Sai Speaks Vol. XXIII (Year 1990)	44.00	510
Sathya Sai Speaks Vol. XXIV (Year 1991)	40.00	540
Sathya Sai Speaks Vol. XXV (Year 1992)	40.00	645
Sathya Sai Speaks Vol. XXVI (Year 1993)	50.00	655
Sathya Sai Speaks Vol. XXVII (Year 1994)	35.00	510
Sathya Sai Speaks Vol. XXVIII (Year 1995)	43.00	620

	Price Rs.	Wt. in Gms approx.
Sathya Sai Speaks Vol. XXIX (Year 1996)	43.00	635
Sathya Sai Speaks Vol. XXX (Year 1997)	35.00	490
Sathya Sai Speaks Vol. XXXI (Year 1998)	53.00	730
Sathya Sai Speaks Vol. XXXII (Year 1999) - Part 1	27.00	370
Sathya Sai Speaks Vol. XXXII (Year 1999) - Part 2	27.00	370
Sathya Sai Speaks Vol. XXXIII (Year 2000)	39.00	495
Sathya Sai Speaks Vol. XXXIV (Year 2001)	38.00	462
Sathya Sai Speaks Vol.XXXV (Year 2002)	40.00	525
Sathya Sai Speaks Vol.XXXVI (Year 2003) - Part - 1	29.00	–
Sathya Sai Speaks Vol.XXXVI (Year 2003) - Part - 2	23.00	–
Sathya Sai Speaks Vol.XXXVII (Year 2004)	36.00	–

SATHYAM SIVAM SUNDARAM SERIES:
(LIFE STORY OF BHAGAVAN SRI SATHYA SAI BABA)

Sathyam Sivam Sundaram Vol. 1 (Birth to 1961)	44.00	500
Sathyam Sivam Sundaram Vol. 2 (1962 to 1968)	40.00	410
Sathyam Sivam Sundaram Vol. 3 (1969 to 1972)	48.00	425
Sathyam Sivam Sundaram Vol. 4 (1973 to 1979)	39.00	375
Sathyam Sivam Sundaram Vol. 5 (1980 to 1985)	55.00	–
Sathyam Sivam Sundaram Vol. 1 to 4 (Deluxe Edition)	245.00	3 kg

SUMMER SHOWER SERIES :
(DISCOURSES ON INDIAN CULTURE AND SPIRITUALITY BY BHAGAVAN SRI SATHYA SAI BABA)

Summer Showers in Brindavan 1972	15.50	230
Summer Showers in Brindavan 1973 (New Enlarged Edition)	46.00	–
Summer Showers in Brindavan 1974 Part - I (New Enlarged Edition)	36.00	360
Summer Showers in Brindavan 1974 Part - II (New Enlarged Edition)	38.00	380
Summer Roses on the Blue Mountains (Ooty) 1976 (New Enlarged Edition)	37.00	360
Summer Showers in Brindavan 1977	17.50	175
Summer Showers in Brindavan 1978	46.00	510
Summer Showers in Brindavan 1979 (New Enlarged Edition)	34.00	–
Summer Showers in Brindavan 1990	20.00	275
Summer Showers in Brindavan 1991	22.00	285
Summer Showers in Brindavan 1993	23.00	200
Summer Showers in Brindavan 1995	19.00	280
Summer Showers in Brindavan 1996	19.00	205
Summer Showers in Brindavan 2000	34.00	460
Summer Showers in Brindavan 2002	25.00	300

CHILDREN'S BOOKS:

Chinna Katha-Part I	25.00	350
Chinna Katha-Part II	42.00	385
Chinna Katha Illustrated	17.00	80
My Life is My Message	17.00	115
Stories for Children : Part I	13.00	190
Stories for Children : Part II	28.00	325
Divine Stories Vol 1 (Human Value Stories)	37.00	–
Divine Stories Vol 2 (Human Value Stories)	32.00	–

OUR OTHER PUBLICATIONS:

Baba - The Breath of Sai by Grace J. Mc Martin	46.00	485
Bhagavad Gita (Part - I and II)	69.00	820
Birthday Blessings of Bhagavan	25.00	325
Grama Seva is Rama Seva	20.00	255
Conversation with Bhagavan Sri Sathya Sai Baba by Dr. John S. Hislop	29.00	375
Fundamentals of Sri Sathya Sai Educare Vol. I - Compiled by Ranvir Singh	52.00	–
Fundamentals of Sri Sathya Sai Educare Vol. II - Compiled by Ranvir Singh	50.00	–
Fundamentals of Sri Sathya Sai Educare Vol. III - Compiled by Ranvir Singh	49.00	–
Fundamentals of Sri Sathya Sai Educare Vol. IV - Compiled by Ranvir Singh	62.00	–
Finding God by Charles Penn	50.00	705
Gems of Wisdom	50.00	690

Title	Price Rs.	Wt. in Gms. approx.
Guidelines to Active workers of S.S.S.S. Organisations from Bhagawan Baba	17.00	195
A Recapitulation of Baba's Divine Teachings by Grace J. Mc Martin	35.00	485
A pioneering attempt at child labour elimination-		
A tribute to Sai Baba, The Ultimate Motivator	35.00	335
Seva: A Flower At His Lotus Feet - Grace J. Mc Martin	29.00	325
Spirituality and Health by Dr. (Mrs) Charanjit Ghooi	60.00	725
Bhakthi and Health by Dr. (Mrs) Charanjit Ghooi	40.00	270
Benedictory Addresses (21 Convocation Discourses by Bhagavan as Chancellor from beginning up to 2002)	26.00	350
Easwaramma The Chosen Mother (Enlarged edition)	24.00	–
End of the Endless Search by P.P. Arya	28.00	265
Sathya Sai Education in Human Values	25.00	280
Garland of 108 Precious Gems (108 Holy Names of Bhagavan)	20.00	170
Journey to God - Part II - J. Jagadeesan	86.00	645
Loving God - by N. Kasturi	52.00	725
Love of Conscience	26.00	305
Life is a Game Play It - Joy Thomas	42.00	465
Life is a Challenge Meet It - Joy Thomas	26.00	330
Life is Love Enjoy It - Joy Thomas	28.00	345
Life is a Dream Realise It - Joy Thomas	32.00	335
My Baba and I - Dr. John S. Hislop	32.00	455
My Beloved - Charles Penn	35.00	395
Nama Mahima	13.00	160
Namasmarana	8.00	55
Ocean of Love	500.00	1865
One Single Stream of Love	41.00	210
Pathway to Peace Prasanthi	21.00	235
Purifying the Heart - John Goldthwait, Ph.D	20.00	215
Sadhana - The Inward Path	41.00	475
Sai Baba - The Ultimate Experience - Phyllis Krystal	32.00	435
Sai Baba - The Holy Man and Psychiatrist - Dr. Samuel H. Sandweiss	58.00	440
Spirit and the Mind - Dr. Samuel H. Sandweiss	46.00	545
Sai Bhajanamala	45.00	570
Sai Baba's Mahavakya on Leadership (Hard Bound) - Lieut Gen. (Retd) Dr. M.L. Chibber	42.00	460
Sai Advent - Compiled by Harendra Singh	11.00	–
Sai Study Circle Manual	20.00	–
Sri Sathya Sai Gita – All about Spirituality in Qs & As - P.P. Arya	45.00	–
The Glory of Womanhood	17.00	205
To my Father - Justice Padma Kastgir	24.00	165
Sai Echoes from Kodai Hills	20.00	235
Quiz on Bhagavatam	10.00	50
Quiz on Mahabharata	10.00	50
Quiz on Ramayana	10.00	50
Quiz on Bhagavad Gita	7.00	35
Quiz on Divine Life of Bhagavan Sri Sathya Sai Baba	6.00	65
Sai Baba and You - Practical Spirituality - Mark and Barbara Gardner	25.00	295
Seeking Divinity - Dr. John S. Hislop	27.00	385
Thought for the Day	26.00	215
Divine Discourses on Easwaramma Day	22.00	225
Divine Memories - Diana Baskin	47.00	485
Universal and Practical Teachings of Bhagavan - Prof. K. Anil Kumar	26.00	305
Unforgettable Baba - Joyce Darlene Barker	40.00	–
Aura of the Divine	40.00	435
Sree Gurucharanam (A Compilation of Guru Poornima Discourses)	11.00	145
Prema Dhaara Vol. 1(Letters Written by Bhagavan to His Students)	16.00	130
The Light of Love	18.00	225
The Wish-Fulfilling Tree	44.00	545
The Mind and its Mysteries	16.00	–
Truth is Only One	32.00	370
Prasanthi Nilayam Information Booklet	10.00	110
The Dharmic Challenge	25.00	335
The Direct Flight to Divinity	22.00	230

	Price Rs.	Wt. in Gm. approx.
Dasara Discourses 1997 (Senses for Selfless Service)	15.00	160
Dasara Discourses 1998	19.00	200
Dasara Discourses 1999 & 2000	25.00	280
Dasara Discourses 2001	18.00	220
Dasara Discourses 2002	13.00	160
Dasara Discourses 2004	6.00	–
Message of the Lord	185.00	1575
Sathya Sai Parenting - Rita Bruce	30.00	390
Sri Sathya Sai Anandadayi - Karunamba Ramamurthy	48.00	550
Siva Sakthi Swarupa	13.00	130

FOR SALE ONLY IN INDIA

	Price Rs.	Wt. in Gm. approx.
Transformation of the Heart - Judy Warner	23.00	285
Reconnecting the Love Energy - Phyllis Krystal	25.00	265
Taming our Monkey Mind - Phyllis Krystal	25.00	340
Suggestions for Study Groups and Individuals use of the Ceiling on Desires Programme	6.00	75
A Catholic Priest Meets Sai Baba - Don Mario Mazzoleni	34.00	490
Pathways to God - Jonathan Roof	26.00	360
With Love Man is God - Samuel H. Sandweiss	115.00	–

Rates indicated are the prevailing rates. They are liable to change.

INLAND / OVERSEAS BOOK ORDERS & SUBSCRIPTION FOR MONTHLY MAGAZINE SANATHANA SARATHI

Books are despatched by Regd. Book Post only subject to availability. Indents and remittances within India should be received by Money Order/Indian Postal Order/Account Payee Cheques/Bank Drafts.

REMITTANCES

Remittances from Overseas towards Book Orders / Sanathana Sarathi Subscriptions (English & Telugu) can be sent by A/C payee Bank Cheque / Demand Draft / International Money Order in **FOREIGN CURRENCY ONLY AND NOT IN INDIAN RUPEES.** Sending Cash Currency is liable to be confiscated by Government.

All remittances should be in favour of **THE CONVENER, SRI SATHYA SAI BOOKS AND PUBLICATIONS TRUST, PRASANTHI NILAYAM, ANANTAPUR DISTRICT, ANDHRA PRADESH, INDIA, PIN CODE - 515 134,** payable at State Bank of India, Prasanthi Nilayam (Branch Code No. 2786) mentioning full address in capitals with Area Pin Code, Zip Code No., where the books are to be despatched.

The approximate postage + packing + forwarding charges for Overseas Sea Mail and Inland per packet are indicated below:

Wt. of Packets	Overseas		Inland
	APPU Countries	Others	
Upto 500 gms.	Rs.78/-	Rs.82/-	Rs.37/-
Above 500 gms. - Below 1 kg	Rs.93/-	Rs.100/-	Rs.42/-
Above 1 kg - Below 2 kg	Rs.109/-	Rs.118/-	Rs.52/-
Above 2 kg - Below 3 kg	Rs.135/-	Rs.150/-	Rs.72/-
Above 3 kg - Below 4 kg	Rs.162/-	Rs.180/-	Rs.82/-
Above 4 kg - Below 5 kg	Rs.188/-	Rs.212/-	Rs.92/-

N.B. Maximum weight allowed per packet is 5 kgs. Weight of packing materials *per packet* to be added to the weight of books – Overseas – 300 gms.

Inland up to 2 kgs – 100 gms. Above 2 kgs and up to 5 kgs – 300 gms.

APPU Countries: Afghanistan, Australia, Brunei, Cambodia, China (People's Republic), Fiji, Indonesia, Iran, Japan, Korea (Rep.), Laos (Rep.) Malaysia, Maldives, Myanmar, Naura, Papua New Guinea, Philippines, Solomon Island, Sri Lanka, Thailand, Vietnam, New Zealand, Singapore.